SAFARI PRESS

# Bowhunting for the North American Twenty-Eight

# Bowhunting for the North American Twenty-Eight

## Hunting All Varieties of North American Game

by

Gary Bogner

with

Jim Van Norman

Safari Press

Bogner, Gary

First edition

Safari Press

2008, Long Beach, California

ISBN 1-57157-288-0

Library of Congress Catalog Card Number: 2007929255

10 9 8 7 6 5 4 3 2 1

Printed in China
Readers wishing to receive the Safari Press catalog, featuring many fine books on big-game hunting, wingshooting, and sporting firearms, should write to Safari Press Inc., P.O. Box 3095, Long Beach, CA 90803, USA. Tel: (714) 894-9080 or visit our Web site at www.safaripress.com.

# Table of Contents

# Foreword

Gary Bogner is unique in the world. Through the years, many things have been said about him, but they all add up to one thing—passion. Gary is a totally passionate person . . . and the hunting world is better for it.

Some people might suggest that I am an unlikely person to write the foreword to Gary's book since few would identify me with bowhunting. They would be wrong. A guy named Fred Bear introduced me to bowhunting. Then, after a fifty-year hiatus from bowhunting, Gary Bogner re-introduced me to it, making possible the placement of the last piece in the complex puzzle that brings us all to this point.

As fate would have it, I was a member of the staff at Safari Club International during Gary's ascendancy to the presidency (and then his two consecutive terms as president) of that prestigious organization. Interactions during that period have given me rare insight into all that is Gary. To get the most out of this book, the reader must first understand Gary Bogner.

There does not exist, indeed could not exist, a more passionate hunter than Gary Bogner. It is that simple. It is so ingrained, I am thoroughly convinced, that it emanates from the DNA level. What contrasts Gary from others is that he is, paraphrasing a now-archaic title, the "complete hunter." The physical act of hunting in the wilds is only a part of what Gary really is in the hunting world.

The actual act of hunting may be the common thread that unites us all, but it would not, could not, exist absent the hard work and long-term investment of Gary and those who are even remotely like him. Gary has put his money where his mouth is, supporting all kinds of activities in the hunting world. Gary has invested more than a career's worth of time and effort into the hunting world. He epitomizes the concept of "First for Hunters." In fact, he is "first, last, and foremost for hunters."

In case it hasn't been obvious, I touched on "bowhunting" initially and then have continued by mentioning merely "hunting." There are reasons for this. First, Gary's legacy benefits ALL hunting. Second, I am a gun person, and so I bring with that moniker the credibility to suggest that this book as well as Gary's many other writings are both relevant for and valuable to anyone who hunts, including those whose implements of the sport go "bang" at the moment of truth.

Speaking as a member of the old guard in the firearms industry, I can say unequivocally that without the things Gary Bogner has done, the gun business would be less for it, for Gary's actions have helped preserve hunting itself. In large part, the hunting tradition continues today because of this man. Yet Gary will be the first to insist that neither he nor any other individual could have accomplished such things. But someone had to be in the driver's seat to help steer things down the right path and keep the reins tight when the road was bumpy. Gary was there, both in good times and bad.

In all of humanity, hunters were the first to use the written/graphic "word" to communicate with others. Symbols that comprise cave drawings witness this fact. That means this book, by its very existence, continues the tradition of hunting.

In that sense, I invite readers (whatever implement they use when hunting) to enrich their own overall hunting experiences, even if only vicariously, through the adventures that have helped define the life of one of the greatest hunters who has ever pulled a string or squeezed a trigger. It is not for us to try to copy Gary's accomplishments. Rather, we can benefit from his experiences, knowledge, and commitment.

In the end, this book is relevant not only to all hunters but also to all people. Hunting, after all, is among mankind's oldest activities. Yet it is not what makes us human but rather what bonds us as humans. Which brings us back to Gary Bogner. Much of his successes in life have come because of his ability to understand, fundamentally, that we all have hopes, dreams, and goals. With this understanding comes the realization that it is when we share these common aspirations that we are able to rise above the din and do something truly significant. When I think of these things, I think of Gary Bogner. As surely as there are Happy Hunting Grounds, we all share the cosmic hunting camp. This book allows us to share the camp personally with Gary. In doing so, we may salute him. But we also join with him. That's what makes us hunters.

If reading this book does nothing else, I hope that it will impart to the reader that, indeed, it is possible for ordinary people to accomplish extraordinary things. Gary, like most of us, did not start life with a silver spoon. Yet through hard work and determination resulting from unrelenting passion and commitment, Gary took all twenty-eight species of big game on the North American continent, and a whole lot more.

Each hunt in this book can stand alone, valid in its own right. Enjoy the adventures. But keep in mind that each hunt also is a part of a greater whole. Take a moment to reflect upon how these hunts compare with your own experiences. Then take the larger step and imagine how, when the final tally is made, your own efforts both individually and collectively will have contributed to both your own fulfillment and the furtherance of the hunting heritage.

Finally, I hope that after finishing this book, all readers take with them the sense that they, too, can contribute their passions to the heritage of hunting. Gary would want nothing less, and has accepted nothing less for himself.

Steve Comus
Director of Publications
Safari Club International

# Remembering . . .

Another memorable November day is ending in the deer woods of Michigan. Blue-orange flames lick at the stacked hardwood logs that pop and spark within a soot-blackened hearth. This warm room bears the commingled aromas of wood smoke and freshly cooked supper. But for the moment, our food can wait. Standing fireside, sock-footed and red-checked from the autumn cold and heady excitement of our evening's hunt, Tom and I are babbling to Gary and Merle about the big bucks we'd seen and the easy shots we'd passed. Our patient and gracious host simply smiles and nods, listening, genuinely interested. And because he has been there, done that himself, Gary is—like us—momentarily sated with the satisfaction of our collective return to this unique yet universal deer camp where each tomorrow's hopeful dawning whispers its welcome on a restless wind that rustles the frost-curled leaves near our favorite stands.

I have come to discover that sharing any hunting camp with Gary Bogner is always special. I have also discovered that there is something truly extraordinary about returning to where it all began, to hunt snowy-rumped bucks that are the descendants of the same deer we pursued in our youth all those long decades ago. And I find it especially comforting to hear Gary, this worldwide journeyer, this woodland dreamer, this man of such great leadership ability and positive actions and hunting successes, so readily admit that the ubiquitous white-tailed deer remains an eternal challenge and a personal favorite. In that regard, we drink from the same cup.

You see, Gary and I arrowed our first deer in 1963. It was by pure happenstance that we both chose, instinctively, to shoot with recurve bows. And although we didn't know each other in those early days, that soon changed as our mutual passion for bow-and-arrow hunting caused our paths to cross, again and again.

As a journalist, I would write of his organizational involvements and personal accomplishments. I would eventually share with others the news of his Sheep Slam and Super Slam and of his successful Africa and Asia adventures. But as his friend, I would increasingly grow to admire how this gentle man—and gentleman hunter—always represented me and every American sportsman and sportswoman as an ethical, responsible, and law-abiding hunter and concerned conservationist. I, for one, am convinced that we sorely need more Gary Bogners in today's outdoors world.

And now, thanks to his belated but most welcome book, you can get to know Gary for yourself. I predict that you will find reading these North American adventures to be time well spent. I also envisage that you will come away with a better appreciation of Gary's considerable hunting skills and the gritty determination required to accomplish what only a mere handful of archers have ever achieved.

So, toss another log on the fire and freshen up your branch water. Then sit back and enjoy the musings of an extraordinary man and his personal recollections of some remarkable hunts. It's the next best thing to being there.

M. R. James, founder
*Bowhunter* magazine

# About the Author

Gary F. Bogner has been an avid hunter and wildlife conservationist for more than fifty years. Born in Muskegon, Michigan, in 1942, Gary graduated from Muskegon Heights High School in 1961. Being the son of a Michigan game conservation officer, Frank W. Martin, Gary quickly developed a deep love for the outdoors. His passion for archery was extraordinary.

As life would have it, at an early age Gary had a stepfather. His stepfather, Herman Bogner, did some hunting with both firearms and archery, but he didn't share the same passion for hunting and the outdoors as did Gary. However, their next-door neighbor, Dick Miller, a lineman for Michigan's Consumer Power, became a very special guy in Gary's life. Dick often invited Gary to go hunting with him and his family, which included his father and brother. By age twelve Gary was hunting small game and tagging along on hunts for Michigan whitetails every chance he got.

Gary's parents allowed him to skip school for deer season. The first time that happened the Catholic nuns at Gary's school were furious. When he returned to school, one of the sisters paraded Gary to the priest for a reprimand. The priest looked sternly at Gary, told the nun he would handle the situation, and dismissed the sister. When the door had closed, the priest stooped down and excitedly asked, "Did you get one?"

It turned out that the priest was an avid hunter himself, and they spent the next half-hour exchanging hunting stories. The priest's name was Father LaPrey. Gary had little trouble skipping school during hunting season after that.

Gary hunted deer with both bow and rifle in those days. His first bow was a forty-pound Black Hawk recurve with cedar arrows and Bear two-bladed broadheads. Thirty-yard shots were Gary's outside limit back then. Gary's first rifle was a Stevens bolt-action .30-30. Gary shot his first deer with a rifle in 1958 at the age of sixteen. His experience with a bow proved a lot more difficult.

By age seventeen, Gary's love for archery inspired him and a childhood friend, Bill Childress, to open an archery shop. They built many arrows for local archers in those days and spent a lot of time shooting in archery contests.

Gary actually started anodizing arrows back in 1959 while operating the archery shop. His mother worked in a factory where they anodized aluminum parts on an assembly line. Gary was always annoyed by the way raw aluminum (the way arrows came in the old days) made his hands black. He got the bright idea to anodize arrows so that the black aluminum color wouldn't come off when an archer or shop owner handled them. He had his mother show him how the process worked. With the permission of the factory owner, Herb Kersmen, his mom and the employees figured a way to anodize arrows in different colors. Gary figured to make them both easier to find and to blend better with natural colors. After quite a bit of success with the process, he decided to send a letter and a sample to Easton, the main arrow manufacturer in the country, to suggest his idea. The owner of the company, Doug Easton, wrote a nice letter back saying: Thank you, son, for the idea, but there is not that much of a need to make them cleaner to handle or prettier to the eye. Gary and his friend Bill stayed in the archery business for three years.

Gary would pursue whitetails until age twenty-one before getting his first bow kill. His persistence would pay off one day while in a ground blind not far from a family cabin near White River. In those days tree stands were illegal. The ground blind was near the intersection of two deer trails. Shortly after sunrise a big doe came by and stopped within range. Gary put an arrow into her vitals. Although the penetration from his primitive equipment concerned Gary, she went only a short distance. He was so proud of finally getting a deer with a bow that he put her on the car and paraded her to all his buddies' houses. The bowkill was a long time coming, but "Boy, she was a dandy!" This type of unwavering persistence has shown itself time and time again throughout Gary's bowhunting career.

All of Gary's hunting back in those days was within sixty miles of home, and most of his trips were within thirty miles. Little did Gary know what lay ahead. Gary spent as much time as he could outdoors and at the family cabin. He decided, after the archery shop fell on hard times, to go live in God's country near where he hunted. He bought an option on a grocery store in the area for one year but quickly found the grocery business wasn't for him.

Well, life grabbed hold, as it does for all, and before Gary knew it he had entered flight school and had begun pursuing a whole new career. There was the occasional local hunting trip, but hunting soon took a back seat to family, kids, and work. However, once Gary gained seniority as a captain in the airlines, he returned to his first love—hunting.

One of the other things that made hunting possible was Gary's financial investments while flying for the airlines. "While my associates were buying fancy cars and big homes, I was investing in real estate. I was lucky, and things have worked out well. The harder you work, the luckier you are."

# Introduction

Having just completed the African Big Six that afternoon, one of my professional hunters and a good friend, Natie Oelofse, the whole hunting crew, and I were sitting by our campfire toasting our hard-fought success. We had managed to complete the Big Six in one hunting expedition.

There are few successes in life that do not involve the support of others. In my life I have been blessed with a good deal of support from friendships that often began in small tents and in less-than-hospitable places.

Nonetheless, as we all rested by the fire, filled with a combination of exhilaration and exhaustion, Natie gave me a sort of half-smirk and shook his head. I asked him what was up, and he gave me some words that have stuck with me ever since. He said, "Tall trees catch a lot more wind."

Those words remained with me because I have learned through the school of hard knocks that, for some reason, human nature often casts a suspicious frown on those who do not walk the common path. Natie knew what he was talking about.

We all approach life differently. We each portray ourselves in a different fashion, generally misaligned a bit with our true self-esteem but revealing the way we want the world to perceive us. Our hearts know right from wrong; our minds know good from evil. But it's amazing what happens to those ideals when ego, power, fame, and money come into play. Each of these compulsions can pulse to change us. It saddens me to see what those forces do to some.

It is sometimes disheartening, too, to feel the undertow in the core groups of organizations making serious decisions for the masses. It doesn't matter the organization, for it is present in them all. It took many years for me to understand the politics that afflict people who aspire to make a difference and hold positions of high office, people whose decisions determine the entire fate of organizations. It is all a monstrous chess game because of human nature "under the influence."

And further, those choosing to be "in the thick of things" are required to maintain the highest profile they can stomach to keep their seat in the game. It's a wearisome task; take my word. But even with that said, I will never give up fighting for stronger organizations interested in wildlife conservation and our hunting rights, no matter how arduous it becomes. We have, and I am proud to be a part of, some of the strongest organizations in the world. I hope each day for more unity among people striving toward common goals, setting aside the shallow influences that distort our souls and ideals.

I've judged my peers too harshly at times, and at times they've judged me with a vengeance. Many of those judgments were made while we each postured and misdirected—for a greater cause. The tactics a person uses may be mistakenly identified as reflecting his character. The politics of the chess game can warp a person's judgment.

I have always believed that we all have an obligation to stand up for what we believe. That often means putting yourself in a spotlight. However, you do not always succeed in surrounding yourself with cheering crowds. More often than not, the spotlight puts you in silhouette, and the silhouette makes you a target.

As you read, you will understand that I love bowhunting. It is a passion with me. Coupled with that passion is my appreciation of the meaning of wildlife conservation and the need to ensure the protection of the right to hunt for our children and our children's children, no matter what weapon they choose.

If I have anything close to a patron saint in my life, I guess it would have to be Teddy Roosevelt. He was a president who not only hunted with a professional passion but also dedicated millions and millions of acres in national parks and forests for others to enjoy. He was also a person who did not let others dictate his destiny. Above all else, it was his spirit that has influenced me to keep going when smarter people than I suggested I slow down or quit.

Don't judge too harshly a man who is willing to run the gauntlet for the greater good . . . till you've run it yourself. Theodore Roosevelt said it best:

"It is not the critic who counts, nor the man who points out how the strong man stumbled: or where the doer of deeds could have done better. The credit belongs to the man who is actually in the arena; whose face is marred by dust, sweat and blood, who strives valiantly; who errs and comes short again and again; who knows great enthusiasms, great devotions, who spends himself in a worthy cause; who, at best, knows in the end the triumph of high achievement; and who, at the worst, if he fails, at least fails while daring greatly, so that his place shall never be with those cold and timid souls who have known neither victory nor defeat."

I've done my best to help preserve our hunting heritage and conserve wildlife. I will continue to do so until too weary to play chess any further. That day will come when my life has passed! It's up to you to do the same, at whatever capacity you can, or watch our hunting heritage fall by the wayside.

I have written twenty-seven stories of my North American bowhunting experiences. Some hunts were successful; some were not. Some provided me with new friends and everlasting memories—others, with reality checks.

I have elected to tell my stories because I am convinced that there are innumerable others in America, and the world, just like me: ordinary people who can achieve the extraordinary goals we set for ourselves if we are willing to take the risk.

I have learned a great deal from hunting about both people and life. What success I have had can be measured by laughter and tears, especially the laughter and tears of others who have influenced my life through hunting. Many of them have often inspired me to keep going.

If you really want to get to know a man, share a hunting camp with him. Since hunting with each of you is an impossibility, I hope that you will get to know who I am as you read. As you hunt with me, I hope you will enjoy our new friendship.

I trust there is knowledge here that you will carry with you when you take your dream hunt. It is my further hope that after you read my stories, you will seek your own hunting stories. Set new goals and make it happen. Believe me, you will not regret your time spent with nature and man. Good hunting.

# Acknowledgments

To put together a book like this is no easy task. Many people have influenced my hunting life and made it possible for me to relate these stories. Although there is not enough room here to acknowledge them all, I will name a few who have influenced me most.

I thank my children, Gary and Chris, for their love and respect as I pursued my hunting passion.

To the family of friends I live and work with each day, who have encouraged me and supported me in many ways, I send my thanks. My friend and legal counsel, Thomas Andrews. My friend Merle Shepard: young, yet so wise for his years, who taught me, among other things, so much about the conservation of wildlife and how to meet the challenges of preserving the tradition of hunting. I must acknowledge his untiring and relentless efforts on behalf of all hunters and the conservation of wildlife. A very special thank you!

Bill Childress: a childhood friend and hunting partner with whom I shared many first-time hunting experiences in the woods of Michigan.

Rich, Al, and Albert Miller, my neighbors, who befriended a young boy and nurtured his passion for the outdoors, hunting, and fishing.

Paul and Cathy Donohoe of Nye, Montana. I've hunted with them for twenty years and feel I've become part of their family. I learned a great deal about many things from them and will always treasure our friendship.

Bob Easterbrook, Sr., who was instrumental in getting me involved in serving others through Safari Club International.

There is an endless list of very special outfitters, guides, and their support people who assisted me on so many special hunting adventures—adventures that encompassed six continents and seventeen countries around the world. Those people helped make my accomplishments possible.

It pains me that I can't acknowledge and credit every person who helped, but in the space allowed I will acknowledge these extraordinary people:

Alexander Lisitsin, Russia/Asia
The late Natie Oelofse and Pattie Curtis, Africa
Ivan Romo Pavlovich, Mexico

Greg and Fay Williams, Canada
Rick Guinn, Canada
Brian Swift and Glen Venus, Canada
Sam Fejes, Alaska
Butch Thompson, Texas
Paul and Cathy Donohoe, Montana

Special friends in the archery industry:

Jay Scholes and the OUTTECH, Inc., organization
Hoyt USA
Easton Companies
Simms Vibration Laboratory
Scent Blocker/Robinson Labs
New Archery Products
WolfCreek Productions

A special thanks to all who made this book possible.

## Accomplishments

As a commercial pilot for North Central, Republic, and Northwest Airlines during the period of government deregulation and airline cutbacks, Gary was elected by his fellow pilots to serve as their ALPA (Airline Pilots Association) representative and councilman. He represented the airline pilots through two airline mergers and three labor contracts. After eighteen years of flying he was forced to take a medical retirement. His flying experience took him to many cities, and his conversations with hunters further enlightened him and gave him a greater appreciation for diverse wildlife conservation issues facing hunters across the United States.

Gary obtained a Michigan real estate broker's license and a general contractor's license after leaving the commercial air carrier business. He developed and designed both commercial and residential properties throughout western Michigan. He currently owns and operates varied real estate properties, businesses, and investments.

Gary has actively served on numerous hospital committees, corporate boards, and on the board of a publicly owned bank. He continues to be involved in charitable functions within his western Michigan community.

Gary has hunted on six continents and seventeen countries. He has been fortunate enough to harvest more than 125 species of big game animals with a bow. Gary was the number five man among the current eight bowhunters to complete the North American Super Slam (taking all twenty-eight North American big-game animals with a bow). Gary was also thankful to be the eleventh bowhunter to complete the North American Grand Slam of Sheep.

Gary's bowhunting travels have taken him to Africa, where he took the African Big Six: elephant, rhino, hippo, Cape buffalo, lion, and leopard. Gary was fortunate enough to take all six species on one safari, thanks to the hard work and dedication of his PH, Natie Oelofse, and crew.

In May 1991, Gary was the first bowhunter to travel to Russia, pioneering modern-day bowhunting there and teaching the history of bowhunting to all who would listen. Gary made eight trips to Russia. He always brought extra brand-new Hoyt bows as gifts and taught all who expressed an interest in shooting a bow. Gary was the first bowhunter on record to take a Russian Kamchatka brown bear. Gary also had the good fortune to take a Marco Polo sheep in Tajikistan, on a hunt that took place at fifteen thousand feet above sea level and higher. He taught everyone he could about bowhunting and how to shoot a bow.

Of all his adventures, however, Gary feels that one of his greatest accomplishments was taking his first white-tailed deer with a bow. "It was a doe, and she was a dandy. It took me nine years, from age twelve to twenty-one, to figure out how to get one!"

Gary is a life member of Safari Club International/First for Hunters (SCI/SCIF) and has served two terms as president of the SCI/SCIF board of directors. He has served on numerous SCI committees. His past favorite was being chairman of the SCI Alternative Hunting and Archery Committee. He has also been the president of the SCI World Bow Hunters Chapter and served as an SCI Regional Representative for all SCI bowhunting chapters. Gary is also an SCI master measurer.

Gary's memberships include Boone and Crockett Club (B&C); Pope and Young Club (P&Y); life memberships in Foundation of North American Wild Sheep (FNAWS), International Professional Hunters' Association (IPHA), the National Rifle Association (NRA), the Rocky Mountain Elk Foundation, Grand Slam Club, and the Alaska, Michigan, and Lone Star Bow Hunters Associations; and the Alaska, Wyoming, and British Columbia Guides and Outfitters Association.

Right now, Gary's heart is dedicated to SCI, the conservation of wildlife, and the protection of hunting (SCI First for Hunters). One of his strong beliefs is that all sportsmen must work to put back more into conservation efforts than they take. Wildlife is a renewable resource, and hunting plays an important role in wildlife management. He also believes that the heritage and future of hunting depend on sportsmen and their actions and inactions.

"It is sad to see the majority of hunters and outdoorsmen and women stand on the sidelines and simply watch our rights as hunters be challenged every day. It is discouraging to see only a few of the millions of hunters stand up and help take on the antihunting organizations. Just recently People for the Ethical Treatment of Animals (PETA) and the Humane Society joined forces. That organization now has $85 million in assets and $125 million in annual income. We need our masses to stand up and help fight this 'dragon.' At the very least, we need people to join a conservation, prohunting cause and donate their membership and subscription fees to help finance the battle. Get involved. Join the effort in whatever capacity you are capable. Preserving hunting and passing on the hunting tradition also preserves the conservation of wildlife. Without hunting and the donations and fees accumulated because of it, there will be no conservation of wildlife."

In 1995 Gary received the SCI World Bow Hunters Hall of Honor Award for exhibiting the highest degree of integrity, success in the field, and lifetime contribution to the past and future growth of bowhunting and archery. Fred Bear was the first recipient of this award.

In March 2002 a special honor was given to Gary during the 107$^{th}$ U.S. congressional session. The Honorable James Barcia of Michigan in the U.S. House of Representatives recognized Gary as the international ambassador of bowhunting and presented him with a reading of his hunting and archery accomplishments into the Congressional Record.

In spite of Gary's many awards for service to the archery and hunting world, his major interest still remains spreading the word nationally and internationally about bowhunting, wildlife conservation, and preserving the hunting heritage for generations to come.

Chapter 1

# Patience and the Mystical Peak Dwellers—Dall Sheep

I had dreamed of hunting sheep since the days when I chased rabbits in the back woodlot as a kid. Back then I read every outdoor magazine I could get my hands on, cover to cover. I paid particular attention to stories about hunting wild sheep in the Northwest Territories. The Northwest Territories! Just the name made it sound like a frontier far beyond my reach. What few pictures were in the magazines displayed mountains that looked unreal. My imagination and those few pictures would do the country, I learned later, very little justice.

As life would have it, it was many, many years later before my wife, Nanette, and I attended our first Foundation for North American Wild Sheep convention. Although I had continued to read all I could about sheep hunting, including many of Jack O'Connor's adventures, I had no idea that the seed planted years before was about to grow so wildly—a seed that would sprout sheep hunting adventures and new friendships around the world.

At the show we met Greg and Fay Williams of Nahanni Butte Outfitters, a couple who outfitted for Dall sheep in the Mackenzie Mountains of the Northwest Territories. A new friendship was born, and I booked my first Dall sheep hunt.

I took my first Dall sheep with a rifle, and the trip was one of the most memorable experiences of my life. Even though I sustained a major knee injury, I was able to take a beautiful 39-inch ram, thanks to the dedicated help of Greg and his professional guides. But what amazed me most was the scenery. The country filled me with awe. Until you lay eyes upon the cathedrals of the Northwest Territories, you truly have no concept of how magnificent and vast that world is. It is a world away from the world, a place of endless majesty. Truly, it is a place everyone should visit to

*As the sheep went down, emotion ran high, and I gave thanks.*

reinforce an awareness of the power and beauty of nature. I simply couldn't stay away.

Consequently, I booked another hunt with Greg and pursued the wild white sheep again. This time, however, I took both a bow and a rifle. Greg decided to fly me in to an area where he figured the sheep had never seen a white man. It was so far north of Greg's main camp that we had to stop at a fuel cache Greg had hidden. The mountains were wide-open slopes with few rock outcroppings and very short grass.

The country there made stalking sheep extremely difficult. There was very little cover, and after many days and a final, frustrating stalk on rams just out of bow range, Greg suggested that I take one with the rifle. We were down to the last few hours, so I agreed. I put my bow down and took my second Dall sheep with a rifle. As fate would have it, two rams then returned and stood at fifty yards, watching us prepare to pack out the fallen sheep. I could have arrowed either one.

I still couldn't get enough of hunting the white rams of the Northwest Territories, so I called Greg and booked yet another trip with archery equipment. Greg took me out again, to another remote area of the Territories, to find sheep virtually undisturbed by man. On that trip, unfortunately, I wounded a good ram with my bow and had to borrow a rifle from Greg to finish the job. The sheep was a beautiful, mature ram that, at the time, would have ranked well up in the record book. I was extremely glad to have recovered the wounded ram but felt bad about the poor shot. I attributed it to finger drag on the string. Some years earlier I had cut three of my fingers badly with a snow blower and had to have them sewn back in place.

We had stalked that big ram most of the day while crawling through heavy, wet snow. By the time I'd crawled up behind a small spruce within twenty yards of the sheep, my fingers were so stiff that I could hardly let go of the string. There was no doubt I had acquired a handicap detrimental to my shooting ability (a physical handicap in addition to the mental one my wife claims I have). Right then and there I vowed to start shooting with a release. Be that as it may, I wounded the sheep. It was my responsibility to put him out of the misery I'd caused, as quickly as possible. Greg was a friend and understood completely.

Then, out of sheer determination, or bullheadedness, I booked yet another sheep hunt. My wife just shook her head and mumbled something under her breath. I didn't ask her to repeat it.

That fourth trip proved to be an effort in futility. Try as we might, we just could not get into position for a shot. Don't get me wrong; it was a great trip. How frustrating it was, though, to be so close, time and time again. Those confounded rams could pick the very best places to bed—places where no cover existed for a stalk and the wind was in their favor. Their eyes seemed sharper than normal on that trip, too. Biologists say that Dall sheep have visual acuity the equivalent of a 10X binocular. I believe it's every bit of that, and more. The sheep on that trip were positively mystical, I swear. Stalk after stalk turned out impossible. Many times we would spot a big ram in a group of rams in the evening and come back the next morning to find all the rams but the big one, which had somehow vanished. We spent countless hours glassing basins with no luck. Then, typically, just when we were about to give it up, a band of sheep would appear out of nowhere. And when we thought we finally had them where we wanted them, having made the perfect stalk, they would disappear without a trace. To top it all, after ten days of hard work we finally did get into position—and I missed the shot.

I was beginning to get seriously annoyed: not at my guides and outfitter, as they always did a superb job, but at myself and those seemingly unattainable sheep. I left the Territories feeling pretty inadequate, with the conviction that as a bowhunter I didn't have enough stealth to take a sharp-eyed, mystifying Dall.

Greg telephoned the following winter, encouraging me to return and refusing to let me give up. With some reservation, but still determined, I set 12 July 1995 as the day I was to begin yet another adventure in the Mackenzie Mountains.

I was starting to get quite used to the complicated procedure of traveling from the airport, upon my arrival in the Northwest Territories, to a sheep camp on a high plateau somewhere overlooking the world. Each trip, although outwardly the same, was always a different adventure. Here's how a hunt begins with Nahanni Butte Outfitters, and how my next attempt developed.

After I had arrived at Fort Simpson for the fifth time (the fourth time with a bow), another hunter and I were picked up at the airport for a two-and-a-half-hour drive to Blackstone Park. Blackstone sits on the banks of the Nahanni River. Once in the park, we loaded our gear onto a riverboat piloted by a local native and were transported upriver to the Indian village of Nahanni. The two-hour boat ride was treacherous. Not only was the water very high and muddy from the spring runoff but, in addition, debris that the locals called "dead heads" was floating in the river. Deadheads are stumps, logs, and sometimes entire trees submerged and afloat. The murky water made those obstacles nearly impossible to detect until the boat was almost upon them. You can imagine what might happen if a boat, running hard upstream, ran into a submerged tree coming down the swollen river. In addition, many shifting and hidden sand bars made navigation tricky. In several instances, the "pucker factor" was 9.5! Although the river was wide and slow, it was powerful. To give you an idea of how large the Nahanni River is, Nahanni Falls, which was upriver a good distance from our position, is second in size only to Niagara.

In addition to the river hazards, the air was infested with mosquitoes and black flies. We were at risk of being lifted off the boat and carried away! Gallons of Deet bug repellent, a bug jacket, and a head net were required apparel. The bugs were unbelievable!

*Gary's fourth Dall sheep hunt and his first Dall ram taken with a bow. Mackenzie Mountains, Northwest Territories, July 1995.*

We reached the village and base camp without incident, although a small group of rare wood bison threatened to tip our boat over during a short stop along the way. Greg was waiting to greet us as we docked the boat. It was old home week for me as we got reacquainted. Greg told us that there were two other hunters and a couple of guides coming upriver, and that camp would soon be full for the opener. The first hunt would consist of four bowhunters and two rifle hunters. Greg's outfit was becoming well known for guiding bowhunters to Dall sheep, and I was hoping for the best. We had arrived on 13 July and would have another day to get ready before the opening on 15 July. These hunts take place early because winter has set in solidly by late September in the Territories. Nobody wants to be in the Mackenzie Mountains after the first of October.

After a great dinner prepared by the camp staff, most of us drifted out to the bunkhouse and began repacking our gear into our backpacks. Greg's trips are backpacking affairs. He provides a good equipment and clothing checklist ahead of time, suggesting the weight a hunter should carry while hiking and the total weight to be carried on board the plane.

Freeze-dried food, a few canned goods, and spring water were the norm. The water was generally gathered at a seep not far from the campsite. Greg would then fly hunter and guide, in a modified Super Cub, to a given area for a ten-day hunt.

The next morning we were up early with anticipation over the approaching hunt. But Mother Nature had other ideas. First she sent the wood bison to camp to ransack the place during the night—their damage included tipping over garbage cans and rubbing against Greg's airplane. They bent a wing strut and punctured the fabric on the plane's fuselage in several places, requiring some work by Greg and me to fix it. On top of that, she blanketed the area with a heavy fog and no wind. It would take half the day for the fog to burn off and flights to begin into the mountains.

It took two trips out and back for each hunter, plus guide and gear, and the flights varied from thirty minutes to two and a half hours, depending on the area being hunted. It was decided that our camp would be the last to go. The other hunters and I assisted with loading the plane, and after it took off some of us fired a few last-minute practice shots with our bows. My guide this year would be Mike Ukrainetz, who had guided several bowhunters to the largest rams taken in the last two years. Deep within me began to grow an exciting anticipation of another Dall sheep hunt.

As our turn to fly out approached, so did the roar of the wind and a fast-moving weather front. We could see the disappointment on Greg's face when he returned. There would be no more trips until the weather cleared. That meant spending another night in base camp and losing at least one day of hunting. I had learned over the past years of sheep hunting—and my many years as an airline pilot—that there are only three things called for when bad weather like this sets in: patience, patience, and still more patience. It wasn't all bad, though, as we had a great and long overdue talk that evening about past adventures.

At five o'clock the next morning the wind was still howling. Our departure would again be delayed. However, by evening the breeze had relented, and Greg decided to see if he could get over the first big mountain range. He took Mike and a small fly camp in case things looked good. I was told to be ready to leave in about an hour. Greg was soon back with good news. Mike was setting up camp. We threw my gear in and were off! During the forty-five-minute flight we observed a good number of sheep. I could feel the anticipation building.

Our camp was situated on a mountain plateau, allowing us to travel the top and hunt down the many timbered fingers and slopes. There wasn't as much cover as I like for stalking, but the country was definitely to my liking. In past years we had spotted sheep where the terrain was much too demanding for me: The chances of my getting to the sheep were good but of getting back in one piece, slim. I welcomed the opportunity to hunt gentler country.

Mike had set up camp nicely. Water was only a few steps from the tent, which is a luxury in that part of the world. He had also spotted some good rams just a couple of miles away. It couldn't get much better! Greg's parting words were, "Remember, patience. Wait until they get into a stalkable position."

In the north at this time of year, the hours of daylight are long and the hours of darkness short. That's a good thing when it comes time for a fatigued guide and hunter to head back to camp: Darkness isn't much of a problem. However, it's hard to sleep because of the extended daylight. Of course, anticipation of what the next day may bring adds to that problem.

We quickly spotted the sheep that Mike had seen the previous evening. There were two mature rams in the group, and we decided to go after them. The sheep fed from the valley floor up into a boulder field, where they bedded in front of a boulder the size of a garage. We needed to get to a better spot, so we worked our way around to a position just above them. A short evaluation showed that a stalk was out of the question. The sheep had picked a great place, from their standpoint, and were bedded in such a way that they could see 360 degrees. There was nothing to do but wait for them to get up again and bed where they could be stalked. We waited all day. They moved several times, but always they bedded in open terrain.

Dall sheep are notorious for hanging a bowhunter out to dry. You plan a stalk, get into position, and the sheep have moved when you get there. Or they have vanished completely. Another common disappointment is that you get to where you want to be and find that there is a hundred-yard space (which had looked like thirty yards from a distance) between you and the sheep, and there is absolutely no cover. Consequently, you are pinned down, sunburned (I should say cooked to a crisp), tired, and

*Gary poses with his first Dall sheep taken with a rifle in 1986.*

thirsty. You either give up, spook the sheep, and walk away, or the rams amble over the next mountain range. Slightly exasperating? Those are not the words I'd like to use!

We decided to take a look at one more pocket before going back to camp—and we ran smack-dab into a group of sheep. We hit the ground and began glassing. What we saw was a bunch of ewes and lambs and eight rams, several of which were mature. The rams were only 150 yards away but presented no opportunity for a stalk. We eased back out of the little basin and made a plan for the next morning.

Back in camp, while watching the water boil to bring our freeze-dried supper to life, I thought of how many trips I had made in pursuit of these impossible critters. It seemed harder this time, somehow. Maybe I was a bit panicky about being able to pull this off. I gazed up at the heights above our campsite and wondered what really had brought me here once more. Was it just the burning desire to be among the select few who have succeeded in taking all the North American sheep with a bow, or was it something else, something within? A doubt about myself, maybe? A doubt that I needed to put to rest? Or was I simply here to take in all that nature has to show, to catch a little piece of what the hunters of long ago had experienced, and to get away from the lunacy of the real world? Maybe it was all of those things. I truly wasn't sure, but I had a feeling that one day the true reasons would come clear.

The following morning we checked on the group of rams we had stalked the day before, but again we found them in a poor position to stalk. We were almost back to the spot where we had seen the other sheep when we ran headlong into the ewes and lambs—again. The rams, however, weren't with them. We managed to work our way around the group without being seen, and upon reaching a high point from which to glass, we began our search for the missing rams. Much to our surprise, we found that we had walked right by them while sneaking around the ewes and lambs. Frustrated, we raced back down the ridge. Then, peering over a small knoll, we found them just below us—as usual in a bad spot. To add to our problems, a single small ram was lying between us and the mature animals, with no way around him.

To keep from being winded, we backed away and found another spot on higher ground. It was time to reach down for some more patience, and we waited for a stalk to develop. After a considerable time, the sheep began to feed. The small ram fed within twenty-five yards of us and pinned us down with his sharp eyes. Mike and I lay motionless for what seemed like hours. I had time to become intimately familiar with the moss on the rocks my face was pressed against.

Our bodies were beginning to cramp when, finally, the little whelp turned around and lay down facing away from us. The big rams were feeding toward us, and they looked as though they might pass within range just below. Even if they did, though, we couldn't move unless the young ram moved. To top things off, a big thunderstorm had moved in and begun drenching us. But we weren't moving for anything!—that is, unless a lightning bolt tapped us on the shoulder.

We waited for at least another hour. Finally, the little ram got up and made its way down the slope in the direction in which we had last seen the other rams move. We inched our petrified bodies out onto a ledge and spotted the big rams directly below us, but still out of range. They got up again and began feeding in the opposite direction. Suddenly, the little ram ran in and tried to join the big boys. The older sheep would have nothing

*A happy bowhunter headed for camp and some sheep steaks.*

to do with him and began to run. We watched them circle the mountain, stopping only momentarily to grab a few bites of grass, until they at last reached the far end of another ridge, four miles away. Frustration is not the word! Devastating defeat is more like it. Neither of us could believe our eyes or understand why that had happened.

The walk back to camp was the longest I'd ever remembered. Over hot tea and another freeze-dried supper, we spoke very little. When we did speak, it was to try to explain the events of the day. As always, we second-guessed ourselves and went through the "what we should have done" riddles. I reassured Mike that there was nothing we could do about any of it. It just wasn't my time. Silently, though, I thought, *Maybe I'm not meant to get a Dall ram with my bow.* I slept very little that night. My mind replayed the day's events a hundred times.

The following morning we slept in and ate a quiet breakfast. It was only the third day, but we were pretty tired, both mentally and physically. We decided to check the basins we'd explored over the last few days before trying some new country. Upon crossing the flat where Greg had landed his airplane, we spotted two rams on top of a ridge just ahead. They were two of the rams we had been after previously. We backtracked until we couldn't see the sheep and made a two-hour trek around the mountain. The rams had fed farther out onto the plateau, allowing us to come in behind and above them. Again, it was time to wait. And wait we did—all day while the sheep napped and fed. Although not quite offering us a stalk, they were nevertheless making their way around the base of the ridge toward us. I was starting to grit my teeth a little, but I heard Greg's parting words once more: "Patience!" I knew that was the only way, but this was hard.

Along toward evening, the rams got up and began feeding in our direction. We discussed a few tactics but decided to stay put. As the time slowly passed, we realized that we were going to have to make a move before we ran out of light. While carefully making our way around a knoll, we bumped two other young rams that we hadn't seen. They ran toward the rams we were stalking. Looking skyward, I shook my head. Mike had a few choice words for the situation, too. The only thing left to do, though, was to continue and assess the damage. We bellied toward the edge for a look.

Mike crept into position, then turned back with a thumbs-up. He motioned for me to stay down, as one of the rams was looking our way. He reached carefully into his coat and pulled out my Leica Geovid binocular/rangefinder. I felt a surge of excitement and swallowed hard. Mike turned his head in my direction, slowly, and whispered the range. It was a lot farther than I liked. I needed to think.

I had spent the previous months honing my skill at shooting long distances—hoping I'd never have to. I was proficient at those ranges, though, and felt confident. Longtime friend Jay Scholes had loaned me his bow, a Hoyt Defiant Fastflite, before the hunt because of its speed and flat shooting ability. It was the newest and the best. Again Mike whispered the range and probed, "What do you want to do? We aren't gonna get any closer." I closed my eyes, said a quick prayer, and nodded my head.

Ever so slowly I pulled my legs up and under me, allowing me to rise up on my knees while sitting back on my heels. I needed a good, steady platform from which to shoot, yet I had to maintain a low profile. Mike suggested that I come to full draw before rising up. We would rise up together so that he could range the closer big ram. We both began to rise, only to find the sheep glaring at us. Mike quickly relayed the range, and mentally I tried to calculate the allowance for our elevation difference. I was also concentrating on settling down when suddenly the arrow was gone—flying over the big ram's back. I nocked another arrow as the group of sheep took a couple of quick bounds and started milling. When they stopped for another look, Mike whispered a range of eighty yards. Miffed at myself now, I brought the bow back smooth and easy this time. I anchored, rock solid, behind the big ram's front shoulder, gritted my teeth, and let fly. The ram bolted and began to run hard. Mike hollered, "You got him!"

A crimson spot on the side of the sheep's chest began to grow with each stride, and he tumbled after a short sixty-yard sprint. Neither of us could believe we'd finally done it. It was a triumph that had begun to seem impossible. But there he lay. The emotions ran strong, as they always do when an accomplishment comes so hard. We congratulated each other with a hearty handshake and a sizable hug.

And what a ram this was. His sweeping horns were almost identical and measured 37 inches and change. He would score somewhere in the neighborhood of the mid-150s. But that was irrelevant to me now because at last I had taken a mystical white ram of the Northwest Territories with my bow. I had a mature ram. What more could this sheep hunter ask? We spent some time reviewing the day's events and discussing the hazards of a sheep's life in the wilderness. And then we admired this magnificent trophy Dall sheep some more.

I slept like a rock that night and awoke more rested than I had in weeks. The first thing I did (like a little kid) was to run over to where we had buried the cape and horns. We'd buried them the night before to hide them from the many grizzlies roaming the area. I had to make sure they were still there, as well as to confirm that this wasn't just a dream. Mike and I uncovered the sheep and began fleshing the cape for the trip home in a few days. As we were salting and rolling the cape, we both stopped to listen. The faint drone of an airplane engine wafted through the basin. A low pass and a wave of wings told us that Greg was going to land. We grabbed the horns and raced for the top of the hill where Greg had already landed and was headed in our direction. I held the ram's horns over my head and shouted. Greg sported a big smile and congratulated both Mike and me. He said, "I figured you would get it done sooner or later. I sure hoped it would be this year."

*A spike camp situated at the base of the mountains, where there were lots of grizzly bears. Nahanni Butte, Mackenzie Mountains, NWT, 1990.*

As our plane cleared the end of the high plateau I thanked the Almighty for the many blessings and good fortune He had given me. I also offered thanks for having experienced the Northwest Territories more times than any man should have a right to. But, more important, I thanked Him for the lifelong friendships developed, and the many people who were instrumental in making my Dall sheep hunting dreams come true.

Now, as to why I push myself so hard in these quests, I can't quite find a handle. All I know is that it becomes a spiritual issue, a challenge to a man's inner soul and hunting skills. It is the hunter against himself, the hunter against the elements. The hunt defines a man in certain ways that I don't yet fully understand.

Chapter 2

# Michigan White-Tailed Deer

*In the first chapter of this book I shared with you one of my most difficult challenges with a bow, the Dall sheep, in order to give you an idea of what is to come. That adventure, however, could never have taken place without the hunts that follow.*

I was born of a young mother, Ardeen Parker, whose parents came from farms on the Muskegon River near Maple Island, Michigan, and fathered by a young man, Frank Martin, who had a deep love for the outdoors, having been raised in the Bear Lake area. So it is no wonder that I was stumping the fields with my bow in search of pheasants and rabbits at the age of twelve. In addition, my parents bought a small log cabin on the banks of the White River while I was still very young. It was only twenty-five miles from home, and I spent every possible minute there, exploring the surrounding woods, fishing, and hunting.

From lawn care with a push reel mower to bicycle repair at the local Gambles hardware store, I had some type of a job for as long as I can remember. The Gambles store carried some sporting goods, such as hunting and fishing equipment. I purchased my first deer hunting rifle there—a bolt-action Stevens .30-30.

Whenever I didn't have to work or had finished just enough homework to stay out of trouble, I was outdoors in the summer shooting my bow and fishing, and then hunting for the entire fall season. I even hunted rabbits right up to the close of the season in the deep snow with our trusty black-and-tan hound Prince—anything to prolong the seasons.

When I was about twelve years of age, I bought my first real manufactured cedar arrows. I was thrilled. Before that I had made my arrows out of wooden dowels from Gambles.

*This is Gary's first whitetail, taken with a rifle when he was sixteen, near Horseshoe Lake, Holton, Michigan, 1958.*

At the age of fourteen I could start whitetail hunting legally with my bow or gun. I could pursue that passion, however, only when my parents chose to go to the cabin—until the age of sixteen. Then I was allowed to drive there alone.

I can remember the fall that I turned fourteen. My birthday is 10 October, so I had missed only the first weekend of the archery season. I still remember the anticipation and excitement. I couldn't sleep, and I hardly ate a thing.

I hunted alone that weekend, as my parents were busy with other grown-ups who had come out to the cabin. The gathering was nothing fancy, you understand, all just hard-working people looking to get away for a while. I tried as hard as I could that week just to see a deer. I sat at the base of an old pine tree dressed in green for hours. Then I tried to tiptoe through the still, green forest. I saw little other than the occasional rabbit or grouse. Once in a while I'd catch the flash of a whitetail at a great distance. Those animals must have wondered what "it" was, what "it" was doing there, and if "it" were lost. Fifty years later, I think that many critters are still thinking the same thing.

But I didn't give up that season, even though I didn't get close to a whitetail. You must understand that tree stands—or getting off the ground while hunting—weren't legal at that time in Michigan. I don't believe there were manufactured blinds in those days, either. The only scent control I learned about, some years later, was putting pinecones in a bag with your clothes, and placing pine and spruce cones around where you sat. That was real stealth technology back then, according to the experts.

For some years I worked a lot and was able to bowhunt only on Sundays or maybe on a day off. Although it was easier to get a few days off for the traditional 15 November whitetail firearm season, that lasted only fifteen days or so. Michigan had close to a million hunters back then, and they called them the "Red Army."

In November of 1958 I was rifle hunting with special friends and neighbors Rich, Al, and Albert Miller at Horseshoe Lake, just south of our cabin. I was also hunting with a young man my own age from Holton, Michigan. The weather had turned very wintry, and we were slowly following some deer tracks in a heavy snowstorm. A small eight-point buck walked out in front of us about one hundred yards away, and we both fired at the same moment. When we got to the buck, there was only one bullet hole from our .30-30s, so we divided the meat and both took credit for the kill. It was the first buck for both of us.

In those days I also hunted and fished with a high school and neighborhood friend, Bill Childress. We started a small archery shop together when I was seventeen, and we were able to borrow enough money to purchase the inventory. By the 1960s I had a couple new bows. Both were made by a local man, Glen Wilson. We sold his custom bows in our shop. I had a 36-pound-draw target bow and a 45-pound hunting bow.

As I recall, it wasn't until I was twenty-one or so that I got my first shot at a white-tailed deer from a ground blind with a bow. It was at my maximum shooting distance, approximately thirty yards. I was so excited when the small doe came by that I must have shot three feet over her back. The arrow was so high over her back, in fact, that she didn't spook. She just looked around with an expression that seemed to say, "What was that?" Then she wandered off, probably to tell the other animals about the strange things flying around the woods. Despite all my practicing and my being so

*The Bogner cabin on White River, Hesperia, Michigan, October 1958.*

confident, I had missed by a mile. But nothing prepares a person for buck fever—or doe fever, in this case.

It wasn't until 1963 that I finally shot my first whitetail. It was late October and almost the end of bow season. I was hunting the property surrounding the folks' old cabin. It was a Sunday morning, and I had driven up early to be there before daylight. I crept into an alfalfa field and followed the edge of the woods line to a small strip of trees separating the field from another meadow. I had a brush blind built about twenty-five yards off a deer trail. Reaching the blind without making noise wasn't easy because of all the dry leaves. The surrounding oak, maple, and poplar trees had laid a carpet of leaves, in addition to which there had been a good frost. After I'd perched for a while on my knees, I got up to stretch. I sat back down on my frosty old bucket and thought that I should have been dressed a bit more warmly. I was starting to shiver when I heard something coming in from my left. It sounded as though it was on the trail I was watching. My heart began to race until I could hear the pulse in my ears.

I nocked an arrow and took off my right-hand glove. I was using a "Can't Pinch Finger Tab" back then. It seemed like forever before I got a glimpse of what was coming. I suddenly realized that it was a nice white-tailed doe. It wasn't a buck, but that was all right. *Maybe this is the day,* I thought. There was almost no wind; the feather hanging from a string on my bow confirmed that. The deer finally reached my shooting lane and was in no hurry. I felt sure she didn't know I was there. The anticipation was building, and when she stepped into the lane and looked away, I could not wait any longer. I drew the 45-pound Wilson recurve and anchored. When the sight picture looked right, I released. The Easton arrow tipped with a Bear Razor went on its way. This time it was true to the spot, and the deer bolted.

I sat for about thirty minutes, shivering and trembling. Finally, deciding I'd waited long enough, I crept quietly over to the trail. I proceeded down the path about ten yards before I found what every bowhunter is looking for: pink-reddish blood on the leaves. I continued to move slowly down the trail, looking ahead and watching the ground. After about 150 yards I found my first white-tailed deer. It was a nice, big doe, and I was proud of her—and I do mean proud! I didn't have a camera, so I took out my trusty knife and took care of things. I was eager to get her out of the woods and loaded onto my car so I could take her back to town to show my friends. The venison was great eating, too.

It was four or five years later before I got my next white-tailed deer, a small and unusual three-point buck. I was on the Muskegon River flats, hunting where my good friends, the Millers, had taken me so many times as a youngster. I'd had to go up the river several miles in a small boat in the dark and get around three or four logjams. It was risky all by myself, but it was a great spot. I saw very few people up there that time of year, too. I was sitting just off the ground on the fallen trunk of a large, old cottonwood tree, where I had built a small three-sided screen made of brown burlap bags. My stand was back from the riverbank about forty yards or so, and a game trail ran parallel to the river, some five or ten yards from the bank.

I had been sitting for less than an hour on that late-October morning when I heard the deer coming. It didn't have any idea I was there, and I felt

*After fifty-two years of hunting whitetails, I still experience the thrill of the hunt and love the challenge. The 2005 hunting season.*

lucky that morning. I was still shooting the 45-pound Wilson recurve and the aluminum arrows that I had made almost ten years before. Now I also had a state-of-the-art three-finger glove.

As the deer approached, I drew. I couldn't hold too long because I hadn't been doing a lot of practicing that year, because of work. I was just about at my endurance limit when the young buck went by the last big tree on the trail, entered a good shooting lane, and looked toward the river. I released the string and watched the Bear Razor tip go into his chest cavity. The turkey feathers disappeared just behind the front leg.

I had been calm up to that point, to my surprise, but the shakes hit me hard as I watched the deer bound up the trail. This time it was a very short run. I never lost sight of the buck all the way to the ground. I was out of my blind in a bolt and running. This white-tailed buck, my first with a bow, wasn't going to get away from me, no matter what.

When I got to him, less than fifty yards away, he was stone-dead. I remember quietly saying, "I got him." With each repetition of those words, my voice became louder. I suddenly realized that I was almost shouting.

I took care of things, pulled out my archery tag, and put it on my first white-tailed buck. I was going to drag it back down the trail along the riverbank to where I had tied up the boat, but I finally came to my senses and realized that I could bring my boat upriver, right to the buck. For a moment I wasn't sure I wanted to leave him there while I went for the boat. Better judgment prevailed, though, and I retrieved the boat, loaded the deer, and headed back downriver to the Giles Road boat landing. I remember seeing a couple guys at the landing and being real proud showing them my buck. They congratulated me and wanted to hear the whole story.

I will never forget those early days, when life was much simpler. Money was tight and I had a new family and responsibilities, but life seemed more manageable and to move at a slower pace. I was thankful for the success, and the meat was going to be handy on our tight budget. What a day to remember.

*******

One thing I learned in the early years was that I was not a born woodsman. Success always came hard. Also, because of family and work, it would be some years before I got the next buck—but that was OK. I knew that someday I would be able to have more time and more opportunities to hunt, as well as be able to participate in the management and conservation of whitetails. And, with any luck, maybe I'd hunt and help manage even bigger game in faraway places. If only I had known what life had in store.

I must spend a few words here to thank my old friends the Millers, whom I haven't seen in years; I need to look them up before it's too late. I would also like to thank others like the Hannahs and the Burtons. Those people, and our adventures together, made big and lasting impressions on a young boy. Thank you for all of those wonderful hunting and fishing trips you shared with me. And God bless.

Chapter 3

# Mule Deer

My first trip mule deer hunting was in 1979, with a friend of mine and older hunting partner, Joe Verschueren, a veterinarian. Joe and I had hunted several times together, including a trip for moose and caribou early in both of our hunting careers. Joe was twenty years my senior and a great guy to hunt with. He had been invited on a hunt out West, and someone in the group had canceled: He wondered if I wanted to fill the spot. It was a combination deer and elk rifle hunt on a ranch owned by Arnold George. We went with the group in 1979 and 1980.

The next year we weren't invited back, so we looked for a hunting spot close by. We had both enjoyed the country and the people out West, especially Arnold and his wife, and the cook there, Noel, had told us about a neighboring ranch operated by Arnold's daughter and her husband, Paul and Cathy Donohoe. Noel said that Paul was starting a hunting operation and was a good hand. He had done quite a bit of hunting and had a lot of experience with packstrings for the Forest Service in Montana.

I called Paul and asked if he had space left for four. He said he had plenty of room. I asked about the first week of the season, and he replied that we could have that slot if I sent a $500 deposit right away. The first week of the rifle season in Montana is generally the third week in October. I asked if we could have that first week—for life—if we left a standing deposit and then paid in full each year. He agreed, and that is how our relationship began.

Of course, we really didn't know what we had in the way of an outfitter, and they didn't know what kind of dudes they were getting hooked up with. I picked one of my friends, Dr. Gordon Heller, to be a part of the group, and Joe picked one of his, Franky Thomas. The fall of 1981 proved to be a tough

*Cathy Donohoe, Dr. Peirpont, David Russell (patient), and Tom Demoupolous (left to right). David is eating a sandwich while Dr. Peirpoint sews him up.*

year in Montana because of drought and hot weather. We saw a few elk, but none of the group got one. We did get our mule deer, though, and everyone was happy about that.

Paul was sure, though, that we were upset about the results of the hunt, and he figured we would never be back. When we left, we reassured him that we certainly would. He said later that he'd had his doubts whether we really would be back. That first trip was the beginning of a twenty-year relationship. The only year I missed was 1983.

In 1982 I was invited to attend a branding on the Donohoe ranch. That was quite an education for a city kid. Then, a couple years later, I went out in the fall and helped with the roundup of cattle from BLM and Forest Service lands in the mountains. We gathered cattle with all the surrounding ranch neighbors—another good education for a Michigan dude. I also took a few spring trips to Paul and Kathy's place over the years on spring bear hunts. I was lucky enough, one year, to get in on a bear tagging and trapping program with the Game and Fish Department.

*First mule deer taken with a compound bow, Nye, Montana, 1990.*

*Hunting party at the Donohoe's ranch (from left): Dr. D. Peirpont, Pete Metros, Chris Bogner, and Gary Bogner. This was a very successful season, Nye, Montana, 1988.*

I didn't start taking my bow on those yearly hunts until 1986. That year was a special one for me because it was the first year that my son Chris came along. He generally didn't hunt, but once he'd gone to the Donohoe ranch he made it an annual trip. I was elated to have him with me. We've savored some good father-and-son memories there.

My bow of choice for that year, and the next, was a Hoyt recurve. Man, I was green, I realize now, thinking back over some of the unsuccessful attempts I made at stalking mule deer. Elk, too, evaded me with ease. In 1990 I brought along my first Hoyt compound bow.

One morning on that hunt I sneaked to the edge of a bowl-like basin, just over the top of a ridgeline where the Donohoes had planted some alfalfa. Depending on the year and whether there was rain, the alfalfa might draw a lot of deer, and sometimes elk, down from the hills. It was hard to get into the bowl without being seen, but it could be managed if you stayed low and followed some weedy old fence lines and irrigation ditches. The grasses, in good years, were three feet tall and provided good cover.

That morning lots of deer were feeding in there, and several were bucks. I lay in the grass and watched as the bigger bucks filtered out of the basin early, in the direction of their bedding areas. Two of them went up into the rocks, and some of the others went into the tall willows along the draw. There was no way to stalk in the willows because they were too thick.

One nice buck stopped short of the willows and bedded down. I watched him for quite a while before deciding to go around behind him on an old two-track road. I would come over the top, find him, and start my stalk. It took quite a while to get into position, and when I finally peeked over the edge, pine trees and boulders blocked my view. It must have taken me another hour to work my way down to where I thought the deer was bedded.

I wasn't too stealthy in those days, either. I remember stumbling around with two left feet and cussing myself as I tried my best not to make noise. There were two huge boulders the size of cars standing on end near where the deer had been bedded the last time I saw him. I made it to one of those boulders and started trying to locate the buck. When I found him, he was up and feeding again. I needed to get to the other boulder to be within range. There was no cover between the two rocks except grass about a foot tall. So I crawled on my belly each time the deer looked in the other direction, and surprisingly, I made it to the second boulder unnoticed.

I remember standing with my back against the boulder and getting nervous. My heart was racing a hundred miles an hour, and I was beginning to shake. The deer was right there, and I wondered how I would ever pull this off. How was I going to draw without being seen? To make matters worse, the deer was to my right and behind the rock. That setup is a bad deal for a right-handed hunter. I couldn't get a clear shot without being fairly well exposed. But I nevertheless nocked an Easton 2117 arrow and began moving away from the rock to make sure the arrow and bow would clear. I knew that deer was going to spot me before I could get into position.

I kept inching around until I was totally exposed, but the deer was nowhere to be seen. I figured that he had either heard me or caught my scent and left. I decided to go back around the way I'd come and check the other end of the rock. When I peeked around the other side of the boulder, there he was, staring at me. I quickly ducked down, thinking, *Maybe he didn't see me.* I knew very well he'd seen me. I didn't know who was a bigger idiot, him or me.

I was a little disgusted with myself and knew full well that the deer would surely be gone. Nevertheless, I drew and raised up to find him still there, wondering what I was. He was facing me head on, but I let fly anyway. We all know that's a poor shot opportunity, but back in those days I didn't know any better. The buck took off on the run and disappeared behind the boulder again. I ran to the other end to see where he would come out. I tried to nock another arrow as I ran, but I banged it against the rock, dropping the arrow onto the ground. I thought, *Man, you are one stealthy outfit! You'll be lucky if you don't run an arrow through your own gizzard!* I reached the end of the rock just in time to see the buck fall on the side of the hill across the main draw. I had just taken my first mule deer buck with a bow.

I hoofed it back to the cabin and got the truck. I returned to the deer, dressed it out, and threw it in the back. I was waiting when everyone returned. I was as proud of that mule deer buck as I had been of my first whitetail—the white-tailed doe that had taken me nine years to get.

*The author snapped this picture of his son Chris with his nice deer. It was a proud moment for both father and son, Montana, 1985.*

*First trip to outfitter Paul Donohoe's guest house, located in Nye, Montana, October 1981.*

That buck and my solitary success helped to propel me on a quest that I never dreamed I would experience, hunting the North American Twenty-Eight. More important, the Donohoe family and mine formed a friendship that has lasted for more than two decades. We feel that we are part of the same family—not just in the fall but throughout the year. Hunting is secondary, these days, to the chance to get the families together, to enjoy talking about the old days, and to catch up on family news. The relationships I have developed on my hunting adventures far outweigh my hunting accomplishments.

Mule deer hunting is where I began to develop my relationship with Jim Van Norman, the ghostwriter of these adventures you are reading. I met Jim through a mutual friend, Tom Nelson of the *American Archer* television show, at one of the old AMO archery shows somewhere back East. Safari Club had an auction at the show, and I was the speaker. Jim bought one of the hunts, which included a ride in a stunt plane owned by the donator of the hunt. We struck up a conversation about the hunt, and I learned that Jim was also a pilot. We talked about my career as an airline pilot and his

*Who says you can't take a nice mule deer with a bow during gun season? Gary is shown with his friend and outfitter, Paul Donohoe, Nye, Montana, 1994.*

early career as a flight instructor and charter pilot. I soon found that Jim had a passion for hunting, just like me. He was also an outfitter and had a great place in Wyoming for hunting mule deer. To make a long story short, I ended up booking a hunt with Jim a few years later. Here's how it went.

Jim met me at the airport in Casper, Wyoming. I had decided to film the hunt for an upcoming video and brought along a cameraman. I had had a hard time finding a cameraman that September until one of the firms doing my videos, Wolf Creek Productions, volunteered a new photographer they had just put on staff. The gentleman had a lot of experience on the camera, but this would be his first chance to film a hunt.

As we left the Casper airport, the cameraman started hollering, "Stop the car! Stop the car!"

Jim asked, "What for?"

Our cameraman replied, "To take some film of those deer right there!"

Jim rolled his eyes and mumbled, "We're in serious trouble."

The deer our cameraman was so excited about filming were pronghorn antelope. Instead of being distressed like me, though, Jim was simply amused. (The cameraman, by the way, is still with the firm and has developed into a good hunting cameraman and production assistant. He has figured out the world's different game species, too.)

We had a great hunt that week and put together a pretty decent film. In fact, the film contributed to the video called *Passport to North America, Deer and Friends.* I took a real nice mule deer buck in Wyoming and saw some huge deer that turned out to be a lot smarter than we were. We enjoyed several stalks on good-size deer but couldn't quite get into position before they caught us in the act—or the wind got us.

One scorching afternoon during the hunt, we crawled into the shade under a sand-rock overhang to eat our lunch. Jim and I began visiting about my hunting adventures in Russia and the people I'd met. I mentioned that it would be good to get some of my hunting excursions documented in a book,

*The author took this mule deer on the Van Norman ranch, Casper, Wyoming, September 2000.*

*Outfitter and writer Jim Van Norman during mule deer hunt in Casper, Wyoming, September 2000.*

or books, someday down the road. Jim had written two books on mule deer hunting and several chapters in various books for a variety of publishers. We briefly discussed putting our heads together and making a book a reality.

Jim and I seemed to develop a friendship a lot faster than normal. We found we thought a lot alike on many subjects when it came to philosophy of life and hunting. So we kept in close touch over the next few years and spent some time together on a few hunting trips. One day I decided that it was time to make the book deal happen. I asked Jim to be my ghostwriter, and he accepted—and here we are, many long hours of discussion later. Best wishes to you for several hours of good reading.

Chapter 4

# Polar Bear

The land of the midnight sun. For many years, this place and the people who live in it have fascinated me. An opportunity to go there, let alone to have a chance to see a polar bear, seemed as if it would be a dream come true. As destiny would have it, I was about to realize that dream. Not only was I going to see the Arctic, but I would also hunt the "great white bear."

The trip was set up through the booking firm of an acquaintance of mine, a firm called Expeditions by Ron the Guide. Ron also planned a meeting with Jerome Knapp of Canada North Outfitting. Jerome was well known for his ability in the North Country. Both Ron and Jerome were surprised when I announced my choice of weapon. The date was 1987, and the Whitetail II (draw weight: 55 pounds) was Fred Bear's latest-technology compound bow. Ron and Jerome commented that a polar bear hunt with bow and arrow would be a huge challenge, but it was possible. We immediately began to discuss when and where the hunt should be, and which of the well-known guides were best suited for a bowhunt. The hunt was booked for the spring of 1989 and would cost $12,000, which was a lot of money.

During the next eighteen months I worked hard preparing. In doing some research I found that a good friend of mine, Archie Nesbit, had spent some of his younger years in the Northwest Territories of Canada. He coincidentally was planning a trip to the Arctic Circle in the very same year. Archie was a dedicated sportsman and conservationist, and at the time he was the president of the Foundation for North American Big Game, headquartered in Calgary, Alberta, Canada. Archie and I began wearing out the phone lines comparing research on equipment and clothing. After months of such talk, Archie's hunting date finally arrived, and he was off to the Arctic.

*Blocks of snow were stacked to insulate the tent from wind and snow whiteouts. Located on ice some twelve hours from Resolute Bay, NWT, April 1989.*

One of the great things about this situation was that Archie would return from his hunt before I left on mine. I would have the benefit of his experience, the better to prepare for my own trip. I eagerly awaited his return and the chance to hear his story. Meanwhile, I continued to shoot daily and to ready my equipment.

Archie came home from his adventure with a polar bear squaring nine feet and a good muskox. During the remaining three weeks, I gleaned as much knowledge from Archie as possible about the Arctic Circle and the details of his hunt. Having the benefit of Archie Nesbit's experience was invaluable to me. One of the most important facts I learned was that all the clothing and boots we had chosen would be useless in the Arctic environment. The Inuit would provide me with what I needed. Another interesting fact, among many, was that feathers were the only choice for arrow fletching. Vanes were too brittle in the severe cold.

Finally, my departure date, 10 April 1989, arrived. I flew to Resolute Bay on Cornwallis Island in the Northwest Territories, just two hundred miles south of the magnetic North Pole. I stepped from the plane in the early morning hours and was hit in the face with air that was thirty below zero. Your first intake of Arctic air makes you wonder if you are truly ready for such an adventure.

After listening to some successful hunting stories by the heater that evening, and after a fair night's rest, I felt ready to go. My Inuit guides, a father-and-son team—David and Adam Ooingoot—arrived early the next morning. David Ooingoot was one of the oldest and most experienced Inuit hunters in the area. He had guided more than a hundred polar bear hunts personally and had himself taken many bears. However, he had never taken a bowhunter.

They had brought with them a complete handmade caribou-skin suit consisting of knickers, pants, a parka, boots, and mittens. Caribou hair is hollow and has superior insulation qualities. They also provided sealskin booties to be worn over bare feet inside the caribou boots. The key here: Sealskin is waterproof. No manmade fibers keep out the Arctic elements as well as caribou and sealskin. I also wore a good facemask and a pair of high-quality ski goggles. You simply cannot have any skin exposed, or it will freeze. My goggles were tinted to combat the extreme glare of the sun on the snow and ice.

At the time, only two other people had attempted to take polar bear with a bow out of Resolute Bay. The first was unsuccessful, and the second was my friend Archie Nesbit. David Ooingoot was eager to take a bowhunter and to get a polar bear. Even though he could speak no English, I managed to glean by listening to the others that David, being an elder, was insulted for not having been asked to guide the two other bowhunters. A man's hunting ability in the Arctic is sacred and is a huge part of his status in the eyes of his peers, as well as among other Inuit villages. David was a loner, living well outside the village with his family. He possessed the face, as well as the presence, of a well-seasoned Inuit elder. You could tell just by looking that this Inuit hunter had faced all that a life on the ice could deal out . . . and survived.

By early afternoon we were packing the dog sled and sleigh with gear and food. A sixteen-foot sleigh carried most of the supplies, pulled by a snow machine. There is a rule in the Arctic: All hunters of the great bears must hunt from a dog sled and are not allowed to use motorized vehicles. You can pull supplies with a machine, but the nonresident hunter

*The skull of Gary's polar bear measured 26⁰/16 inches. His Bear Whitetail II compound bow was set at 55 pounds, Resolute Bay, NWT, April 1989.*

must hunt from a sled. The huskies were whining with excitement and the desire to move out.

Our sled ride was rough. The ice was either bare or had up to eight inches of snow on it, and because the wind relentlessly drives the snow, it was packed like concrete. Also, there were ice ridges and small drifts, and that sled hammered me, jarring every bone in my body and rattling my teeth. The cold was almost unbearable, even with all the caribou clothing. David and Adam knew that the white man isn't used to such severe cold and punishment, and they would stop every two or three hours for tea or instant soup. They understood how important it is to rest and keep fueling the body at frequent intervals to fight the cold.

In some Arctic areas bears come right into the villages in search of food. In other places you can see fresh bear sign only an hour or two from the village. But, generally speaking, you are in prime bear hunting country within three to four hours via dog sled. Polar bears hunt basically whatever moves. Life on the frozen sea is tough, and the large carnivore must hunt continuously to survive. Although seals are their main source of food, polar bears also eat seabirds, lemmings, caribou, muskox, walrus, white whales, and narwhals. The polar bear is at the top of the food chain and isn't particular. Anything on the ice is fair game, man included. In fact, for a white bear to hunt and track a man is not that uncommon. Many Inuit stories tell of men being dragged from tents or ambushed coming out of a cabin or igloo. And many didn't live to tell the story. Like other bears, in the summer the polar bear will eat berries and other plant material, but 99 percent of a polar bear's diet is meat. There are about ten reported attacks per year on humans in the Arctic. Without question, the great white bear is the most dangerous bear on earth.

David had chosen a hunting area that took us eight hours to reach. As soon as we arrived, the snowmobile pulling our supplies broke down, and to top off the difficulty, the winds kicked up, causing a whiteout of frozen ice crystals. We spent the next two and a half days weathered in our tent. Let me tell you, two and a half days in a small dome tent with two guys you barely know tests your resolve.

The visibility was down to less than fifty feet at times. Our shelter consisted of a small double-walled dome tent heated only by a Coleman cookstove. There is just enough room for three people, and not an inch more. The temperature averaged between 25 and 40 degrees below zero, but, of course, the wind made it feel a lot colder. The only time I felt really warm was when I was inside my twenty-pound down sleeping bag.

On the afternoon of the third day the wind finally subsided. It was nice to be able to stay outside of the tent and see a fair distance through the cold, clear air. I also got my first look at Nanook that day. Nanook is the name the Inuit give to the polar bear. Adam explained that the name means "wanderer" or "roamer." The Inuit named him well because these white bears are, for the most part, continuously on the move hunting. An adult bear can stride across the ice in an unorthodox-looking shuffle at a steady 2½ miles an hour. Many times, the bear's acute sense of smell will drive it to cover huge distances on just a scent of food. They are magnificent animals, and I broke out in goose bumps the size of measles every time I saw one.

Each day we broke camp and traveled the sea ice in constant search of a wandering polar bear. We also spent some time in search of meat for the eleven-husky team that pulled our sled. The main source of dog

*This picture of a black pirate flag sitting atop a white schooner's mast was taken on the eighth day of the author's polar bear hunt, Resolute Bay, NWT, April 1989.*

food out on the ice is harp seals. The Inuit guides would follow ridgelines in the ice and look for small mounds of snow resembling what I thought of as miniature muskrat huts. These mounds were where seals had air holes in the ice. Generally, seals follow these ridges and have an air hole every two hundred yards or so. They surface for air about every fifteen minutes. David or Adam would take an ice knife, resembling a machete, and enlarge an air hole enough to allow a seal to be pulled out. Then they would drape a blanket over their heads and the hole, to block the light, and wait. When a seal came to the surface, they would either harpoon or shoot it with a .30-30 rifle, then quickly use a large and sturdy hook to keep the seal from falling back down the hole.

The ice in the Arctic is between eight and twelve feet thick, so it is important to hook the seal as quickly as possible to prevent its being lost. I had an opportunity to cover my head and look down into one of the holes. I was astounded at what twelve feet of ice looks like, compared with the mere eight to twelve inches I was used to seeing while ice fishing at home.

After seven days on the ice and seeing many polar bears on the move, I was getting eager for an opportunity to stalk one. Also, the constant cold was beginning to wear on me. There was no way to escape it, except for the few hours we spent in the tent of an evening. Not every bear you see is in a position to stalk. Many times the wind is wrong, the bear is on the other side of a lead of open water, or it is on the wrong side of "rough ice," a place where the ice has been pushed up and frozen, creating an almost impassable field of obstacles. There is hardly a way to walk through rough ice, let alone get a sled through. Polar bears use those areas to hide and rest; the jumbles serve as windbreaks and also provide a suitable place to ambush prey.

On the eighth day we came across a large and reasonably fresh track. It was decided that Adam would unhook the snow machine and go in search of a high vantage point from which he might spot the bear. David and I would proceed in the direction the track was headed and search for fresher sign. It wasn't long before David and I found another track.

Suddenly, the weather began to change rapidly. Our focus quickly went from finding a bear to worrying about Adam's being out on the ice with no food, no shelter, and no rifle! The approaching whiteout overtook us with a fury. Visibility at times was less than twenty yards. There was no way Adam would find his way back in such a storm. We fought our way back to the dog sled. Then we located a thirty-foot-high hill of ice close by, climbed up, and stuck a harpoon in the top with a black plastic sack tied to it. The harpoon and sack looked like a pirate flag atop a white schooner's mast. We hoped the visibility during the storm would improve from time to time and Adam would catch a glimpse of the flag.

David and I secured the dogs next and then set up our tent to weather the storm. I could tell by the look on the old man's face that the situation was grim. He may have spoken no English, but I didn't have to understand Inuit to know that he was very concerned. Adam was at the mercy of the storm and in serious danger from the many polar bears in the area—especially if his machine were to break down. Adam had promised to stay close, but then the weather had changed so very rapidly. . . .

Every now and then we could hear Adam's snowmobile getting closer but then fade into the storm again. After two long hours of zero visibility, the whiteout let up just enough for us to be able to see about fifty yards.

*Sled dogs anxiously await a feeding of seal meat while out on the ice, April 1989.*

We climbed the ice hill to look and listen for Adam. To our amazement, as we peered out into the blowing snow, there was an eight-foot polar bear moving through the ice ridges a short distance away. David indicated that the bear was a sow. We watched the female move out of sight, but within ten minutes another bear appeared. This one was a big boar. Although David was racked with worry, he gestured and said, "Big, big bear! Let's go!" His words may have been in his native language, but any hunter would have understood.

I grabbed my Bear Whitetail II from the sled and took it out of its case. Unbelievably, during the trip my sight frame had gotten bent at a 45-degree angle. Quickly I tried to bend the frame back as straight as I could, expecting it to snap off in the frigid cold. My confidence level sank about three notches because I had no idea whether the pins were where they needed to be. There was no time to stand and wonder, though, because the bear was getting farther away by the minute. By the time we got the dogs organized, the bear was out of sight. We proceeded in the howling wind and blowing snow, ducking between ice ridges. We had ridden the sled about half a mile when David spotted the bear and immediately turned loose the dogs.

Now, it is important to understand that when an Inuit turns his dogs loose he expects you to hotfoot it along right behind him and the dogs. There are two reasons for that: One is that if you lose track of the dogs, you have no transportation, and there is no guarantee they will come back; the other is that if the bear kills any or all of the dogs, you have little or no transportation. In other words, peril is imminent! Put another way, you will be an ice cube before anyone finds you. The dogs are paramount to the Inuit and to survival in the Arctic. The Inuit people put a tremendous amount of work into their dogs, and they are proud of them. It is important to get to the bear as quickly as possible, before he gets mad enough to start killing dogs.

After running a good distance, I shed the caribou parka. I was down to a windbreaker by the time we could see that the dogs had the bear at bay. When I say a windbreaker, by the way, I mean a heavy, fleece-lined, man-made parka with wind-breaking material on the outside. It felt like a windbreaker in more ways than one. I was exhausted from the running and the weight of my remaining clothes. I wondered if I would be able to shoot well with all the bulky clothing I still had on as well as breathing so heavily. To add to the difficulty, the wind was blowing about thirty to forty miles per hour. We worked our way in slowly as the dogs distracted the bear.

As I nocked a shaft, a typical Easton 2117 with a three-bladed, 125-grain Thunderhead, several thoughts raced through my mind: *Are the sight pins all right? How will the bow react when I turn loose of the string in such cold? Will the string snap back in place, thus launching the arrow correctly? We'll be in big trouble if it shatters like glass. Can I draw without any interference from my clothing? Can I get a good release with the deerskin gloves I'm wearing? Where should I hold the sight pin in all this wind?* It is amazing how quickly your mind spins when you're under pressure.

It soon became evident that we weren't going to be able to stalk any closer than thirty-five to forty yards. So I raised the 55-pound bow and released an arrow toward the huge bear's vitals. When the arrow struck the

*There is an art to taking a seal to feed the sled dogs while out on the ice, Resolute Bay, NWT, April 1989.*

bear, I saw immediately that it was too far forward. It had lodged in his chest cavity just in front of the shoulder but angled back into the vitals. I didn't know if my sight pins were off, or if I had pulled the shot because of all the heavy clothes. Whatever it was, I now had wounded the "king of the ice."

Luckily, the big bear made a run for some rough ice not far away. The dogs did their best to keep up, but they were getting tired. David wanted to shoot the bear with his rifle. And what a rifle it was: a rusty old Winchester .30-30. But I talked him out of it, wanting one more chance with the bow. I ran after the bear and followed it into the craggy, frozen terrain. The visibility was now down to forty or fifty yards at best, and I knew this was a dangerous situation. The bear was mortally wounded, but I had a responsibility to get another arrow into him. After climbing and peeking carefully over a small mound, I spotted the bear just below me, twenty-five yards away. Quickly ducking back down, I drew again, rose up, and this time sent the arrow into his vitals. The great white bear walked only a few yards and then went down for good.

Mixed emotions flooded through me. I was elated about getting the polar bear but upset with myself over my poor first shot. I had put our lives in jeopardy, as well as David's prize dogs. I apologized to David as best I could for my mistake, but to my surprise he was extremely happy. He was both happy for me and proud of the fact that he had just successfully guided his first bowhunter, after having guided more than a hundred successful polar bear hunts with a rifle. The Inuit elder lit his pipe and gave me a big smile, even though I could tell that he was still very troubled about his son.

His pleasure was short-lived, though, as he knew that we had our work cut out for us. Not only did we have to skin a 1,000-pound, 9½-foot polar bear before he froze solid, but in addition we needed to find Adam. The concern for his son began to show heavily on the old man's face. We skinned the bear completely in about forty minutes, except for the skull and paws. They were frozen by the time we had finished the rest of the bear. We also cut two quarters from the bear to feed the dogs. Those were the coldest forty minutes of my life. I would have been much better off if my caribou parka and mitts hadn't been lying on the ice somewhere. The poly liners and deerskin gloves I'd used for shooting weren't much help at those frigid temperatures.

David and I backtracked our way to the sled. On the way through the blowing ice crystals, I was glad to spot my parka again. We quickly reconnected the dogs to the sled and went back to the kill site for the hide. Polar bear hides, with the skull attached, weigh somewhere in the neighborhood of two-hundred-plus pounds. We tied the hide behind the sled and let the dogs pull it back through the blizzard to our emergency camp. We then rolled the hide, knowing that it would soon freeze solid.

David's full attention soon turned back to his son Adam. Climbing the ice hill where we had placed the harpoon and flag, we listened and watched carefully. I could only imagine what must being going through the Inuit father's mind. I imagined what it would be like for me if that were my son out there. I immediately began to feel a panic deep inside. It is a feeling only fathers can relate to.

One of the longest hours of my life idled by as I agonized and prayed for the elder and his son. This trip would become a nightmare if we lost that boy. A little more than an hour later, we both heard a faint murmur. David and I glanced at each other. Was it the wind, or was it Adam's machine? Soon there was no question that we were hearing a snowmobile.

The visibility had improved just enough for Adam to spot our flag. When the young man dismounted, he had tears in his eyes. His father embraced him, and the tears began to flow from him, too. The boy was lucky to be alive. He had made a grave mistake by not taking any supplies or a rifle with him. Both men knew that Adam had heard the whisper of death in the Arctic.

Once back in the tent, we celebrated the success of the hunt as we warmed up. Sleep came easily that night as the stress of the Arctic quest partially dissolved. We still had to make it back to civilization in one piece, but I had decided as I prepared for bed not to think about that. The next morning we went back to the polar bear carcass and retrieved more food for the dogs. In addition, we took another seal to ensure that we would have enough dog food for the long trip back to Resolute Bay.

As the sled bounced along the frozen terrain, I thought of the Inuit and their ability to survive on the endless ice. How did they learn to handle the isolation, the daylight that lasts forever, the continuous cold beyond most men's imagination? Or the loneliness, or the many perils they faced each day? I thought of how insignificant I was in the whole scheme of the Arctic, and I pondered the many explorers and Inuit people who had lost their lives here. Without question, the fortitude of the Inuit people is beyond comprehension. Their lives are a continuous adventure, and I was here only because they had permitted me to be a part of that adventure.

I was thankful to have survived the Arctic with honor and to have accomplished the task of taking of a polar bear with a bow. But more than that, I had shared a perilous and humbling experience between father and son, and had been an intricate part of an Inuit elder's quest to maintain his sacred status as the finest hunter in the land of the midnight sun.

Chapter 5

# Stalking Black Bear

In the fall of 1993, I made plans to hunt Roosevelt elk with Larry Dugan of Trophy West Guide and Outfitters. Since Trophy West also offers some of the best spring bear hunts around, I decided to try a black bear stalk while awaiting the fall elk hunt. The hunts on Vancouver Island are all spot-and-stalk, and I was looking forward to the new challenge. Apart from meeting the outfitter, I especially value a chance to visit a new area.

The following spring my wife and I were off to Vancouver Island and the little town of Campbell River. I was surprised to discover that Larry Dugan had sold the operation to a man named Don Rose. It's always a concern when you find that there is a new outfitter—especially when you hadn't heard about it in advance.

Don immediately approached and explained the situation. He expressed his concern about my deposit for the planned fall Roosevelt elk hunt, as none of his crew had had much experience with bowhunting elk. He didn't want any problems and would be willing to cancel the hunt if necessary. I appreciated his businesslike manner and his willingness to work things out, and I agreed to take the hunt anyway and make the best of it. He assured me that there were plenty of bears for this hunt and that a few of the crew had guided bowhunters on spot-and-stalk hunts before. It wouldn't be easy, but it could be done.

Campbell River was a nice place with a resort atmosphere. It reminded me a lot of Aspen, Colorado. It had a quaint Western look, to my surprise, and provided a neat getaway for a good number of tourists. Trophy West Outfitters rented a nice lodge with a series of cabins on the water for their headquarters. The accommodations were top-shelf and the food was excellent. We dined on seafood, wild game, and other delicacies.

*Gary and outfitter Don Rose, Vancouver Island, June 1993.*

A black bear hunt on Vancouver Island allowed a hunter two bears because of the huge bear population. There were six other hunters in camp, including one other bowhunter. Each had a guide to himself and would leave early in the morning for a separate hunting area. My guide was Mike Moss. Mike had some experience with bowhunters and was confident that we would get a shot. Mike also worked as a taxidermist on Vancouver Island.

The various hunting areas were generally an hour or so from camp. We hunted primarily clear-cuts and slash piles along active logging roads. We had to keep a sharp eye out for huge logging trucks coming down the mountain. There was no way those big trucks could stop if we were in their way. It was a bit scary on each corner we came to; a couple of log truck encounters had me on the edge of my seat.

The clear-cuts were primarily on southern slopes. Skunk cabbage, all sorts of green plants, and an abundance of grass grew wherever the sun reached the ground, and the bears were out in force looking for greens to get their systems functioning again after the long winter's hibernation. It is interesting how a bear eats vegetation. Elk, deer, moose, and the like pick the tops from plants and eat about half of the plant. Bears, on the other hand, eat the vegetation right down to the ground. Once you know what to look for, it's easy to tell if a bear has been grazing.

The bears were also looking for the occasional winter-killed elk or deer carcass to work on. In addition, the boars were searching for sows in heat. Boars wander continuously in their drive to mate. On occasion they will kill and eat any cubs with a sow so as to bring the sow back into heat. The boars come out of the dens first, and the sows follow later with their cubs. The sows then try to take their cubs to feeding areas where they are not likely to run into a boar. What Mother Nature had in mind here is hard to understand.

The American black bear is found only in North America. These bears live in forests as far south as Florida and northern Mexico and as far north as the forests of Alaska and Canada. In northern Labrador, where there are no longer grizzly bears, black bears range out onto the open treeless tundra.

Most black bears are four to seven feet long and stand about three feet at the top of the shoulders when on all fours. Wild male black bears of breeding age usually weigh between 125 and 500 pounds, depending upon age, season, and food supply. Very well-fed bears can be heavier. The record is 880 pounds, taken in Craven County, North Carolina; a close second from northeastern Minnesota weighed in at 876 pounds. Wild females usually weigh between 90 and 300 pounds, with the heaviest known weighing 520 pounds, taken in northeastern Minnesota on 30 August 1993.

Bears see in color and have good vision up close. Their hearing exceeds human frequency ranges and probably has twice the sensitivity, and their noses are extremely good. More black bears have been recorded to attack people than any other bear species. That is partly because black bears live so close to human settlements, and partly because there are so many of them. If a black bear does attack, it is generally to eat you. The advice to play dead is not a good idea when a black bear attacks; it is better to fight back. At least, this is what most experts say.

There are several ways to hunt black bears. The most common way is out of a tree stand. Tree stands are used mostly in extremely thick conifer forests where the cover is almost impenetrable for humans and where there are few openings in which to spot a bear. Bait is used as an attractant. Dogs are also used in many areas, and for the same reasons. Spot-and-stalk, although the most difficult method, is very effective.

Spot-and-stalk hunting involves doing a major amount of driving, walking, and glassing for bears feeding in the clear-cuts. The normal method is to glass long distances and then find your way along logging roads to the bears. In my case, getting off the logging trails while stalking was difficult. The terrain was so rough and uneven it was unbelievable. The stumps and slash—not to mention the big ravines and gullies in the clear-cuts—made it almost impossible at times to find a bear again after we had gotten to its location. Getting within range of a bear was an arduous task because of the fickle winds and poor footing. A bear's nose is as good as that of any animal alive. The wind was a huge factor, as I would find out on many blown stalks.

We saw lots of bears that first day. If this had been a rifle hunt it would have been over quickly. Most of the stalkable bears we saw were small or young, lanky boars. I enjoyed watching several bears climbing trees to amuse themselves. There seemed no other reason to climb except for entertainment, for there certainly wasn't any food up there. Many times they would climb, only to fall asleep twenty or thirty feet up.

I stalked several animals without success. Because they were on the move constantly in search of food, it was common to find a bear a good distance from where it had last been seen. The new location often presented no stalk, or the variable wind got us.

On the fourth morning, just after daylight, we spotted a bear walking on a long, dead snag. Comically, it was using the logs and stumps as a bridge over the rough terrain. The roads on this particular mountain went around in rings about a quarter-mile apart, and this bear was one road below us. We made our way down to the next road, being careful not to get busted, and found him again. But during our ensuing stalk through thick vegetation, we completely lost him. So we trekked back up to the logging road and began glassing again. Sky-lining was our biggest worry because the country was so steep. The many snags, stumps, and treetops scattered throughout the clear-cut made glassing tedious. We had to pick apart every suspicious clump of clutter to find the bear again.

After several tense moments we spotted the bear moving up in our direction. It looked as though it was going to go past on our right, and

*Gary and his large Campbell River bear that measured $18\,^{4}/_{16}$, Vancouver Island, June 1993.*

we made a decision to angle down the slope and cut him off. Mike stayed back, to minimize the noise, and I moved across a small ravine to get a shot. The big boar came through exactly as planned and turned broadside at forty-five yards. The downhill angle was extreme, and it was a good thing I had practiced from the top of my garage and knew which pin to use for such a radical angle. I had done a good amount of practicing at steep angles, up and down, at ranges up to fifty yards. Also, thanks to my sheep hunting experiences, I felt confident.

When the bear ducked under an overhanging log and disappeared, I drew. My heart began pounding as I anticipated the shot. When he came out, though, he was a different color. This was a different bear altogether! I let down in total confusion. This one looked like a small sow. *Where in the heck did she come from?* I thought. She worked her way slowly in my direction and eventually passed by at fifteen yards. She stopped for a moment and stared at me. Let me tell you, it's a lot different being on the same level with a bear than it is watching from a tree stand.

Finally the big boar emerged, but he stopped and tested the air at seventy yards. He slowly followed the sow but took a different route. My heart began to pound again as he closed the distance. When the bear turned broadside at fifty yards, a puff of wind hit the back of my neck. I knew that the jig would shortly be up. It looked like he was now as close as he was going to get and in a matter of seconds would catch my scent. I quickly drew and released an arrow. In my excitement, though, I forgot to allow for the downhill angle, and my arrow struck the big bear in the spine. He went down immediately. I jumped up and nocked another arrow, but before I could shoot again the bear had crawled forward and disappeared.

Mike had seen what happened, and the two of us converged on the bear's location. The big boar had found a hole something like a bear den: a ten- to twelve-foot-deep crevice covered with deadfalls. He had pushed his way into the hole so far that we could barely see him. The crevice was almost like a bunker. By this time the excitement had hit me full-tilt. I was trembling, the way I always do after a shot. But this was a potentially dangerous situation. If that bear got mad and came after us, my bow wouldn't be much protection.

After we'd spent an hour trying to get the bear to move, he finally made a small movement and gave me a marginal shot. My first arrow stuck in a log. The range was only ten yards, and I hadn't allowed adequately for the short distance. My second shot hit home. I nocked another arrow as quickly as I could, in case he decided to come out, but the big boar was finished. The next chore was to get him out.

When we had finally managed to get him up out of the crevice, it was amazing to me to note the build on that big black bear. There didn't seem a lot of difference between his build and that of a human. The muscle structure is similar, although gigantic compared with a man's. No wonder they are at the top of the food chain.

My black bear squared seven feet and scored well up in the Pope and Young and SCI records. It was quite an accomplishment for me at the time to stalk a bear of any kind. The number of bears we saw was just phenomenal. I wondered how many I would run into during the coming elk hunt. Bears definitely appeared to be something to keep an eye out for while sneaking through the brush.

I hunted a few more days but didn't see another bear as large as the one I'd already taken, so I decided not to take another. Letting some of the smaller boars grow up to a ripe old age would make the hunting better next time.

Many of the guides became interested in what it took to become a bowhunter, once they saw that it could be done. The challenge fascinated them. The next spring, when I came back for another bear hunt, I brought a new group of bowhunting friends, including Jay Scholes, Andy Simo, and Randy Schoech. I also brought new bows for the guides. I left behind me a bunch of excited new Robin Hoods. Much to my satisfaction, they all became very accomplished bowhunters and have remained great friends over the years.

Chapter 6

# Bright Lights and Pronghorn Antelope

I had taken a few antelope with a rifle in Montana over the years but had never pursued them with a bow. There weren't a lot of antelope among the vast wheat fields and low-lying farmlands where I hunted in Montana. The chance of getting within bow range in that type of country was limited as well.

I got serious about taking an antelope with a bow in 1991, when I met Wayne Cronister at a Sheep Foundation convention in Las Vegas. He told me of an area where the chances of drawing a permit were excellent and the possibility of getting a good buck was above average. Wayne had an operation called Silver State Guides. He was an electrician by trade, but he also outfitted for both desert rams and antelope. I booked both a desert sheep hunt with him and an antelope hunt. Although I never did draw a desert sheep permit in that area, I was successful in drawing an antelope permit the first year I tried.

When I told people that I was going to Vegas to hunt antelope, they all raised an eyebrow, chuckled, and said, "Yeah, right!" When I arrived in Las Vegas, having been there only one other time many years before, I was stunned. The place had exploded with construction. My first thought was, *Why, with all this noise and thousands of people, would an antelope want to be within miles of this place?*

Here's a little information on antelope not many people know: The pronghorn is not a true antelope but in a family by itself (Antilocapridae). It is native only to North America. The pronghorn is the only North American big-game animal that has branched horns, from which fact comes its name. Pronghorns have true horns derived from hair—not antlers. The horns have an outer sheath of fused, modified hair that covers a permanent bony core. Pronghorns shed the hollow outer sheath each year in October or November and grow a new set of horns by July. Both bucks and does have horns, but

*A meager tent camp in 90 degree desert weather, Lincoln County, Nevada, August 1993.*

doe horns are shorter and more slender. Adult pronghorns stand three feet at the shoulders. Bucks weigh about 110 pounds, does about 80 pounds. Pronghorns have a bright reddish-tan coat marked with white and black. The buck has a conspicuous black neck patch below the ears that is not present on the doe. Their white rump patch is enlarged and conspicuous when they are alarmed. Also, just above the rump patch there is a gland that expands and flairs the hair when the animals are alarmed. That white flash serves as a warning signal to other pronghorns and is visible at long distances. Pronghorns currently have a scattered but widespread distribution throughout western North America.

In the early 1800s, when the Lewis and Clark Expedition recorded the presence of large herds of pronghorns, the total population across North America was estimated at thirty-five million. In less than one hundred years, however, intensive market hunting brought pronghorn numbers to a low of approximately thirteen thousand. Quick action by conservation-minded leaders saved the pronghorn from possible extinction, and in the late 1800s and the early 1900s most Great Plains state legislatures passed laws making it unlawful to kill, ensnare, or trap pronghorns. In fact, pronghorns were given complete protection for nearly fifty years. In the 1940s and 1950s limited hunting was again permitted, and pronghorn hunting seasons have been held ever since in most Great Plains states. Populations have shown a notable increase over the last two decades. Trapping and transplanting programs to re-establish pronghorn populations by state wildlife agencies, along with proper management and protection, have been major factors in the pronghorn's recovery.

Wayne warned me to expect some hot temperatures and dry conditions: The temperatures while hunting would be 100 to 110 degrees. He had received permission to hunt from a rancher whose place was four to five hours from Las Vegas. We would be hunting from ground blinds and a windmill over water in the desert. Wayne had seen a large buck in the 16- to 17-inch class at the windmill on a scouting trip, and he really hoped I'd get a shot at him.

We set up a meager camp on the desert. And when I say meager, I mean it! All we had was a small dome tent, a card table outside, and two chairs. I was a little disappointed at the whole setup, to be honest. I had expected better accommodations, based on what I'd been told. The blinds left a lot to be desired, too, in my opinion, but I decided to make the best of things. I was already there, and a few antelope in the distance bolstered my hopes.

I had never camped in the desert before and imagined all sorts of scorpions and rattlesnakes crawling into our tent. Wayne laughed when he saw me dumping my boots upside down each morning before I put them on.

After looking at the windmill setup, I decided that I would rather sit in a ground blind. The windmill didn't look all that safe, and the heat would have melted me down to a blob. The ground blind was not a pit blind, but set above the ground and made of wire and desert vegetation. The possibility of rattlesnakes slithering in to visit didn't thrill me much, but still it beat falling out of a rickety old windmill. A storage tank and trough provided water for livestock and the antelope. To be honest, with all the thorns in the vegetation on the blind and the sparse cover, this Michigander couldn't see how this was remotely going to work.

That first morning we didn't get up in time to be at the blind by first light. Wayne dropped me off at the ground blind, and he scouted from the windmill. All I saw that day were a few does and fawns. They did come to the water, but they didn't stay long and they looked extremely nervous. The next morning I was there at dawn. Not long after sunup a few does and fawns proceeded toward the water with a good buck following. The does suddenly stopped, though, and began pacing back and forth at around seventy-five

*A rough, homemade ground blind looking toward a water hole, Lincoln County, Nevada, 1993.*

yards. The wind was right, but they had definitely seen something they didn't like. After a few tense moments, they turned and walked away.

Wayne had seen the big buck from the windmill the day before, and it would have been a thirty-yard shot for him if he had been hunting. I began to think that I should have sat up there, regardless of how hot or dangerous it looked.

About 11:00 A.M. the same group of antelope returned and decided to come to the water. One at a time they came nervously in to drink. The big buck, though, hung back at sixty yards and was staring at the blind. The rest of the antelope began drifting away from the water. The big buck turned broadside, and it looked to me as though he was not going to drink. I quickly guessed the yardage, drew, and let fly.

The buck jumped, but I couldn't tell where I'd hit him. I did see a puff of dust behind him, so I knew the arrow had passed through. He ran a short distance and then stopped. I scanned his body with my binocular, but I couldn't see a mark on him anywhere. The rest of the antelope ran over to him and, much to my amazement, they all walked off together.

I couldn't believe that I had missed. I thought for sure that I'd seen the arrow hit him. I wanted to jump out of the blind and head after him, but

I knew that would be senseless. So I forced myself to stay in the blind for forty-five minutes more. I began thinking that if he had been hit and died just out of sight, the 110-degree temperatures would be baking him right now. I sneaked out of the blind and went to where the buck had been standing. A few specks of blood confirmed that I'd hit him. I scanned the desert floor, but he was nowhere to be seen. Finding the arrow was the next step. I located it quite a distance from where he'd been standing, and it had good blood on it.

I nocked another arrow and began following the scant blood on the hardpan desert floor. I was worried about jumping him out of his bed, but with any more time in the hot sun he might make like a hot-air balloon and float away. As I came around a small rise in the terrain I could see him, stretched out flat. He had gone about a hundred yards after I had lost sight

*Gary and his Nevada antelope, whose $14^{1}/_{2}$-inch horns scored $76^{0}/_{8}$ inches (SCI/PY), 7 August 1993.*

of him. It was great to be able to find him so quickly. I could only imagine what it would be like to chase a wounded antelope across the desert in this blistering heat. He proved to be a better buck than I'd thought. It was all very exciting now that he was down. The camp and the blinds didn't seem all that bad, either. Funny how that works.

The antelope was definitely starting to bloat in the heat, and I decided to gut him at once. But then I realized that I had no way to clean the blood up or take any decent pictures. So I dragged him back, being careful not to break the hair on the cape. I pulled him around behind my blind in a bit of shade and decided to wait for Wayne. The only problem was that Wayne and I had discussed staying out all day, till dark. With this heat I'd hoped that he would change his mind. Luckily, about an hour later Wayne's truck came bumping up the road. We dowsed the buck with water to get some good photos, cleaned him out, and we headed for camp.

It is amazing how bleak we humans can make things look. But when the animal you are after settles to the ground, things don't seem half so bad. It is important to trust your outfitter when he comes highly recommended. There were a few things that might have been better, but most of my dissatisfaction was the result of my inexperience hunting antelope, and hunting in the Nevada desert. We both agreed that there was no sense in staying in the desert another night. We loaded our little camp in a flash and were out of there. It was great to have a good antelope. The buck measured 76 inches—a nice buck in anybody's book.

Chapter 7

# Snow-Bound Lion: The Culvert Trick

I had shot a mountain lion with a rifle in Montana in the 1970s. That particular lion had been killing livestock on a ranch owned by a friend. I hadn't yet taken a lion with my bow, however, so I was keeping my eyes open for a good lion hunt. I met Mark Condit through the Wild Sheep Foundation. Mark's father was a big outfitter from Dubois, Wyoming, who specialized in sheep, moose, and elk. Mark had followed in his dad's footsteps, offering many of the same hunts his father did, including black bears and lions. For several years I had had a bowhunt for mountain sheep booked with Mark, but I could never draw a Wyoming sheep permit.

Then, in 1991 at a Wild Sheep Foundation convention, Mark suggested that I come to Colorado and hunt lions with him. The hunt was to be through a Colorado friend of Mark's, Bruce Nay of Book Cliff Outfitters. Mark worked for Bruce during the mountain lion season, and he told me they had some huge lions there. Bruce operated on ranches that were having trouble with lions killing domestic sheep. It sounded good to me, so I put down a deposit for a hunt in 1992.

Here are a few interesting facts about mountain lions: In the past, mountain lions had the most extensive distribution of all American terrestrial mammals. They ranged from coast to coast in North America, and from southern Argentina and Chile to southeastern Alaska. Today the big cats in eastern North America are nonexistent, except for a small population of Florida panthers. Hunting pressure in the old days and habitat destruction later on began restricting their once vast range to relatively mountainous, unpopulated areas. In recent years, as a result of wildlife conservation, populations have begun to expand into areas of human habitation, especially in the western United States. Mountain lions are now fairly common in

*This is the irrigation dam where my mountain lion was hiding, Routt County, Colorado, January 1992.*

suburban areas of California and have recently been sighted as far east as urban Kansas City, Missouri, where several have been hit by cars.

Mountain lions use a wide variety of habitats, including montane coniferous forests, lowland tropical forests, grassland, dry brush country, swamps, and almost any other areas with adequate cover and prey. Dense vegetation, caves, and rocky crevices provide their shelter.

A mountain lion may live as long as twenty years in the wild; they may live slightly longer in captivity. Mountain lions are solitary animals. Population densities vary from as low as one individual per eighty-five square kilometers to as high as one lion per thirteen square kilometers, depending on the density of prey and other resources. Mountain lions mark their territories by depositing urine or fecal material by trees marked with scrapes. You can also find territorial scrapes under rock overhangs and cliffs. Males are found together immediately after leaving their mother, but rarely as established adults. Mountain lions are primarily nocturnal.

These furtive animals are carnivores, their main prey being ungulates—moose, elk, white-tailed deer, mule deer, and caribou. They also eat smaller

*This is a good size for a Colorado lion, Routt County, January 1992.*

creatures such as squirrels, muskrats, porcupines, beavers, raccoons, striped skunks, coyotes, bobcats, other mountain lions, rabbits, opossums, birds, and even snails and fish. They may also prey on domestic livestock, including poultry, calves, sheep, goats, and pigs. Lions in urban areas will eat dogs and cats. Yearly food consumption is about forty-eight large ungulates per lion per year. Although mountain lions are secretive and generally avoid humans, about four humans per year fall prey to mountain lions. These are generally small adults and children traveling alone at dawn, dusk, or at night. Mountain lions are top-notch predators.

On New Year's Day Mark telephoned to say that conditions were perfect for cat hunting and that I should come down as soon as possible. The snow was deep and the weather prime. They had already taken several hunters out after the big cats and had killed some good lions. What's more, they had seen several other big cat tracks in the area.

I hadn't expected a call that soon, but I rearranged my schedule and flew to Denver on 5 January. I rented a car and headed out to meet Mark.

The outfitter had rented an old house near the hunting area for use as a base camp. Mark was a real horseman and had some big, stout horses ready for this hunt. Some were workhorse crosses, and it was a good thing they were tall and tough. The snow was deep and the going difficult. The only trouble I was having was trying to reach the stirrups. These horses were monsters!

That first morning we drove the roads looking for tracks. It wasn't long before we crossed a fresh lion track and turned out the dogs. We unloaded the horses, saddled up, and followed. We rode for what seemed like hours before the dogs bayed "treed." The snow was belly-deep on the horses, and the trees were covered with fresh snow. It was tough keeping dry because snow fell continuously from the branches down my neck and into my lap. In many places the horses had to lunge to push through the drifts. You can imagine what it was like for a greenhorn to stay aboard.

When we finally caught up to the dogs, they were baying where half a dozen big fir trees grew tightly together. Try as we might, we could not find the cat. We looked everywhere, but the trees were so tall and thick, with heavy snow piled on the branches, that a lion could have been in there almost anywhere. We looked around the group of trees, thinking that maybe he'd jumped, but there was no track to be seen. We spent about an hour looking for that cat. If he had gone to the top of any one of those trees, finding him would be out of the question.

We finally gave up and started gathering the dogs for the long trip back to the truck. We had a tough time getting the dogs to leave. In fact, three of the dogs just wouldn't go. The trip back to the truck was miserable because of the blowing snow, and the temperature had dropped to 20 degrees. We arrived back about 9:00 P.M. It gets dark around 6:00, so a lot of the trip was in the dark. We loaded the horses and made our way back to camp down some dangerously icy roads. With a load of horses in the truck bed, the road conditions made for some white-knuckle driving.

The next morning before daylight we were out looking for tracks in some lower country, hoping that the snow there wouldn't be quite so deep. Soon, we found another big cat track and turned out two dogs. Two would get the chase started, as we knew we were going to be short on dog power. We still had to go back sometime that day to find the three dogs we had left the previous night.

Mark listened to see which way the dogs were headed and then turned the truck around. The cat was headed to an area where another road crossed. Rather than unload the horses there, we proceeded by truck to a place where we could listen for the dogs again. No sense in riding any farther than necessary in the deep snow.

When we stopped and listened, the dogs were headed in our direction. Mark turned out a couple more dogs. We decided to proceed on foot, hoping that the cat would tree in short order. After we'd walked a short way, the dogs began barking at bay. About halfway to the dogs Mark and I found a fresh mule deer kill. Very little of the deer had been eaten. We hadn't gone much farther when we found another deer kill. So much for the myth that mountain lions kill only enough to survive. It is common knowledge among lion hunters that the big cats many times kill just for the fun of it. Some guides have followed a lion for many miles to learn all they can about how these animals hunt. Those guides have sometimes found several kills along a big cat's route where the lion has killed a doe deer just to eat her milk bag, then left the rest untouched.

The dogs were at bay above us and about a quarter of a mile away. It was taking a long time to wade the deep snow uphill, and we began to worry about the cat jumping before we could get there. As we closed the distance, the barking began to subside. We looked at each other in disgust, figuring that the cat had jumped the tree. When we made it to the dogs, however, there were no sizable trees. The dogs were milling around, barking once in a while, and a couple of the dogs were lying down.

The only nearby cover was small trees, with some low brush here and there. As we worked our way up a creekbed, we could see an old cement dam of some sort. When we got closer Mark recognized it as an old headgate used to divert water for irrigation. Cemented in the dam was a culvert that extended downstream twenty feet or so. One of the dogs kept going over to the end of the culvert and barking. We looked in there and could see the lion at the very end. Board slats used for diverting water covered the opening on the cement end of the dam. They were frozen in the mud. Each time we looked into the culvert, we would hear a low, rumbling growl. The culvert acted like a megaphone of sorts, amplifying the lion's warning, which was pretty impressive. In fact, the sound made the hair stand up on the back of my neck.

The open end of the culvert was lying flat on the ground, and I tried to figure out how to get a shot. I lay on my sides, both right and left, got back a good ways, and pondered the prospects of being able to slip an arrow up the culvert and into the cat. There was no way to get it done from that end, it seemed. It was dark in there, too, except for a sliver of light that entered through a crack in a board on the cement end. Placing a lethal shot would be pure luck. While we were concentrating on the problem, one of the dogs kept trying to dive in the end of the culvert after the cat. Mark dragged the dog out by its tail each time.

We didn't have any tools with us with which to dig the board slats out of the frozen mud. Finally, however, we found some old tree limbs and a broken post or two. We used them to break one of the wooden slats. That opened a hole through which we could see the cat when he pressed his body against it.

Mark went around to the other side and made some noise so the cat would come to my end. I had backed off about fifteen yards and hid behind a bush, hoping for a shot when the big cat pushed his body against the opening again. The first time he came back, all I could see was part of his head and his breath, which rose from the hole in the slats. He disappeared again but was back in short order. Although his chest was not visible, I knew where it had to be. Taking careful aim, I let fly. There was an old steel fence post in the middle of the hole—and wouldn't you know, I hit it dead center. The arrow made a huge clang, and the cat disappeared into the darkness. How's that for being dead on!

Disgusted and disappointed, I quickly nocked another arrow as Mark made more noise down at his end. The cat immediately showed at my end again. This time I put an arrow perfectly through the hole. There was a startling growl and a lot of snarling inside the culvert. Mark stood ready on his end in case the cat came charging out, and I nocked another arrow. After a long silence, Mark shone his flashlight into the culvert. The big cat lay motionless. But in the midst of the excitement and congratulations, it dawned on both of us about the same time: How were we going to get it out?

We decided to try to remove the rest of the boards from my end of the dam, but there wasn't any way to budge them. They were frozen tight. The only option was to crawl up the culvert, grab hold of the lion, and drag it out. I wasn't volunteering, right off, for the task. In fact, I thought the idea bordered on lunacy. But it seemed the only way, without going back to camp and getting some tools. Mark decided to shed his heavy clothes so that he would be small enough to shimmy up the pipe.

Much to his surprise, once inside he found half a deer carcass stuffed in there, too. Mark had to crawl over the decomposing carcass as he made his way toward the cat. Suddenly he saw something move. His light revealed it was a skunk. After some anxious moments, he determined that the shadows from the light had made the skunk only look as if it had moved. It was actually dead, and it stank to high heaven. Mark crawled over the dead skunk, too, to reach the lion. This was going way beyond the call of duty, as far as I was concerned.

When he backed out with the cat in tow, he dragged out a portion of the decaying mule deer and the skunk. You can just imagine what he smelled like. But we had my cat. The lion was a large male weighing just under 180 pounds and stretching 7 feet, 10 inches from the tip of his nose to the tip of his tail.

Chapter 8

# Fort Chimo Caribou—Quebec-Labrador Bull

Finally 31 August 1993 arrived. Archie Nesbit and I had wanted to hunt for Quebec-Labrador caribou in northern Quebec for quite some time. We both needed the species for the North American Slam. When the call came from Trophy Connection, we were ready.

The Akuliak Caribou Camp in northern Quebec was normally booked solid from year to year, but Wes Vining of Trophy Connection had called with news of a cancellation. If we wanted to go, we'd have to hurry and call back. The open slots wouldn't last long. We sent in our deposits and began planning.

We flew into Montreal and then to Fort Chimo; the Inuit name for Fort Chimo is Kuujjuaq. This Inuit village, not far from the Arctic Circle, reminded us of Indian villages in the United States in that almost all of the housing was the same. Each house was about six hundred to eight hundred square feet, was very simply constructed, and had a large heating oil tank attached.

The airport was primitive, with only a few hangars and an old fuel truck sitting alongside the taxiway. The remnants of two airplane crashes were visible not far off the taxiway, perhaps an old Beaver and a Cessna of some kind. It reminded me of my career as an airline pilot and the many hair-raising moments I had experienced before retiring. Thankfully, I had survived my close encounters.

The weather up in this part of the world is fickle, especially toward the winter months. Bad weather in this part of Quebec begins in August, and any flight here could turn into a disaster. It's just the chance you have to take. Because I have a lot of flying experience, I was acutely aware of some of the wild things the pilots I flew with accomplished with their

*The author took this Quebec-Labrador caribou in northern Quebec, September 1993.*

machines—in a word, they scared the begeebers out of me. I would have enjoyed the trip a whole lot more if I had known nothing about flying.

The flight from Fort Chimo to the Akuliak Caribou Camp was a long one. We flew in one of the workhorses of the North Country, a Twin Otter. Many Otters are equipped with floats for water landings, but this one had wheels. The Akuliak Camp had a dirt runway. I'll call it dirt, but there were an awful lot of rocks, too. When we landed I wondered why the water was so far from camp. There was nothing but one hundred yards of boulders to the water's edge. *Surely,* I thought, *the tide doesn't go out that far!* Well, the tide *does* go out that far. The tide there rises and falls some twenty to twenty-five feet. Some days the water was two hundred yards from camp.

Camp consisted of small, four-man plywood cabins with heating-oil stoves, fueled by a fifty-five-gallon drum set horizontally on a wooden rack outside. There was a cook cabin, shower, privy, and meat house, as well as a few other storage buildings. The camp was impressive.

We soon met all the cooks, guides, and helpers. To our surprise, two from the group were from the United States, Cliff White and Kraig Brawly. It was nice to have someone in camp who spoke our brand of English. A group of Frenchmen was in camp when we arrived. Cliff and Kraig relayed to us that the crew had specific orders to make certain the Frenchmen were taken better care of than anyone else. Much of the future business of this camp depended on the satisfaction of those guys. It wasn't long, though, before we began to feel like second-class citizens.

The crew waited on those Frenchmen hand and foot. The equipment their guides used was the newest, their cabins were the largest and most comfortable. We didn't let it bother us at first, but as the trip progressed it got worse. We tried not to let this situation dampen our excitement for the hunt, but the truth was it was irritating.

My first stalk on a Quebec-Labrador caribou surprised me considerably. I had wondered about all the footage I'd seen in which the caribou stream past a guy hiding in the bushes and he is able to pick the one he wants. It was obvious that this hunt would be a greater challenge than that. Hunting caribou here was like stalking whitetails.

The Quebec-Labrador is one of the largest caribou species, taking into consideration antler growth. Caribou are the only deer species in which both males and females have antlers. Their antlers, which are shed every year, have long, sweeping main beams up to five feet wide. Each side has one or two branches, and each branch may have several points. The George River and Leaf River herds together currently number over a million animals.

The average lifespan of an adult caribou is eight to ten years. They reach maturity after about three years. As with most deer species, male caribou fight each other for a harem of five to forty cows.

Caribou feed on sedges, grasses, fungi, lichens, mosses, and the leaves and twigs of woody plants such as willow and birch. Although some herds stay on the cold tundra all year, most caribou have distinct summer and winter ranges. The large northern herds migrate long distances, frequently crossing large, swift-running streams and rivers; consequently, even the caribou young are extremely strong swimmers.

Caribou were once essential to the survival and livelihood of the native peoples of the Arctic. Natives used caribou meat, milk, and

*Inuit guide in northern Quebec, September 1993.*

organs for food. Hides provided material for clothing and shelter, and bones, antlers, and sinews were used for making tools, tableware, and handicrafts. However, although caribou remain a subsistence food resource, other uses have declined as native populations have become more technologically advanced.

Archie and I each had a guide, a guide's helper, and a boat to ourselves. Although the boats and motors were ancient and worn out, we did manage to get around the various bays and glass for caribou without too many difficulties. Boat motors quitting now and then and a few leaks were all we contended with, to start.

The wind blew hard the first two days, making the caribou nervous. I stalked within fifty yards of a good bull, but the wind was blowing so hard I missed. We had a couple of other stalks, but I wasn't able to get a shot. The biggest trick was to survive the boat ride back to camp every evening. The ocean was rough once the wind started blowing, and we were never positive that the boat wouldn't capsize or come apart. One evening Archie came in and seemed surprised that he had made it in alive. They had been among waves so large that he was thrown into the air. When he came down, he broke the boat's seat. On our way home another night, we found Archie and his guides stranded in a bay with a dead motor. They were trying to paddle to shore, without much luck. We threw them a line and towed them to camp. Several of those boat rides gave us a good scare. Even though we had life jackets (of a sort), if the boat had capsized we would never have made it to the shore alive because of the extreme cold. A person might last ten minutes in the water there.

Several days into the hunt the wind finally subsided. We were making our way along the shoreline and spotted some caribou swimming in a bay. If you have never seen caribou swim, take it from me that it is astounding how far they can go. I remember watching from afar as a bunch of caribou jumped into a bay and headed for the other bank. That other bank, mind you, was a mile and a half away. I thought for sure that I'd see some caribou drown. Not a chance! They swam the distance, shook the water off, and trotted away.

This latest herd split in the water and headed for land. My guides were sure they knew where the caribou were going, so we ran the boat a good distance ahead of the animals and ducked into a bay. We beached the boat, ran over a hill, and hid behind some big rocks by a well-worn caribou trail. As soon as we were situated, the caribou swam around the corner and headed for the beach. There weren't any really big bulls, but since this was my first crack at a Quebec-Labrador I picked one and waited for him to get on land. As he shook the water off, I put an arrow through his vitals. It hit a bit farther back than I'd planned, but the bull was bleeding badly. He made a running half-circle out through the rocks and came back to the water, where he went down. He was floating when we reached him.

While we were tending our caribou, Archie was stalking bulls on the other side of the bay. We glassed over to see if he was doing any good, but we couldn't see him. He ended up stalking within range of a huge bull and took him at what would be quite long yardage for most bowhunters. (Archie is very skilled at great distances. He puts in a lot of practice time to maximize his opportunities.) That bull turned out to be the largest the camp had taken in several years.

*We watched the incoming tide at our base camp in northern Quebec, September 1993.*

We were each allowed two caribou, but the weather took a turn for the worse, and we changed our minds about fighting the waves. The remainder of the trip was spent holed up in our cabin relaxing, enjoying some reading, and snoozing.

Chapter 9

# The Clear-Cuts of Vancouver Island—Roosevelt "Olympic" Elk

North America has three species of elk: the Rocky Mountain, the tule, and the Roosevelt. The Rocky Mountain elk is the most widely known, the tule the least known. The Roosevelt is widely spread in Alaska, Oregon, Washington, and Vancouver Island in British Columbia.

For some years I had hoped for an opportunity to hunt the oversize Roosevelt. It is the largest of all the elk species, and a mature bull will weigh between seven hundred and eleven hundred pounds. Their antlers are generally more massive than those of the other species but tend to be shorter in tine and main beam length. They also tend to be narrower. The fourth tine on a Roosevelt bull many times will be webbed and hold three or more points forming a cup or crown, something seldom seen on the other species.

Don Rose of Trophy West Guide and Outfitters, out of Campbell River on Vancouver Island, has two nonresident permits available per year, and he offers some of the best elk hunting in British Columbia. Vancouver Island is a little larger than the state of Florida. It is covered with huge mountains, timber, and lots of foliage. The island presents some of the most difficult terrain and the wettest climate in the Pacific Northwest. At the time of my hunt, 1993, a healthy elk herd of approximately three thousand animals roamed there. There is no special season for the archery hunter. The season opens around the first week of October, and you have to compete with a number of lucky resident rifle hunters.

I made my hunting plans with Trophy West, but the hunt itself would not take place until two years from the booking. Since Trophy West offers some of the best spring bear hunts around, I decided to try a bear hunt while I waited. Besides meeting the outfitter, I'd have a chance to visit the area.

*Gary's Roosevelt elk scored 264 2/8, Vancouver Island, British Columbia, October 1993.*

Therefore, the following spring my wife and I were off to the island and Campbell River. The Roses were great folks and looked forward to the challenge of an archery hunt for black bears. I took a good one on the second day of the hunt, and the following three days were spent fishing and sightseeing. We did see some Roosevelt elk, some black-tailed deer, and cougar. We left the Roses' camp feeling good about the new friendships, and I was all fired up about the next year's elk hunt.

October of 1993 found me en route to Vancouver Island with high hopes. My guide was Glenn Venus, a local lumber camp manager whose second love is elk hunting. Glenn took vacation time every year from his job to guide one nonresident elk hunter. To our advantage, I soon discovered that Glenn had lots of friends headed for the field on opening morning. They shared their preseason scouting and promised to relay any opening-morning sightings. I was advised that we would see a lot of elk and a good number of bulls. Although I was Glenn's first bowhunter, it didn't take me long to see that luck had brought me a good choice in a hunting companion.

A small but comfortable motel called Salmon River, in Sayward, BC, was to be Don's base camp for our hunt. Its central location allowed us to cover the entire hunting area with a minimum of driving time. "Minimum" is a relative term, though, as it still took anywhere from thirty to sixty minutes to get to the hunting areas. Traveling the switchbacked logging roads to vantage points high in the mountains made possible a better view of the vast valleys and high clear-cuts.

The island offers plenty of awesome elk habitat. Each hunter in camp would have his own guide and transportation, but walking and climbing were definitely on the agenda. Walking in this country is extremely difficult. The mountains are covered with boulders and rocks of every shape and size, and the brush is thick and tangled. The tree cover and undergrowth are almost impenetrable. When you attempt to cross a clear-cut, rocks, slash, stumps, and "jack pines" fight you every step of the way. You have to be careful, or a broken leg or ankle might put a fast end to your hunt.

The next day was opening morning, and the excitement in camp was growing. The local community was also buzzing with the prospects of the season opener. It's great to travel and meet new people in places where hunters are welcomed. Different cultures have always fascinated me.

Mixing with people in the small town was a chance to glean some local flavor, something I look forward to in all my travels.

We checked my bow and discussed the equipment we would need for the first day. Some evening scouting revealed several beautiful bulls. Glenn didn't know which special spot he wanted to try at first light. He said that he would sleep on it. As always, sleep came in fits and starts for me the night before the hunt.

The guides and hunters shared a big breakfast the next morning and discussed tactics. We wished each other the best of luck and headed for our secret spots. Glenn and I went to a river drainage low in the valley. He had scouted a number of bulls there, including an unusually large one. We would be walking into the river flats in the dark. Although risking the chance of running into a feeding elk herd, we needed to be in position before daylight.

Shortly after leaving our truck and descending a trail to the river, we heard a bull bugle and some cows talking. After a few more steps we smelled the elk. Quietly backing out, we took another path, which brought us out of the cover farther downstream. Still walking in the dark, we arrived at the river and found a good hiding place. Some uprooted stumps would break up our silhouettes perfectly as we waited for daylight.

We began to hear several bulls talking from different directions. Suddenly elk were splashing in the river. As the darkness lifted, we strained to see . . . nothing. "They must have winded us before crossing," Glenn whispered.

We agreed to backtrack and take another trail upriver. Upon intersecting the other trail, we again heard and smelled elk. Another few yards revealed a cow and calf crossing an old logging road just ahead. There were other elk moving through a stand of small jack pines behind them. We tried to sneak closer, but a calf caught us moving. After a long stare-down, the calf moved on. We decided to make a new plan.

Glenn felt that the main herd, with the big bull, had been up in the jack pine thicket feeding and were heading back to the river flat to bed. He thought what we had heard in the river earlier had been some satellite bulls. The new plan was for me to backtrack halfway to the river and find a place to hide within easy range of two crossing trails we had found. Glenn would go around and make a silent push through the thicket. It wasn't long before the action began.

Elk began streaming from the thick trees, and flashes of tan glided through the cover in my direction. The wind had been in my favor, but then something changed because the elk began to split and pass on either side of me. I was tempted to move, but within seconds five cows filtered from the cover fifty yards to my left, and I could hear more elk coming. Suddenly the sound of antlers hitting branches rang loud and clear. My heart began racing. I raised my bow and tried to calm myself. *Breathe deeply and pick a spot!* I cautioned myself. Just then a glimpse of antlers caught my attention. It was the bull that Glenn had told me to watch for. There was no mistaking this bull, and he was going to walk right out in front of me. The moment of truth was close at hand.

The distance to the crossing was farther than I liked but within my range; anyway, it was too late to move. I got another glimpse of the big bull before he emerged at fifty yards. But a cow stood between us, blocking the shot. The bull paused for a moment, displaying his majestic rack. He was at least a 7x7 and crowning. The cow slowly began to move, presenting the bull broadside. I drew carefully, but the bull began to move, too. With the long range and a moving target, I let down. Catching my breath, I clenched my teeth—so close and yet so far!

In the middle of mentally replaying what had just happened, I was brought back to reality by brush popping behind me. When I turned, a good five-point bull was staring down my neck a mere twenty yards away. He was behind a small pine, with only his head and neck exposed. We glared at each other for a long time, until I made a small move to draw. Then he bolted through the trees and crossed the trail in hot pursuit of the others. As Glenn came out of the brush, I reflected on the excitement: Two close calls within the first hour of daylight! That's pretty good hunting in my book!

The next few days brought some more great hunting but no opportunity to unleash an arrow. On the sixth morning we returned to our original spot on the lower river. Elk could be heard across the river and in the swamp. We crossed the water and entered the swamp in an attempt to get downwind. The undergrowth was thick and noisy, but we were able to advance surprisingly close to the wily cows. They chirped and fed nonchalantly. The wind began swirling, so we couldn't pressure them enough to see if there was a bull present. We quietly left the area before they winded us. In reviewing our experiences here, we decided that a blind along the river would be a good

*Packing the bull out of the clear-cut, October 1993.*

strategy for an evening hunt. After constructing a makeshift hideout, we carefully noted the yardages to the different heavily used crossings. I felt good about the possibilities.

In the meanwhile we decided to head for a clear-cut where one of Glenn's friends had reported another good bull. Once we had reached a good vantage point via a winding mountain road, Glenn immediately spotted a group of elk just under the timberline. We set up the spotting scope and found that there was a good herd bull in the bunch. So we piled into the truck and raced back down the switchbacks. Then we left the truck low in the valley and began a climb up another old logging road.

By this time the elk had moved and were feeding in a lower clearing, next to a thick swamp. From our position the wind was good, and the terrain would allow us to stay out of sight. We quickly began to close the gap. What we didn't know was that hidden just ahead of us were elk we couldn't see. In the process of working down and around the mountain we ran into three young bulls. Both Glenn and I knew that we had blown the stalk, but we decided to keep going.

Upon reaching the last ridge, we spotted a couple of cows feeding near the swamp. The wind had changed and was marginal at best, and the remaining distance to the edge of the ridge was through a noisy, tangled clear-cut. Step by arduous step we made the last three hundred yards disappear. The wind was getting squirrely. It hit us on the back of the neck once, exasperating both of us. Glenn whispered, "We've come this far—if we blow them out now, so be it."

When we made the edge of the ridge, we began crawling. Peeking over the ridge revealed two cows at seventy-five yards. They were up feeding, but testing the air suspiciously. We froze to the ground for what seemed an eternity and waited until they appeared content. Another ten yards would allow us to see into the bottom and perhaps find the rest of the elk, and an old stump just ahead would offer some cover.

It had taken two and a half hours to stalk to this point, and our bodies—at least this body—were feeling the fatigue. But with the excitement mounting, the aching seemed trivial. We finally reached the stump and relaxed. Lying face down in the grass brought the smell of good, clean dirt to my nostrils. A scent of straw from the grass reminded me of my younger days, belly-crawling to get a shot at my first deer. Back in those days any deer seemed a trophy to me.

The seconds seemed like minutes, and I wanted to say, "Well?" But I knew better.

Finally, Glenn's smiling face told me what I wanted to know: The bull was still there. Glenn motioned for me to move in behind the stump and take a look. The ground beyond the stump quickly fell off into the swamp. I felt totally exposed trying to see, but the two closest cows were still feeding and content. Directly below us was a big 6x6 Roosevelt bull, bedded and quartering away. The rest of the cows were scattered along the hillside. The bull's attention was focused on the cows. To get even an inch closer would be an impossible task.

When I dropped back behind the snag, Glenn indicated that I should go for it. I silently mouthed the yardage and rolled my eyes.

Glenn again said, "Do it!"

Over the previous several years, I had dramatically increased my shooting skills at long distances and had prepared extensively for a situation just like this. But, man, this was going to test my ability. It took several minutes to make up my mind and pull myself together. While shifting to a good shooting position, I nocked an Easton 2413 XX75 arrow tipped with a Thunderhead 125. The bow was well tuned and the arrows carefully matched. If this shot was to be a good one, everything would have to be done perfectly. At full draw, I slowly raised the Hoyt ProVantage Fastflite up and over the stump.

A faint breeze hit the back of my neck as I steadily brought the bow into position. There was no stopping now—I was in plain sight. When the last cross hair on the Fineline sight came to rest on the big bull's chest cavity, I concentrated on a spot. The arrow was suddenly off like a rocket, and the release felt good.

Glenn had picked a spot on the bull's chest where he thought the arrow should be placed, and he was watching it through his binocular. When the arrow didn't show up immediately, he quickly looked up in the sky. He spotted the arrow in flight, and his first thought was, *What in the hell is he shooting at? It's way too high!* Just as he focused back on the bull, though, the bright fletching merged with the bull's chest cavity, exactly where he had been looking. All I had seen was the arrow's initial departure. When I turned to Glenn in question, his big smile told the story.

Unbelievably, the big bull never moved a muscle. He just lay there. *What happened?* I wondered.

The arrow was imbedded is his chest cavity almost to the fletching! Confused and exhausted, I dropped back to the ground. Glenn shrugged his shoulders and shook his head, bewildered too.

The cows had all jumped up and run down the slope into the swamp. The bull never moved, except to lay down his head. There was no way to close the distance for another shot, if it was needed. Wait, watch, and let the broadhead do its work was the only option. Within twenty minutes the cows came back from the swamp and began feeding. The bull suddenly got up and walked ten yards, but then it quickly lay back down. The arrow appeared to have gone through both lungs, with only the fletching visible. But something was wrong, or this was the toughest bull we had ever seen.

A few minutes later, out of the swamp emerged two 5x5 bulls. The larger one scent-checked some of the cows and walked within fifteen feet of the big bull. He raked a small tree for two or three minutes, walked over, and clacked antlers with the old bull, which didn't even get up. The young bull turned, gathered three cows, and disappeared into the timber. The big 6x6 then got up again and staggered a short thirty yards before lying back down. The young bull soon returned and butted the old bull around a bit, gathered the rest of the cows, and left.

It was hard not to feel sorry for the old monarch as he laid his head to the ground. If a hunter has any compassion and respect for the animals he hunts, a situation like this is not enjoyable to watch. Why he didn't die within seconds was beyond us, and remained to be explained. As darkness closed in, the old bull struggled to his feet and staggered into the tangled swamp. We knew that he wouldn't go far, but to avoid pushing him deeper into the cover we decided to come back in the morning.

We called Don Rose and told him of our success. He was elated about his outfit's first bowkill and said that he would be out before daylight to give us a hand. The following morning Don, Glenn, and Rob, another guide in camp, accompanied me to the swamp. The blood trail was scant, with small specks of blood here and there. The bull had crossed a little creek and headed for the heavy brush. We were amazed at the lack of blood, considering the arrow's penetration. My heart skipped a beat or two as I worried about the possibilities.

Within fifteen minutes, we found him lying beneath a huge fir tree. He hadn't really gone far. Upon closer investigation, we could see that the arrow had penetrated only one lung—sometimes that's the trouble with a quartering-away shot. I prefer a broadside any time. The tree was one of those gargantuan firs decorated with light-colored moss. It had to be over one hundred and fifty years old. I would imagine that the bull had spent many an hour under the protection of such trees during his lifetime. To me it was a sacred sign that his spirit would be well taken care of in the afterworld.

We spent several hours quartering and packing the bull to the pickups. Everyone was excited about the Roosevelt bull. Not only was this the first elk with a bow for Trophy West Guide and Outfitters but also the bull would remain high in the Pope and Young and SCI record books for some years.

Chapter 10

# The Bison of Antelope Island

To hunt wild buffalo the way the American Indians used to do it was one of this bowhunter's ultimate dreams. I had been putting in for a bison permit for many years. There are several areas in the United States today where Plains buffalo are considered free roaming by Pope and Young Club standards: Antelope Island in Utah, two areas in Arizona, and one each in California and Alaska. There are a couple of wild herds in Canada, too. One that comes to mind is the herd in the Pink Mountains of British Columbia. Wood bison are wild in parts of the Northwest Territories, too, and are the largest of today's buffalo.

The odds were higher for drawing a permit on Antelope Island than in any other area. The permit is a "once-in-a-lifetime" license, and I finally drew one in 1995. The hunt would take place in the month of November. Antelope Island is near Salt Lake City, Utah. In fact, you can easily see Salt Lake City across the bay from the island. From the mainland, Antelope Island's 28,022 acres appear barren and deserted, but it is home to a variety of plants and animals native to the Great Basin region. The island was without its namesake antelope for many years, but they were reintroduced in 1993 and can now be seen in many areas of the park. Deer, bobcats, coyotes, many varieties of birds and waterfowl, and a small herd of elk also call the island home. But the most famous residents are Antelope Island's American bison, introduced to the island in 1893 and now numbering some six hundred animals. The world-renowned herd is managed by the Utah Division of Parks and Recreation.

The wildlife/range manager for the island, Kevin Sherman, was a little reluctant at first when I told him that I was going to hunt with bow and arrow. Because of the barren terrain and the skittish nature of the buffalo,

*It takes patience to stalk in short grass with a lot of stones, Antelope Island, Utah, November 1995.*

he thought that the task might be impossible. He was also concerned about the equipment I intended to use. He asked specific questions about bow poundage and arrow weight. He finally conceded, though, and was interested to see how bowhunting bison on the island would work.

We would be riding in park vehicles, and the hunt was to be closely monitored. Since a park biologist accompanies all hunters on the island, Kevin was going to participate personally. He could then observe firsthand and evaluate the future of bowhunting on the island.

I hired a guy by the name of Ken Elliot to do some scouting ahead of my arrival. Ken was an outfitter from Alaska who lived in Utah. He would go out with the rangers on the island and locate where the bulls were hanging out.

I had chosen longtime friend and cameraman Ralph Cianciarulo to film this hunt. Ralph and I flew out to Salt Lake on 29 November. The hunt was to start on 1 December, but each hunter is required to attend an orientation program before being allowed to hunt. The orientation included buffalo anatomy lessons as well as information on how the hunt would be conducted and what the country is like. We also took a look at how large the island is and the nature of the bison that live there.

The American bison is called buffalo by most North Americans, but that is not correct. It is not a true buffalo, like those found in Asia and Africa. The American bison and its close relative, the European bison, or wisent, belong to the tribe Bovinea, which consists of the world's cattle, buffalo, and bison.

Bovids are hoofed ruminants with permanent hollow horns and an even number of toes, or hoofs, on each foot. The two middle toes are well developed and support the weight of the body. The two lateral toes (the so-called false hoofs, or dew claws) are either absent entirely or are small and located higher on the foot, where they do not usually touch the ground. These ruminants, or cud-chewers, are plant-eaters with a four-chambered stomach, one of which (the rumen) stores undigested food that is later passed back into the mouth, where it is chewed and swallowed a second time.

Horns are found on the males in all species of bovids, and on females in some species. The horns, which are unbranched, consist of a bony core that is attached to the skull and overlaid with a hard, fibrous sheath. The sheath has the same chemical basis (keratin) as hair, hoofs, nails, and feathers. The same horns are retained throughout the animal's life.

Bovids include cattle, antelopes, goats, and sheep. There are about 138 species. Five species are native to North America: the American bison, the muskox, the American mountain goat, the American thinhorn sheep (Dall), and the bighorn sheep.

After the walrus, the bison is the largest North American game animal. Large bulls can measure five to six feet at the shoulder and can weigh 1,600 to 2,000 pounds, occasionally 3,000 pounds. Females are much smaller, weighing about 900 pounds or less.

Both sexes have a large hump on the shoulders and a massive head that is carried low. The body is rather narrow in cross-section, especially in the hindquarters. The head, neck, and forequarters are covered with a thick, shaggy hair, and there is a short beard. The tail is short and tasseled. The summer coat is a pale yellowish brown; the winter coat is dark brown, becoming almost black on the head and shoulders. Both sexes have short horns that curve out and up from the sides of the head.

The first two days of hunting produced only a few unsuccessful stalks. The closest I got was eighty yards. The terrain was very difficult, and there were only a few scattered boulders and some tall grass to hide an approach. The only way to stay out of sight was on hands and knees. We tried several stalks on lone bulls, thinking we had a better chance one on one, but those smart old loners proved to be the toughest to stalk of all. They didn't let their guard down for a second.

I felt it was important to stalk within fifty yards with my 80-pound Hoyt Alphatech in order to deliver enough kinetic energy to bring down a buffalo. A buffalo has a large "no-man's-land" from the top of the backbone to about two-thirds of the way down the side. A shot in that area would get very little lung. An arrow placed one-third of the way up from the brisket, however, would hit the vitals. I wanted to be close enough to pinpoint my shot and get as much penetration as possible.

A steady drizzle greeted us on the third morning of the hunt, when we arrived at the park headquarters for our continental breakfast. We were glad to see some moisture. The rain would help quiet our stalking. The only concern now was the video camera's health under the wet conditions.

After breakfast we took a back road in a direction opposite to that of the other hunters. We glassed from a vantage point and found six big bulls feeding around an old homestead. The rain had increased to the point that

*Bison are huge. Just imagine the Indians and the equipment they used to hunt these animals. Antelope Island, Utah, November 1995.*

it would help hide any noisy mistake Ralph or I might make. It would also hold down and mask our scent during the stalk. The wind was blowing a pretty stiff gale in our favor, too. Ralph covered the camera as best he could, and we commenced our stalk.

We crawled through the tall grass from boulder to boulder, closing the distance. Then Ralph held up in a good position to film, and I continued. Keeping the lowest profile possible was important, in case the buffalo spotted me. If spotted, I hoped they would think I was a coyote or some other critter out hunting or feeding. Buffalo fear very few predators and generally hold their ground at an approaching animal. The rain came down in buckets as I inched closer. Even though I had my rain gear, I was soaked to the bone.

When I got within sixty yards, the buffalo began feeding in my direction. The bull with the biggest horns fed this way and that, but would never present the perfect shot. Another big bull finally presented himself broadside for a moment but turned and fed away before I could draw. The other bulls began to get nervous. The big bull turned again, this time back in my direction. He appeared to want to come and check me out. The thought flashed through my mind, *What the heck can I do if he decides to freight-train my spindly body?* Chances of getting away would be slim, especially in this rain gear! I quickly erased that thought and concentrated when he turned and presented the perfect opportunity.

The arrow flashed to the mark and penetrated almost to the fletching. The bull flinched as though he thought one of the other bulls had jabbed him with a horn. He ran a few steps and stood still. The other bulls began to mill and sniff the air. They smelled blood. Then they came over to the mortally wounded bull and began blatantly butting him around. They worked him over pretty well and then began to leave. The old bull tried to follow but couldn't. The group dropped just below a little ridge, stopped, and made a half-circle out in front of me. Their backs were the only thing visible. The tremendously tough old bull caught up with the group again. How he stayed on his feet I'll never know. I watched carefully, thinking that I might have to stalk within range and get another arrow into him. That prospect was grim, given that all these bulls knew exactly where I was. It wasn't long, though, before the big bull began to wobble and soon went down.

My first thought was, *Here I am with the most sophisticated equipment known to a modern-day bowhunter. How in the world did the bowhunters of long ago slay a buffalo with the equipment they had?* It seemed impossible to kill such a huge animal with a willow bow, arrow, and stone broadhead. I have always had a lot of respect for the Indians and their skills, but this experience brought home to me the reality of what those people were truly up against.

Then came the task of dressing and skinning such a huge mammal. Rolling one back and forth to get the heavy skin off, let alone the butchering, must have taken the Indians hours. On Antelope Island today, the park officials have a winch truck and a good-size crew to handle the chores. At that, it was still no easy task.

What a majestic icon of North American plains game the buffalo is—actually, the top of the majestic icons, in my opinion. I had most of the meat processed and distributed among some folks at Easton and at Hoyt, and I gave a big percentage to my guide. My family, too, enjoyed buffalo steaks that winter.

Chapter 11

# My Baca Bull—Taken Away

I believe that a big bull elk is a dream of most bowhunters. To take a big bull with a bow is quite an accomplishment. I had hunted elk in Montana with rancher friends Paul and Cathy Donohoe, for twenty years. We rifle hunted there because Paul was too busy with cow work when the elk were in the rut, and he didn't have time to take bowhunters. Today it is a different story, and Paul loves this kind of hunting.

I began researching where to go to have the best chance of: 1) getting a trophy-class elk with a bow and 2) finding an outfitter who knew how to handle bowhunters. A good friend and booking agent recommended the Baca Ranch in New Mexico. He knew the hunting manager at the Baca, a guy by the name of Dave Collus. Dave handled just the hunting operation at the Baca and, strangely enough, was originally from Michigan. He had hunted all over North America and was well known for his ability with both a rifle and a bow. His expertise in bowhunting was extraordinary, and as we found out, his attitude and personality made the Baca experience enjoyable.

The Baca is a huge ranch approaching 100,000 acres in size. It was originally a Spanish grant and had been in the same family for years. The place is still a working cattle ranch but has some of the most pristine elk country there is. Huge ponderosa pine, crystal-clear trout streams, and alpine meadows provide the ultimate habitat. The management practices were also optimum for quality elk, and numbers ran well over four thousand head on the ranch.

I decided to book a hunt for the following year. Andy Simo of New Archery Products hadn't yet shot an elk with his bow, so I talked him into going with me. The lodge at the Baca was such that it would be a

*This is what was left of Gary's bull after the two bears were done, Baca Ranch, Sandoval County, New Mexico, September 1994.*

fascinating trip for our wives, too. The accommodations are first class and the scenery is beautiful. So Andy's wife, Sheree, and my wife, Nanette, accompanied us on the trip.

I booked the second week of September on purpose, thinking that the rut would be in full swing. A lot of experience since then has taught me some other strategies, such as going in advance of the rut to call the big bulls before they have gathered a bunch of cows. That strategy varies, of course, with the area of the country, and each year may be different. But I now prefer to go before the rut.

We put in for the regular drawing in the spring, even though the Baca had landowner permits it could sell us. If we drew a permit, it would save some of the landowner permits for the Baca to sell to hunters who didn't draw one.

Year in and year out Dave Collus managed the elk herd well, making certain that an abundance of quality bulls roamed the ranch. The only thing out of the Baca's management control was that the elk migrated in the winter through an Indian reservation. A sizable harvest could take place on that reservation without restriction, and the Baca personnel never knew for sure how many elk would return to the ranch. So they had to be sure to base their harvest on total numbers of elk actually returning to the ranch in the spring.

When we arrived at the Baca, the lodge was even better than I'd imagined. Known as the kiva, it is a unique circular structure. In the center is the great room/trophy room, with the traditional Southwestern decor and relaxing atmosphere. Separate sleeping quarters surround the big room, and there is a large gourmet kitchen area where the meals, prepared by a chef, were out of this world.

Huge towering pines and alpine meadows were the setting. It wasn't unusual to see elk outside the lodge windows any time of day, but especially in the evening, and the echoes of bugles could often be heard. It was a nice surprise to find some other friends there, too. John Jackson, past president of Safari Club, was back with his wife, Chrissie. John was hunting for another big bull. He had taken a 370-class bull the previous year. Chrissie was hunting a cow. There were several other hunters from different parts of the country. One group from Texas and Arizona had made the trip to the Baca an annual event for many years. Everybody wished the best of success to all the other hunters.

A nice range was set up in the back of the lodge where we could test our bows at distances of up to seventy yards. The range included a couple of elk and deer targets. We tried our equipment and made sure that nothing had shaken loose during the trip.

The elk habitat was unbelievable. If you could wave a magic wand and cast a spell to put yourself in the best elk habitat on earth, the Baca is where you would be when the smoke cleared. The grass was waist deep in the meadows, and there was lots of steep country and heavy timber where the elk holed up during the day. The timber included some old clear-cuts with logging roads winding their way back and forth up the slopes, providing great avenues for roving and calling. Another interesting feature of the area was the Valley Caldera, a collapsed volcano that had created a basin some twelve to fifteen miles wide with a floor three thousand feet below the surrounding peaks. The wide-open meadows and scattered timber on the floor encompassed a world of premium elk habitat. Water was abundant everywhere . . . and so were bugling elk.

*Bubba was a good guide as well and elk caller, Baca Ranch, New Mexico, 1994.*

The first day we encountered hordes of elk. Several satellite bulls came within range, but the big herd bulls either wouldn't leave their cows or would move the whole herd away from our calling. Midmorning the next day we stalked close to a bedding area and spotted a group of elk lying in the timber. There must have been at least fifty, including a big herd bull. A satellite bull kept moving around the outside of the bedded cows but didn't have enough nerve to cause concern to the big herd bull that lay in the shade and watched.

The young bull also kept us pinned down, so we couldn't close the distance on the herd bull. We lay on our bellies for what seemed like forever, hoping for an opportunity to move in. The cows, of course, lay between us and the big bull. The smaller bull was tripping around the herd like a lovesick moose. He came within ten yards at one point. Although he was a younger bull, he was a shooter, but with the cows all around and our lying flat out, we couldn't move.

Finally, the big bull stood and began to tend a particular cow. He moved her back and forth among the other elk. We felt that an opportunity was about to present itself. Sure enough, the elk began getting up and milling on a bench just above us. Soon they began to move away, and we decided that the thing to do was to get to the next little clump of small pine. From the look of the situation, the elk herd's line of sight would be above and beyond our position. The plan was to bolt to the small bunch of trees and get there in time for a shot. If we could make the run unseen, we would be within thirty yards of the herd bull.

We busted out of our hide like two halfbacks out for a pass. In our first few exploding steps we had to jump a log. Well, we both had a little problem, but Bubba, my guide, had the bigger one—he tripped and fell on his face. As the big bull trotted off, he shook his head as if to say, "Where did you stooges come from?" Although the charge was blown, we couldn't help but laugh our guts out.

The evening hunt, however, was encouraging. The bulls were bugling and responding well to Bubba's calls. We had several bulls within seventy-five yards and one spike at twenty. The rut was in full swing, and the prospects looked good for the coming days.

That evening it was quite a treat to eat dinner and listen to all the elk stories. That first day, everyone had experienced close encounters of one

*This caldera was caused by the collapse of a volcanic cone, Baca Ranch, New Mexico, September 1994.*

kind or another. Bulls of every size and description had made the adrenaline surge in every wide-eyed hunter in camp.

The next few days provided many more elk encounters, but no opportunity for a shot. One encounter in particular, however, will stick with me for the rest of my life. Bubba's calling had lured a huge 340-class bull through the thick timber toward my position. As I watched, the big 7x6 canted his antlers back and forth while working his way through low-hanging branches. He was getting closer with every step, and my heart was about to pound out of my chest. As he walked behind the trunks of three big pine trees, I glanced to my left to see where there might be an opening for a broadside shot. But when he walked around the tree trunks, he tilted his head so his antlers would fit between two saplings and faced me head-on at twelve yards. He stared intently, then took a few more steps forward. It was evident he knew something was up. There was no shot, and no way to draw should he turn broadside. A head-on shot at an elk is not an option with bow and arrow in my book.

Suddenly, he bolted. I believe that our scent pool had spread along the ground far enough to reach him because of the calm air. Bubba tried to stop him with a call, but to no avail. A missed opportunity like that can make a man feel like puking. But what a rush! It's the thing we all go back to the elk woods for, time and time again.

The next afternoon, while stalking a patch of timber, we heard the clash of antlers. Judging by the sounds, they were two heavily antlered bulls. There is quite a difference between the sound of massive antlers clashing and two small rag-horn bulls sparing. We stalked the racket, careful not to bust any bedded cows. They are the toughest to get by, as they seldom get distracted the way the bulls do. We eased forward to get a look.

We reached a small opening in the timber and finally got a look at them. Both were well over 300-class bulls. As they pushed and shoved, we closed the distance. Once within range, I waited for a break in the action to get a clear, standing shot at either one. As I waited on my knees, my excitement increased.

Finally, the bulls tangled their antlers in some low-hanging branches and separated for a second or two to get reorganized. While they were jockeying for position, I drew. The bull on the left caught the movement and bolted away. The big bull on the right stepped forward and stared in my direction, presenting a broadside opportunity. When the pin settled on his vitals, the arrow was on its way. The shot looked perfect—until just before impact. The arrow deflected off a twig, hit the bull high in the back, and then bounced back toward us. I hadn't seen that tiny branch. I couldn't believe my eyes.

Inspecting the arrow, I found very little blood. But we spent a considerable time looking for the bull, just in case the hit wasn't what it appeared to be—a superficial wound. Talk about disappointment, but what action! Where else in the world do you get nonstop elk action like that?

After another day of close calls, the fourth day produced the most interesting elk action yet. After hunting most of the morning without any luck, we began walking up a road to an old oil well that Bubba said was one of his favorite "honey holes." We set up every now and then along the road and bugled, hoping for an answer. After several unsuccessful attempts, we walked to the edge of an opening, where Bubba bugled again. After a few minutes we headed across the opening.

*There is a great hot spring in the creek behind this old homestead, Baca Ranch, New Mexico, September 1994.*

When we were about halfway across, a bull opened up right on top of us. We hit the ground, and I quickly nocked an arrow. Immediately the bull emerged from the timber and bugled again. He seemed to be focused beyond and to one side of us. We figured that he was headed for the echo of our last bugle. As he walked within fifty yards of our position, Bubba gave a light cow call that stopped him in his tracks. I drew as he stopped and put the fifty-yard pin on his vitals. The release felt good, and the arrow streaked to the mark. The bull whirled and ducked back into the timber at a dead run.

Things had happened so fast that we were almost in shock. The bull was not quite what I had hoped for, but a good bull at any rate, somewhere close to the 300 mark. Bubba and I were excited about the shot and felt confident that we would find the bull in short order. We thought we had heard a crash in the timber below us. Regardless, we waited a good hour before taking up the blood trail. We quickly found where the bull had been standing and followed the galloping tracks for a short distance before finding blood. The blood trail was sparse, much to our surprise. Before long we were following pinhead-size specks of blood through the dense timber. We began to wonder if we had seen the arrow do something it hadn't really done. Concerned now about what we might find, I nocked another arrow. Carefully, one step at a time, we moved down the steep slope.

We heard a couple of strange noises and thought it must be the bull trying to get up. As we closed in, suddenly there was a long, low growl. We looked at each other wonderingly. I jerked my binocular to my eyes, homed in on the site, and saw an antler with a big black mass of hair standing beside it. A huge black bear had laid claim to my elk!

The bear became extremely aggressive as we tried to run him off. Bubba didn't have a gun, and using an arrow against an attacking bear didn't seem like the best of ideas. After several more unsuccessful attempts to run him off, we decided to go back to the lodge and get a rifle. It was a good half-hour back to the truck and an hour back to the lodge, but there were no other options.

When we got back to the lodge and told our story, no one would believe us. We at last convinced them the story was true and got permission to go back with a rifle. We hoped to be able to spook the bear. When we finally got back and eased into the timber patch—*two* bears were there. The new arrival was a huge brown-phase bear, just as mean as the first.

It was one thing to have to shoot one bear, but dealing with two aggressive bears was a different story—especially given the fact that the ranch didn't allow any bear hunting at all. After several more unsuccessful attempts to run them off, we decided to leave and return the next morning.

In the morning the bears were gone, but unfortunately, so was most of my elk. Luckily they hadn't ruined the cape or the antlers. We caped the bull and cut the antlers from the skull. I had been looking forward to some elk steaks, but there wasn't enough meat left for that. It was also a bit disappointing not to have any photos. Sometimes the top of the food chain walks away shaking his head, having lost a battle. But what an experience—one to be remembered and told around the campfire for the rest of my life. I've already related that story several times to wide-eyed hunters. The tale gets a bit taller each time, but deservedly so. Although I was disappointed at the time, I'm glad to have had that hair-raising experience to add to my collection of hunting tales.

Chapter 12

# Cathedrals of Ashnola—Rocky Mountain Goat

My very first Rocky Mountain goat hunt was up the Stakeen River at Casey's Camp, Mess Lake, British Columbia. Bill Moynihan of Skyline Outfitters had taken me to some rugged terrain, where we hunted grizzlies and goats for two weeks. The country was rough and steep, and some areas were simply inaccessible to me. It was one of the toughest hunts I had ever been on, and unfortunately, I didn't get a shot at anything.

I kept my eyes open for another outfitter and put the word out that I was looking for a good goat hunt. I had always wanted to hunt with Clarence Schneider. Clarence was well known and had one of the best areas anywhere for big goats. I called and asked him to put me on his list for a future hunt. He called the following October, in 1995, after a hunter had canceled. So I shifted a bunch of business engagements and some other hunts to get the chance to go. The hunt was to be from 14 through 22 November.

Clarence's operation is known as Ashnola Guide and Outfitters. He operated out of Ashnola Keremeos, British Columbia. The British Columbia Fish and Game people didn't allow many nonresident hunters in this area because of the huge tourist trade—it seems sightseeing tourists tend not to understand the conservation aspects of hunting. Consequently, getting to hunt in this exclusive area was quite a privilege. To my surprise there were lots of orchards with various types of fruit throughout the valley. There were also some vineyards. The area was spectacular, with huge mountains and many rivers and streams.

The first day we drove halfway up the mountain on an old logging and mining road. We then walked toward the top, where the timber began getting sparse. We quickly found the goats that Clarence and his son Darrell had scouted, but they had moved to the northern slope of a smaller

*Gary's 9-inch billy (45⁴⁄₈) is a good representative of the Rocky Mountain goat, Keremeos, British Columbia, November 1995.*

mountain across the way. The rut was getting started, and the billies were beginning to follow the nannies.

Social structure is variable in mountain goats, and zoologists differ as to whether the males or females are dominant. The sexes seem indifferent to each other except when mating. Nannies and kids are commonly found in herds, and billies are solitary or congregate in small bachelor groups. As the mating season approaches, the males dig rutting pits that they soak with urine, and their sides and bellies become stained by the wet soil. Older males can be identified at a great distance during the rut by their soiled appearance. The males fight each other for mating dominance. They do not fight head to head but instead stand head to rump and strike with their sharp horns against each other's belly and haunches—often with fatal results. Mating occurs from November to January, with births in May and June.

The swirling winds blew hard that day, making stalking difficult. We were getting a few glimpses of goats at thirty to fifty yards—at which point they would catch our wind and take off. Around midday, while switchbacking down a ridge, we made a sharp 90-degree turn in some small trees. Suddenly, four nannies and two billies busted from a trail below us. They stood and stared. The closest was at ten yards, the farthest at fifteen. One of the billies' horns was about eight inches in length, and I was having a hard time turning him down, knowing how hard these critters are to get with a bow. Clarence and Darrell, however, advised against it. We couldn't move a muscle anyway, so getting the shot would have been tough.

They stared for a while and then vanished in a couple of easy jumps. It was amazing how fast they disappeared. The mountain goat is an extremely tough and hardy animal, the most sure-footed mountaineer of any New World ungulate. It is renowned for its ability to climb and jump in rough terrain. It moves deliberately even when alarmed or threatened, although it can run rather well if necessary. Mountain goats swim well, too.

We saw a few others before evening fell, at which point we began to work our way out of the steep slopes. The mountainside with its treacherous footing would be a dangerous place to be in the dark. We made our way back to the pickup and headed for the Schneiders' home, where we had a great meal and plenty of bowhunting conversation. The night went quickly. I slept like a log.

The next morning Clarence had some cow work to finish before the big snows began to fly. Clarence thought that I should go back to the same area. He knew there were some large goats somewhere in that basin. So Darrell and I drove to the same place and hoofed it to the top. We glassed a few billies across the valley, but the terrain was too steep to get to them. We hoped they would end up on our side before the day was over. They were moving toward the females on our side. Rocky Mountain goats are most active in the early morning and late afternoon, and they frequently continue grazing throughout the night. Their movements during the day generally cover several hundred yards, although when they are in the rut and chasing nannies it is hard to say how far they will go.

We moved slowly over the terrain, fifty or so yards at a time, and glassed. Darrell spotted some goats coming up a hogback just below us, and we crouched down behind the trunks of two large pines close together that provided some good cover. The goats proceeded up the hogback, feeding slowly, and it seemed as though they would never get within range. There were seven billies and four nannies, and of the billies, one was close to being a 12-inch goat. There were also two 10- or 11-inch billies, a 9-incher, and some smaller ones.

Of course, I had my sights set on the big one. At one point the he was sixty yards away and broadside. But what with the direction the group was moving in, there was little doubt that a closer opportunity would present itself. The drawback to waiting was not knowing where the biggest goat might end up when the group was in our lap. The other big question: Would I be able to draw without being noticed by the others?

As we waited, the billies changed position several times. The big goats were in front for a while, then the small ones. They switched back and forth for another hour, until I thought I'd lose my mind. Finally, a 10-inch billy moved in close, far ahead of the rest. I whispered, "He's big enough for me, if he presents a good shot." Darrell nodded.

The billy went behind some brush on the side of the hill and disappeared. He topped out just below our position at thirty-five yards and turned broadside. Even though he was looking at us, I drew and let fly. The arrow hit him in the side, and he lunged to his right. He regained his feet and ran toward a ridgeline that dropped into a steep chute. When he jumped off the edge we heard a crash, followed by what seemed like several minutes of tumbling down the shale-covered slide. I couldn't help but wonder what would be left of his horns when we found him.

The rest of the goats spooked for a couple of jumps, then stopped and stared. They were more curious than afraid. A group of nannies came up to where my billy had stood and looked over the edge. The big 12-inch goat followed them and turned broadside at fifty yards. To top that, he looked the other way and presented the perfect shot. What are the odds? But that is how it always works, as you know. The goat gods were watching over him, without question. I pulled the bow back, put the fifty-yard pin on him, and imagined what it would have been like to sink an arrow into his side.

We sat for another fifteen minutes as the other goats milled. They went down the chute where my goat had gone and appeared on the other side. Then they stood for a short while before disappearing over the ridge.

We eased over to the slide and glassed for my goat, but to our surprise we saw nothing. We then dropped below the chute to look up from the bottom. The goat had made it over a huge log and now lay below it. That's why we couldn't see him from above. We labored our way up. The footing was treacherous. The shale was so loose and the slide so steep that for every two steps forward we skidded one back.

When we got to the billy the guide and I saw that he was 9 inches, rather than 10. But it was no big deal. In my book, goat with a bow is a great accomplishment no matter what size it is. Darrell had done a fine job guiding, and we had a good billy. I'd spent two weeks on my other goat hunt and hadn't gotten close enough for a shot. Here success had come on the second day.

We had to dig out a ledge with our hands and feet to get the billy to stay in one place for pictures. We decided to gut him there, too. It would be easier than dragging him to a nearby hogback.

After we had finished getting ready for the hike back to camp, we sat for a few minutes and gazed across the peaks and valleys. This was breathtaking terrain, as far as the eye could see. I wondered what it would be like to live in a place like this, to spend a lifetime here. I looked at the magnificent mountain goat I had just taken and thought about the bit of remorse I was feeling for killing such a monarch of the mountain peaks. I thought of all the perils this goat had faced from mountain lions, wolves, and other predators. Even though it is important to the conservation and

*Goats love this kind of terrain—the steeper the better! Keremeos, British Columbia, November 1995.*

overall health of wildlife to manage herd numbers by hunting, we are not human if we don't wonder about these things. But those thoughts are quickly put to rest when I think of how important the management of our wildlife resources is and how man has affected wildlife since the day he stepped onto the earth. There is no turning back the clock. He will go on affecting wildlife until the end of time. It has always been up to humans to manage wildlife resources and habitat, and we do a far better job today than ever before. I am proud to be a part of wildlife conservation.

Darrell and I packed the entire goat out in one trip and returned to the Schneiders' house by dark. Clarence admired the beautiful goat and commented that he wished we had taken one of the "whopper" billies they'd seen on their many scouting trips. But he was happy we had gotten one. He knew how hard it is to take a goat with a bow.

If any bowhunter, new or old, wants one of the ultimate challenges in the bowhunting world, try Rocky Mountain goat hunting. The scenery is spectacular and the physical challenge is difficult. To take this challenge, a bowhunter must be in top physical condition and prepare for a lot of high-altitude hiking. I dare say that if someone gave me a goat permit at my present age, I would have to think long and hard about going. I might not take it.

Chapter 13

# The Ghosts of Knight Inlet

As we flew from the little town of Campbell River over magnificent scenery toward Knight Inlet, the vast expanse of mountains and water was breathtaking. Waterfalls cascaded from the mountainsides, and tree-covered peaks towered above the water like immense statues guarding the many passages below. The vegetation looked thick enough to smother whatever might lie beneath. Big bears shadowed through my mind as I imagined them lurking under the forest canopy. I wondered what tests I would face down there, and if I could meet the challenges ahead. Was my resolve as strong as I thought? The explorer and pioneer inside reassured me that, regardless of how things unfolded, this would be another adventure of a lifetime.

Having been on three bowhunts for grizzly bear in Alaska without taking a bear, I had sat at my office desk and contemplated where to go next. The guide I would choose for this hunt had to be knowledgeable and fearless, but also understanding of bowhunters and bowhunting. The previous hunts all had been exciting and eventful, but I could never get into position for a responsible shot.

An urgency was building inside me to arrow a respectable grizzly. Being successful this time would inch me closer to a personal goal, the North American Twenty-Eight with bow and arrow. In addition, time seemed to be catching up with me a bit more each year. The spirit may be willing, but the legs lag behind a step or two. The many steep slopes and countless treks into the unknown have tended to slow down my youthful desire for "just one more mountain."

I'd written down several names on a piece of paper, but Don Rose of Trophy West kept coming to the top of the list. I had hunted with Don

*Gary's Columbia blacktail was taken in the riverbottom country of Knight Inlet, British Columbia, October 1996.*

before, taking a big black bear and a nice Roosevelt elk. Don hunted grizzlies out of Knight Inlet along the coast in western British Columbia. Knight is a remote inlet accessible only by boat or plane and renowned for its great density of grizzlies, probably the highest in all of British Columbia. To top it off, Don and his crew were used as a major resource for a bear census run by the Canadian government. Those guys definitely had a lot of experience with big bears.

The grizzlies at Knight Inlet arrive there from fifty to seventy-five miles away, and the trails the bears use are literally hundreds of years old. Generation after generation of grizzlies have made the trip annually, and there's a reason: Enormous fish populations spawn in the streams and rivers flowing into the inlet. In addition, the coastal climate produces huge amounts of vegetation that adds to the bears' diet. The bears of Knight Inlet are some of the biggest on record and rival those of coastal Alaska.

The stage was soon set with a few phone calls, which included hiring longtime friend and video cameraman Ralph Cianciarulo to document the adventure. Don Rose agreed to take me on 1 October—three years hence. That's right, three years! Don was allotted three tags per year, and he could take only a chosen few.

Don and his crew met the floatplane as we stepped onto the beach. Old acquaintances were renewed, and we made some new friends while unloading provisions and gear. We caught up on the latest adventures in the area while we proceeded to camp. Camp there consisted of a cabin rented from one of the small lumber companies still operating in the area. It was a comfortable little place with a good woodstove and plenty of room. Ralph made sure that the camera survived the trip and began organizing camera equipment. I unpacked my bows and arrows, hoping that they, too, had made the long journey safely. Once our gear was checked and arranged, we began to settle in.

With hands in my pockets, I ambled over to the open cabin door, leaned lightly against the doorjamb, and gazed out into the dense jungle. The water in a nearby stream whispered down through the valley floor, and my mind flew to the days when trappers came to this land to seek their fortunes. What did it look like then? How big were the bears? Could there have been an old trapper's cabin on this very spot, laden with furs hanging from the log rafters? I pictured a heavily bearded man sitting in the dim yellow light of a fire, fleshing a hide soon to be stretched and hung to dry, his stern face and dark, vigilant eyes concentrating on the task at hand. What perils did he face? Certainly bears played a large part in his adventures. If only the towering fir could tell the story.

This was still a truly wild place, as new to me as it was to the explorers of long ago when they took their first steps on the beaches there. It was apparent to me that this place, the land as well as the animals, demanded a healthy respect and appreciation. It felt inviting, yet harsh and unforgiving. Certainly those who took this country for granted stood a good chance that their dreams, and possibly their lives, would vanish without a trace.

I slowly strolled back across the creaking wooden floor to my bed, where I'd placed a prototype bow that Hoyt Archery Company had sent me just a few weeks before. Lying beside the bow were my Easton 2413 arrows, tipped with an experimental two-bladed broadhead. In other words, here I was in grizzly country with an experimental bow called the Alphatec and an unproven broadhead called the Spitfire! Even though I had fired the combination time and time again—much to my satisfaction—who was to say that either wouldn't fail at the moment of truth? I seriously wondered why in the hell I had brought them. I had my old standby equipment with me, of course, but I was determined to keep my commitment to the inventors of the new gear. I stepped outside for a few reassuring practice shots.

Bowhunting for grizzlies in the Knight Inlet country presents special problems. Because of the rain forest climate, the cover is so thick that there is only one way to hunt the bears: from elevated positions such as tree stands or rock overhangs along small streams. Every year, Don and his crew have to clear paths through the tangle of brush just to get to the spawning streams. The bush consists of willows, alders, thick ferns, blueberry, and thorny blackberry bushes, to name a few. If you step off one of these cleared trails, you can't see five feet in front of you. The only other "openings" are deer and bear trails, which require crawling on hands and knees. Don said there were a lot of bears in the area and that we should have a great hunt—if the weather held. The weather on the western coast of British Columbia is always unpredictable except for one constant: It will rain. Heavy-duty rain gear is essential.

Early the next morning we awoke to a light drizzle, a condition that would be our constant companion throughout the trip. As we waited for dawn

Ralph and I readied our equipment and put on our hip boots. Hip boots are a must on a trip like this because you are constantly wading. Also, the entire crew put on Scent-Lok suits. Bears possess some of the best noses of all the living beasts, so scent elimination is critical when hunting grizzly.

We had all decided that it made little sense to get to the stands before first light since the chances of bumping into a bear in the dark here were very good. Even though the guide, Bruce Watson, carried an old .45-70 rifle, the bullet would do very little good against an invisible bear in the dark. It would be tough enough getting to the stands without running into one in broad daylight.

A dim light slowly filtered into the foliage outside. Moss-covered trees began to take shape as morning crept into the forest. As rainwater dripped monotonously from the cabin's eaves, the anticipation of the coming day electrified the room, making it difficult to stand still. Imaginary scenes from the day ahead began racing through my mind. Pictures of great bears flashed like still photos through my brain, and the mechanics of drawing the bow and where to hold the pin snapped into my consciousness. Releasing properly and making a clean kill were paramount. Would I achieve these goals? Only time would tell.

I had been here mentally many times before. It is the place where the hours and hours of practice, and the many hunts already experienced, begin to take over and set my frame of mind. But would all of the practice and all the experience be enough for me to make the shot without nerves or age fouling up the works? This is also the place where I wonder if I still possess the "edge."

We followed the trails cleared by Don and his crew, but it seemed that the bears liked those trails, too. The bear beds we came across in the trails looked at times as if a whole herd of grizzlies had camped there. We jumped bears on our way to the stands several times during the course of the trip, and once a bear growled at us from somewhere in the brush as we passed. I turned around on another occasion and learned that a grizzly was following our group up the trail—just ten yards behind us! The jaunts to and from the stands proved to be as tough on our nerves as anything.

Once in the stands, though, I breathed a sigh of relief. At least I could see a bear coming in. In the bush, if a grizzly decided to charge, there

*Gary with his hard-earned grizzly, Knight Inlet, British Columbia, Canada, October 1996.*

would be little time to react. In the stand, there's a better chance of a bear not knowing you're there, and the margin of safety seems better—but not foolproof. A bear might sneak up and tear hunter and stand down; it wouldn't take much effort for a bear. We were using ladder stands, set up in big alders along small streams. We also sat on rock outcroppings just above and overhanging streams.

The locations chosen by Don and his crew were on crystal-clear tributary streams teeming with salmon. Big bears often prefer these smaller streams because there is more cover, the fish are easier to catch, and there is less competition from other bears. Big boars are solitary in nature and prefer not to be bothered. Smaller bears stay in more open areas along the big rivers to avoid bumping into the bigger bears and being eaten. Finding these little streams in heavy cover is key to getting a good, mature boar.

Since the bush is extremely thick along the water's edge and the water is reasonably deep, you would think that a nine-hundred-pound bear would make a significant amount of noise when approaching. Not so! Often I could neither hear nor see anything when a bear came in. I would be looking up the stream, let's say, and when I turned to look downsteam again, there one stood. They drifted in and out like spirits, often appearing in the middle of the stream where nothing had been a moment before. It was as though the riffles and stones had metamorphosed into hulking brown muscle and fur. Every time it happened I stopped breathing and my blood seemed to freeze. It was frightening, yet awesome.

Throughout the course of the trip we had an opportunity to watch several smaller bears fishing in front of or beneath our stands. Several times I had bears walk beneath the overhang on which I was sitting. In many instances bears fished only a few yards from my ladder stand. One particular bear put on a show at one of the stands almost every day we were there. He was such an actor we called him Hollywood. These bears were excellent fishers. They would walk along the bank, reach down and under an overhanging bank or log, and spook salmon into the shallows. The bear would then dive from the bank and run up and down the stream, chasing fish until he caught one. In some of the deeper pools the bears would put their heads under the water and walk through the pool, sweeping their heads back and forth, looking for fish. Once a fish was caught, the bears

*Cameraman Ralph Cianciarulo makes sport of the extremely wet conditions, Knight Inlet, British Columbia, October 1996.*

would take it into the bush, just off the stream about ten yards, and begin eating. Then it was generally time for a five- or ten-minute nap.

Many times the bears would wait back in the bush until they heard another bunch of salmon splashing up the shallow riffles. Without warning they would burst from the brush and dive into the water. A problem that came to mind after watching this was that splashing up the creek in our hip boots on the way to a stand might provoke the same reaction from any grizzly. These little streams were only fifteen to thirty feet wide, and there was a good chance we could suddenly be eyeball to eyeball with a big boar—or, worse, a female with cubs. Neither possibility much appealed to me.

One evening Ralph, my cameraman, and I were watching an average-size bear fishing in front of our stands just a few yards away. About half an hour before dark, the bear suddenly stood up and stared into the bush behind my stand. He then leaped out of the stream and ran headlong into the tree in which Ralph was sitting. The tree shook wildly, and Ralph hung on for dear life. The bear bounced off the tree, stopped, and then looked back. A guttural growl emerged from the bush behind me. The hair rose on the back of my neck as I slowly turned in time to see a huge bear step from the cover. The smaller bear had seemed to know by some amazing mental telepathy—without any physical warning—that something large and omnivorous was sneaking up on him, either to claim its part of the salmon bounty or to ambush the younger bear. The smaller bear left fast, after which the huge bear tested the air, sensed something wrong, and vanished into the brush.

Without question bears have developed some type of extrasensory perception, some mental or supernatural ability that humans do not possess or at least cannot use at will. Both bears knew that something was wrong before the threat presented itself. It's just one more factor in the carnivore's favor and one more reason that the grizzly is a formidable challenge for a bowhunter.

The rain persisted, day after day. Sometimes it came down in sheets, sometimes in a slow, steady drizzle like Chinese water torture. It began to wear on everybody. We were continuously chilled to the bone. Even though we had the best rain gear made, we were never really dry until we shed our gear at night and sat by the woodstove in the cabin. The only other time we got a break was when it rained so hard that the streams became swollen and muddy. The bears knew better than to fish in the murky water and would just quit moving. Then we would trek back to camp and spend the rest of the day drying out.

It was the seventh day of the hunt and things had been going well, except for the continuous rain and the fact that we hadn't yet had an opportunity at a mature boar. Many of the bears were close to being the right size and age, but it was important to take only a large, mature bear as part of the conservation and harvesting policy we had all agreed upon.

As I sat in the stand hour after passing hour that day, I was beginning to fade. I wondered if I had made a mistake passing up some of the bears that had been extremely close to the minimum size. Had I even made a mistake coming to this place? Was the relentless rain a sign that I wasn't meant to get a grizzly with my bow? Was the constant strain of preparing mentally for a shot and being continuously on guard for a grizzly ambush beginning to take its toll? Had the grim possibility of someone being attacked begun corroding my resolve? Given enough time, all these things can wear any man down, mentally and physically.

In weighing how much more of this I could take, I gazed at the raindrops gathering on my bow limb. I watched them slowly merge and trickle to the bottom edge and then drop one by one to the stream below. I was pondering the possibility of this being my fourth failed grizzly hunt when suddenly, in the crystal reflection, there materialized an awesome shadow. I froze.

This was the biggest bear yet! My heart leaped and pounded in my ears. The shakes overtook me, and I knew that I had to calm myself. The shot could present itself at any moment.

The steady drizzle gathering on my face made it difficult to concentrate, and water began trickling from my brows directly into my eyes. But I didn't dare to move. I began to wonder if I would be able to see to make the shot. The big bear scent-checked the air and slowly moved his head from side to side. He briefly looked away, presenting me an opportunity to raise my bow; he then proceeded upstream, quartering away slightly. The bear seemed to be searching the water beneath our rock ledge. As if he knew something wasn't right, he glanced up toward our location—moving just his eyes—several times as he moved. There was no question he knew that something was up. He stopped abruptly, sniffed the water again, and momentarily looked away. I took that as the opportunity to draw. My sight pin wavered all over the bear's massive shoulder as excitement began to get the better of me. Finally, I recomposed myself and settled the pin solidly behind his front shoulder. The string hummed and the arrow flashed toward its mark.

Just at that moment, the big boar took a step backward and turned toward me, all in one motion, before the arrow could reach him. The broadhead struck just in front of the bear's shoulder. My first thought was, *Oh, God, I've wounded a grizzly bear!*

The ponderous creature roared at the arrow as he turned and raced along the water's edge. He crossed the stream, jumped up the bank, and disappeared into the brush.

The emotional roller coaster began immediately. First there was instant apprehension about the shot, then a flicker of hope. The shaft showed good penetration, considering the point of impact. I could hardly believe that the bear had taken a complete step backward while the arrow was in midflight. It was only a thirty-two-yard shot. I could only hope that the broadhead was in a place where it would do its job quickly. I began replaying the shot in my mind, over and over.

As the evening light waned, it became apparent that it was too dark to go after a potentially wounded grizzly. We would have to return in the morning. Leaving the stand that evening required extra fortitude. Not only was the situation disappointing and uncertain but, in addition, there was also a chance that the bear had circled back and was lying in wait along the trail.

We made it back to camp without incident. Sleep evaded me as I replayed the shot countless times in my mind. At times like these a bowhunter begins to hate his own fallibility and the unpredictability of the quarry. The bow and arrow is a lethal weapon when the arrow finds its way to the vitals of an animal. But factor in human error and an animal with a mind of its own—and things can go wrong. Every good bowhunter does his very best to make a clean and efficient kill, but at times like these it's easy to begin to wonder why we are here.

The next morning, as we listened to the downpour on the roof, anxiety hung in the air. We spoke little as we readied our gear. We each knew the perils involved in tracking a wounded grizzly through almost impenetrable bush. We also knew that the likelihood of finding a decent blood trail in this rain would be nil. I silently prayed that the bear had died shortly after leaving the bank of the stream and would be lying only a short way into the bush.

*Knight Inlet is beautiful but harsh country, British Columbia, October 1996.*

We trekked directly to where the bear had stood the previous evening. Bruce Watson stood at ready, with a round in the chamber of the .45-70. Brian Swift, another guide in camp, checked for sign. We then proceeded to where the bear had jumped out of the stream and onto the bank. As expected, there was very little blood. The only blood we could find, in fact, was between two leaves, where the rain had washed it and watered it down. The ground there is covered in moss, and tracks were impossible to find. When a bear steps on the moss it leaves a depression, but the moss quickly springs back into place as if nothing has disturbed it. Once in a great while, however, you might see a slight depression in the spongy surface.

Scant blood on the bottom side of leaves was the only way we were going to find this bear. So we got down on our hands and knees and began trailing. Now, I'm not ashamed to tell you that being on hands and knees in heavy brush, trailing a grizzly, will test your grit. *Is he lying dead at the end of this meager trail, or is he waiting for an opportunity to unleash his fury?* Such thoughts possess you every step of the way. Every unrecognizable noise ahead sent adrenaline throughout my body.

Evidence showed that the bear had lain down only twenty yards from the stream. We found blood there, but not enough to be convincing. Typically, bears don't bleed much on the ground because their hair soaks up incredible amounts of blood. Also, they have huge layers of fat that many times will plug entry and exit wounds, preventing blood from escaping. My heart sank, though, seeing that the bear had gotten up and proceeded on. There was still a chance that the big grizzly had died somewhere just ahead, but it was only a possibility. When we bowhunters unleash an arrow, we accept the responsibility; we owe it to the animals we hunt to follow to the end of the trail, regardless of the risk.

The guides and I inched along on hands and knees, ever vigilant ahead and behind. Wounded grizzlies are noted for circling and attacking from behind. This bear had lain down two more times within a short distance. We had proceeded about two hundred yards when Bruce raised his hand, signaling us to hold up. He glassed intently through the tangled cover, then turned and whispered, "There's a huge brown form just ahead, under that bushy bottomed fir tree."

"It's a bear, bedded down!"

"Be ready for anything!"

We watched intensely for several minutes before Bruce whispered again, "Gary, come with me!"

The wind was swirling a bit, and we needed to get downwind of the bear. The suspense mounted as we circled through a small creek step by careful step, creeping ever closer. My arms began to ache as I approached with my bow and arrow at ready. I found myself grimacing in anticipation of what might happen next.

Once we had stalked to within twenty yards, we looked at each other with question and concern. If the big bear charged at this range, we were in serious trouble. More than one grizzly has played possum, much to a hunter's dismay. At ten yards the huge form was ominous, but remained motionless. Bruce picked up a small stick and motioned for me to draw. He raised his rifle and hurled the stick in the bear's direction. The moment of truth had arrived.

A flood of emotions overtook me when I realized that the big grizzly was dead. We'd done it! The strain of the entire week had finally come to a head, and I felt the last bit of energy drain from my body. I was so elated, yet so fatigued mentally and physically that I actually staggered. I struggled to hold back tears, the way an Olympian does who has just won the gold metal. But inner strength and pride held me at the threshold—along with the need to muster enough energy to skin this huge carnivore and get it back to camp safely.

Obviously, I don't take events like these lightly. All hunts, especially bear hunts, are genuinely spiritual events for me. The effort and teamwork it takes to make a hunt like this a success constitute a major undertaking for all involved. Based on my many humbling experiences, one of the most important facts any hunter should never forget is this: The "Great Spirit" ultimately determines the roles here. Whether I possess the skill and nerve to kill the bear or whether the bear in the end eludes or kills me is only remotely up to me. A huge part of the emotion involved in this experience is the realization that in a grizzly-human confrontation, the human does not stand a chance. But on this day, God chose me! If that doesn't choke you up, nothing will.

Later on, handshakes were exchanged all around as we celebrated the great adventure and admired the grizzly as a truly sacred being. It is no wonder that the bowhunters of long ago worshiped the grizzly.

Because of heavy fog and more rain, the floatplane for the trip home couldn't get into camp. Don suggested that I use the extra tags I'd purchased to hunt a black bear or a black-tailed deer while we waited for the weather to break. The Columbia blacktail interested me. It was another of the North American Twenty-Eight that I hadn't taken. Don and the crew had seen several blacktails feeding along the edge of an abandoned runway not far from camp. There was some green vegetation there, such as clover, that the deer seemed to like. The heavy cover around the old runway was a willow thicket. The runway itself was wide open, and the blacktails liked to bed and feed in the open areas, where they were less likely to be ambushed by the many bears.

We stalked just in the edge of the cover most of the day, peeking out on the runway every little bit. We finally found and stalked within range of two black-tailed bucks. The range was just short of forty yards. Although the bucks were only forkhorns, Columbia blacktails are not easy to come by. Remembering that I had hunted for more than eight years for my first white-tailed buck as a young man, I decided that either was a trophy to me. Fortunately the arrow passed through both lungs of the buck, and he didn't go far. To take two of the species I needed for the North American Twenty-eight on one trip was a real stroke of luck. And now we had fresh venison, too!

We dressed the deer, took him back, and hung him in a shed next to the cabin. Everyone was looking forward to some fresh tenderloins for supper. We were sitting around sipping hot coffee and watching it rain when I noticed, through the window, that the door to the shed was open. Now, keep in mind that this shed was only fifteen feet from the cabin. When I looked more closely, I could make out a big grizzly inside trying to tear the deer from the rafters. My first thought was to run out and chase it away. But when I opened the screen door, I came to my senses and realized what I was about to do. The other guys jumped up and began to holler. One grabbed a rifle and another grabbed a pan and began beating on it. When the bear came out of the shed, we saw that it was a big sow with a yearling cub. We were fortunate she didn't take a stand. Instead, she ran off into the woods with her cub close behind.

The guides secured the deer to the rafters again and reinforced the door. We all remarked at the bear's bravery and disdain for human scent. About an hour later we again heard a noise coming from the shed. The door was still closed, but something was definitely inside making a racket. I have to admit we were a bit reluctant to open the door. When we did, we saw that the big sow had returned, had broken through a window in the back of the shed, torn the deer down, and was trying to push it back out through the window. Luckily for us, it wouldn't fit the way she had it positioned. This time she was difficult to run off. She had laid claim to my deer and wasn't giving up easily. She finally left after considerable effort on our part. We had to take the deer to a new and hidden location. Once again I was amazed at the ingenuity and the mental capacity of these huge bears.

The next morning the weather broke just enough for a single-engine Otter to get in and pick us up. As we flew I looked, still astonished at the majestic scenery below. I silently thanked those powers greater than myself for an unforgettable trip. Equally important, I reflected on the overall outdoor experience, including the camaraderie between men and the time spent with Nature, from her moody temperament to her many glorious creations. I humbly considered the antics and lessons learned from the creatures here. The ways of the animal world are always fascinating. I marveled at the cleansing of the soul that occurs on a hunt. The quest for that kind of experience will continue to take me on many adventures as long as these legs will carry me.

In closing, I wish to thank Don, Bruce, Brian, and Ralph for their part in making my trip a success and for their lifelong friendship.

Chapter 14

# Stone Sheep

Sheep are the ultimate challenge for any hunter. The trophy is as much the adventure as the ram. To be perched on the top of the world looking into some of the most pristine landscapes known to man is a gift all by itself. The grandeur of the scene fills the spirit with awe, and the hardships and danger validate our strength and resolve. At the same time, our ego comes face to face with our mortal limitations. Nature and the mountains do what they wish. If you get in the way unprepared, you will perish. The mountains, the weather, the water, the wind—they decide your fate. If you give them their due and respect their ability to snuff your candle, you may survive. And if you possess what it takes, your shot at a sheep will come.

My second Stone sheep hunt was with a rifle in 1987. Dave Weins of Toad River, British Columbia, was the outfitter, and we hunted a place called Stone Mountain. At the time, I'd booked Dave's first-ever thirty-day sheep hunt. I was bound and determined to get a Boone and Crockett Stone sheep, and I wanted to make sure we had plenty of time. Barry Clark was my guide, and on the twenty-first day of the hunt I shot the biggest Stone ram taken in Canada in seventeen years. The big ram was thirteen years old and presently holds SCI's No. 2 spot. It still ranks very high in the Boone and Crockett record book. This Stone sheep is one of my most prized trophies, and I feel fortunate to have had a one-in-a-million opportunity. But my ultimate goal was to take a Stone with a bow and arrow.

My first Stone sheep hunt with a bow was again with Dave Weins on Stone Mountain. The hunt was scheduled for 1 through 14 August 1992 and would headquarter at the Cabin Creek camp. Dave had two nice cabins built along the creek, and the camp was set up well. My guide, Dave Linguist, his wife, and one of their young children spent most of the summer and fall there. Dave

*Peter Whitlow is cooking the backstraps from our sheep in the rain, Besa River, British Columbia, August 1998.*

knew the country well. There was a little-known mineral lick two hours on horseback from the main camp. The plan was for me to sit there and wait for a ram. The son of the well-known hunter Jimmy Ryan had taken a good ram there the previous year. This mineral lick, though, was situated where you had to glass from a distance and then stalk once the rams came in. The closest shot you could expect was seventy yards. After several days without any luck at the mineral lick, we began to hunt in the mountains around camp.

One of our problems was that wolves had moved into the area, making the sheep scarce. We saw wolf sign every day. The animals were thick enough that one day we spotted two of them walking the trail just ahead of us and our horses. I could have easily shot either with a rifle. Even with the pressure from the wolves, I did get a chance at a good ram toward the end of the hunt. The shot missed, though, when the sheep moved just as I released an arrow.

Dave felt bad about the situation, and he was a real gentleman and offered me another hunt that year if a hunter got his sheep early. He would call and have me come back, as long as they were still up there and had the room. I did get the call, and I went back for the last part of September and a few days in October. The hunting was tough again, but we did manage to get in on a small group of rams. One had a broken leg. He was with two other rams and appeared to be the only legal ram of the three. A ram must be eight years old to be legal. We glassed for a long time, trying to decipher his age. Finally, Dave decided that he was eight, and we began a stalk. The rams were in a horseshoe-shaped bowl with sheer walls around the edges. We stalked within eighty yards but had no chance to get closer. Peeking over the edge and looking straight under the sheer cliff was the only way we could see the sheep. The only option for a shot was to have Dave hang onto my belt as I leaned out over the edge.

The angle was so severe that I held the forty-yard pin on the ram even though the distance was eighty yards. I still overshot it. He jumped up and ran about ten yards and stood broadside. Dave pulled me back and I nocked another arrow. I leaned out again, put the thirty-yard pin behind his front shoulder, and overshot him again. The rams gathered themselves and left the country.

The weather went sour the next day, so we spent the rest of the hunt looking for moose and elk in the lower country. My poor luck held steady, and I missed both an elk and a moose. I must say that I was pretty disappointed

*Water was so scarce that we had to collect rain to use in camp. Guide Will Davis on a mountaintop, Besa River, British Columbia, August 1998.*

in my shooting ability and felt like a bowhunting misfit. Two Stone sheep hunts in one year and both awesome experiences—but no sheep. When hoping for a sheep with a bow, accepting a fair amount of failure is part of the formula. Back to the drawing board!

I didn't get back to hunt Stone sheep until the fall of 1998, when I booked a hunt with Greg Williams. Greg was a friend and hunting acquaintance who had sold his operation in the Northwest Territories and moved to British Columbia. He was leasing an operation from an old-timer he knew from Fort St. John, British Columbia.

I flew in to Fort St. John and met Greg, then drove up to a jump-off point just beyond a place called Pink Mountain. We would then fly to an area called the Lower Besa River. There was also a lower mountain range close by that we would hunt, where there was a small band of sheep that contained a couple legal rams. Greg took only one ram a year from this area, saving it primarily for bowhunters.

We flew in to a valley camp on the Besa River where we would backpack to a higher camp on the mountain. There was no place large enough to land on top, so Greg flew to the upper campsite and dropped some provisions from the plane: the propane bottles and other heavier items that we wouldn't be able to pack in. As it was, we were going to pack around sixty to seventy pounds on our backs to the top of the mountain. Water would be available from small seeps scattered along the slopes around the upper camp.

My guide was a native from the area by the name of Will Davis. Greg had also hired a guide-packer, Peter Whitlow, to lighten our loads and help out generally. The day before the season began we hefted our heavy packs and headed up the mountain. The trip was long and arduous, but the abundance of wildlife kept it interesting. We saw elk and moose at several points along the way. The sixty-pound pack and the cumbersome bow took their toll on me by the time I'd reached the upper camp. I wasn't sure if I could have taken another step. The days of charging uphill "like Grant took Richmond" were long gone for me! We arrived late in the evening, but thanks to the long days at that time of year, we weren't stumbling around in the dark.

We set up two dome tents equipped with rain flies, then located the provision bags that Greg had dropped about a quarter-mile away. But when we went to get some water, we found the seeps dry. It goes without

*Author's camp on the lower Besa River, British Columbia, August 1998.*

saying that was a major problem, and we decided to search for water first thing in the morning. In the meanwhile, Peter volunteered to hike two-thirds of the way back and get some water from a spring we had seen on the way up. When Peter returned, we had some supper and went to bed early.

Sleep came hard in anticipation of the next morning, not to mention that my legs cramped in the night from the long climb. The next morning nature's call forced me out of my bag early. When I opened the tent flap, fog thicker than pudding hit me in the face. Since the others weren't up when I got back, I decided to slip over to the edge of the basin near camp. I was watching my step carefully because of the fog, and it was a good thing. When I peered over the edge of the basin, I was shocked to see a band of sheep that included several ewes, lambs, and a few young rams. I crawled back away from the edge and ran back to camp.

I awoke the guys and told them about the sheep. We all scrambled to get dressed and gather our gear. I grabbed my bow, and we headed back into the fog to see if any legal rams were there. Will Davis eased up to the edge while Peter and I hung back and awaited the verdict. It was tough to evaluate the rams because of the fog, and so we backed off and circled downwind; the sheep, too, were moving down the mountain slope.

The place the sheep had chosen was unusual for this part of the country. The mountain crest was a plateau, open on the top as if the crown had been cut off. It was similar to the Nahanni Butte area of the Northwest Territories. The top was about three hundred yards wide, with canyons and fingers running down from the main ridge.

We peeked over the ridge at various intervals, trying to locate the sheep. As sheep have a tendency to do, they had disappeared. We decided to split up so we might have a better chance of finding them before they got out of the country. Peter and I crossed over to the other side of the drainage to look at the ridge from a different angle and to take a peek into the next basin. Will proceeded down the ridge in the direction he thought the sheep had gone. By the time we'd made the circle it was about 10:30 A.M. Here we were, out chasing sheep around the mountain without having had breakfast or taking any water. Sometimes, first jump out of the box isn't the most intelligent option. We were starting to feel a little gaunt.

The fog began to lift as we headed back toward camp. As we started over a ridgeline, though, we hit the ground at the sight of sheep right in front of us. We almost bumped into them. Peter had me stay back about twenty yards so our pooling scent wouldn't fall off the ridge and spook them. He crawled to the edge for a closer look. There was a good ram in the bunch. He had a full curl, but Peter couldn't tell if he was eight years old. At this distance, he could see only seven growth rings. Although the ram was a full-curl, he was not legal unless he had eight annuli, or growth rings.

After lying there for what seemed like an eternity, Peter decided that we needed a closer look. About that time Will rejoined us. He crawled to the edge for a look and glassed for only a few minutes before he said he was pretty sure that there were eight rings. But before the decision could become unanimous, the sheep began moving. They didn't head down the mountain, though; they paralleled the ridge away from our position.

We watched until they were out of sight and stalked around to where we could carefully peek over the edge. The band of sheep was right below us. The two biggest rams in the group were lying on a bench about forty yards away. After the guys studied the biggest ram for twenty minutes, they agreed he was legal. The plan was for me to draw, rise up, and shoot. But since I hadn't seen the positions of the two rams, a short

*Gary and his mature Stone ram, photographed on the side of a steep mountain, Besa River, British Columbia, August 1998.*

conversation ensued explaining which one was legal and where he lay in relation to the others.

After nocking an arrow, I took a deep breath, drew, and slowly rose. Peter rose behind me with the video camera and Will stood alongside. When I could see the bench, there was nothing but ewes and lambs. They were dropping off the bench and were on a shale trail moving away again, parallel to the ridge. I thought, *Here we go!* But on closer examination, I saw that the rams were not with them.

Suddenly we could hear rocks clicking and shuffling just below a shelf under the bench. We crouched down as several rams emerged from under the ledge, heading single-file away from us. I quickly asked the guys which ram was the one. They looked for a moment and told me he was in the middle. I kept my eye on him and asked Will for a range. I had given him my rangefinder (Leica Geovid) prior to the stalk so I wouldn't have to fool with it myself. He ranged the ram at sixty yards, but the animals were walking at a good clip and there was no shot. Now the ram, with his rump toward me, was getting farther away with each second. Abruptly the group stopped and looked back. The big ram turned and quartered in my direction. Will reported the range at ninety-seven yards. To compensate for the severe downward angle, I decided on the sixty-yard pin. I anchored and put the pin on his rib cage, to allow for the quartering angle, and the arrow was off.

As it arced high in the air, Will muttered, "What are you shooting at?"

On its downward arc, the arrow looked like a missile coming out of the sky. Will had his binocular on the ram by that time and saw the arrow strike the ram at the third rib up from the paunch. The angle of the arrow was perfect to enter the vitals. The ram whirled and slowly trotted back in our direction, to within sixty yards, and lay down. The other rams followed and milled around him. We quickly discussed whether I should shoot again but decided that a miss might spook the sheep—to who knew where. The shale chute and the steep, heavily timbered terrain below were not desirable places to track a ram. We needed to let the broadhead do its work.

Inside a two-minute time span, which seemed like thirty, the ram tried to get up twice but couldn't make it to his feet. It was obvious that the shot was good and he wouldn't last much longer. He laid his head on the ground with his downhill horn pushed into the shale. The horn appeared to be holding him from falling off a ledge. But in his final moments the ram got even. He slowly rolled over and began an unbelievable plummet down the chute. He rolled, tumbled, and somersaulted until he went out of sight. We could still hear him going several seconds later. I just knew that after all these years and all this hard work there would be nothing left of my Stone sheep when and if we ever found him.

Finally the racket stopped. We looked at each other elated but worried about what we would find. It was decided to delay the celebration until we found the ram and had seen what was left of him. We piled all our gear where we were and started off the edge with only my bow and a rifle—just in case. The severe grade in the chute was spooky and dangerous. One slip and we would end up head over heels, just like the sheep. We found the ram three hundred yards below the ridge, snagged on some rocks and small brush. Surprisingly, he was in one piece. He had hardly chipped his horns. The celebration began.

*This happy bowhunter is heading back to lower camp on the second day of the hunt, Besa River, British Columbia, August 1998.*

I'd never, ever, gotten a sheep of any kind on the first day of a hunt, or even gotten a shot on the first day. Talk about luck and a blessing from above! We shook hands and congratulated each other for a job well done. The hardest work, however, was about to begin.

We quartered, skinned, and caped the ram as quickly as we could. The weather had warmed up to the point that we were down to our T-shirts. We had no water with us, so Peter went in search of a seep. He had to go about a quarter of a mile downslope before he found one large enough to fill a canteen. When he returned, we passed the water around several times before feeling refreshed enough to climb out of that hole.

I carried the cape, horns, and a small amount of meat. Peter and Will carried the bulk of the meat. By the time we'd reached the top, our tongues were hanging out. We stopped on top for an hour's rest before we could continue. It was unbelievably steep getting out of there. The canteen was almost empty once we'd reached the top, and only a small amount of water remained back at camp. Finding more would have to be a priority before we started off the mountain.

After the long rest we trekked back to camp. Just as we arrived, a big thunderstorm opened up on us. Immediately, every container we could find, including plastic sacks, was out catching rainwater. Whatever we could catch would help on the trip off the mountain. While the rain came down in buckets we got the Coleman stove going and cooked butterflied sheep loins. We didn't care whether we got wet. They tasted mighty fine, too.

We broke camp in short order and packed the equipment back into the bags that Greg had dropped. We stacked them as a marker, although we had no idea how he was going to get them out. He sure couldn't land there. At least, we thought he couldn't.

The sun came out again, and the weather went back to being hot. We gathered our stuff and started off the mountain. Before I got very far, I turned to look back at the magnificent country, reflecting for a moment. Although I didn't succeed on many of my sheep hunts, the trips were far from unsuccessful. I felt thankful for the blessing of a Stone sheep, and I silently promised that the adventures would stay with me until the day I pass from this earth. As I turned and followed my guides, I also wondered how I would muster enough energy to pursue a Rocky Mountain bighorn and complete the Grand Slam of sheep.

We were about halfway down the mountain when we heard the airplane. We hadn't expected Greg to check on us for at least four or five more days. It turned out that he was on his way back from taking a hunter to another camp and had swung by the cabin to pick up some extra supplies stashed there. We stood on a bare hogbacked ridge and waved our arms off. On his initial approach to the sod landing area, he spotted us. He pulled out of his descent, made a low pass, and wagged his wings when he saw the sheep.

We were pleased not only because we had a ride but also because we weren't going to have to spend another week here before someone showed up. We struggled down the mountain as quickly as we could. By the time we reached the bottom, where the swamp and thick alders awaited, we were played out. Nevertheless, we hurried through the swampy muskeg. The bugs ate us alive, but we cared little. When we broke out of the bush in sight of the cabins, we heard the plane take off. Our hearts sank into our shoes.

We trudged on to the cabins and unloaded our packs. The first thing we did was to find the water barrel and tank up. As we were quenching our thirst, Peter noticed a note on the door from Greg saying that he would be back that night or at the latest the following morning.

Lots of supplies remained, so we fired up the wood stove and cooked a supper fit for a king—macaroni and cheese and fresh Stone sheep. As we finished supper, the distant drone of an airplane topped off a perfect day.

Chapter 15

# Hunting Tule Elk in California Antelope Country

Among the North American Twenty-Eight are three species of elk. The smallest variety, sometimes referred to as dwarf elk and found only in California, is called the tule. The species was reduced almost to extinction in the 1860s because of market hunting and land development. The remaining few tule elk were put on a refuge and protected until the 1940s, when management hunts were allowed to control animal numbers. Around 1964, antihunters were successful in shutting the hunting down, and the hunts were not reinstated until 1988. Tule elk today have reached good, healthy numbers, and they are managed with a limited number of hunting permits on public and private lands.

Although the Pope and Young organization does not recognize the tule as a separate species, Boone and Crockett, SCI, and wildlife biologists do. For me, an archer hoping to get every big-game species in North America, the tule elk was an important step, whether recognized or not.

The quest for a tule took several years because the hunt was canceled twice by the owners of the ranch, the Hewlett Packard family. Because of some indecision among family members and disagreements with California Game and Fish, an opportunity to hunt on that ranch didn't materialize. The ranch had never been hunted, and my hunt was to have been one of the first. The cancellation was pretty disappointing to everyone involved because reports were that the place held a lot of elk, some awesome habitat for stalking, and potentially record-book animals. After the second year was canceled, my booking agent, Wes Vining of Trophy Connection, made arrangements on a neighboring ranch through Larry Heathington.

Larry was a well-known outfitter and agent who had guided and made arrangements for many topnotch hunters: Jack Frost, Chuck Adams, and

*Although the Pope and Young Club does not recognize the tule elk, other organizations such as SCI and B&C do, San Luis Obispo County, California, August 1997.*

Tom Hoffman, to name a few. It was a relief when Larry called to tell me about a group of ranchers who had hunting operations and landowner permits for sale in areas called California Valley and Carrizo Plains. Alex Credal was the outfitter, and his operation was called Carnaza Hunt Club. Alex was an acquaintance of Larry's, and Wes Vining helped arranged everything. Joe Tilton, a former rancher and outfitter, was a partner in Trophy Connection, and he agreed to go with me. Trophy Connection had never sent anyone to this particular outfitter and wanted to make sure he was well organized and capable of handling bowhunters. Joe also agreed to be my cameraman and donate some of his experience with western elk hunting.

We flew in to San Jose and rented a four-wheel-drive vehicle for the week. The hunting area was between Monterey and Santa Barbara. When we arrived at the Carnaza ranch, I was pleased to find that the outfitter, Alex Kuhnle, had taken a lot of bowhunters out for wild pigs. At least he knew a little of what it takes to set up archers and was willing to learn more.

The only concern I had at that point was that the country looked like antelope terrain in Wyoming. It was wide open, with few trees and bushes. The hills were small and rolling, with few breaks or other features that would make stalking more feasible. Here and there was a cutbank in the bottom of a small draw, but that was about it. The grass had grown to three feet in some places and provided some cover, if we were on our bellies. Stalking was going to be tough, no matter.

The hunt began on 12 August. Our intention was to get there at the tail end of the rut, which takes place in July. After our first day it was evident that the rut was over. The bulls would look our way once in a while and squeal a little, but generally they paid little attention to our calling. For one thing, we stuck out like a sore thumb. For another, the temperature was 100 degrees in the shade most days.

There was no doubt that the hunting would be spot-and-stalk only. In addition, I would probably have to attempt a very long shot. Most bowhunters don't have the desire to shoot long distances, which for the most part is a good thing. But part of my shooting regimen had been to practice at extraordinary distances.

We glassed a long way across the wide expanses of the California hills. Spotting elk miles away was new to me. I had spent a lot of time behind a

*The temperature crowded 100 degrees every day, California, August 1997.*

spotting scope while sheep hunting, but I hadn't expected to spend much time with my eye jammed against the "big glass" while elk hunting.

The strategy was to spot elk moving to their feeding and bedding areas in the morning or evening, then set up an ambush. Guessing their destination and having enough cover to stay hidden would test our skill. The middle of the day was spent in camp because of the intolerable heat.

We spotted a group of elk first thing and worked our way to where we thought they might bed. But we guessed wrong. Our calling went unanswered, and the bulls ignored us. That evening we spotted another group and stalked to the only cover we could find. Our hope was to cut the group off as they fed. Some of the elk fed within a hundred yards of our position. Joe and Alex cow-called a bit, but again the bulls hardly looked up. Apart from the fact that the rut was over, there was no question that they could see the four of us trying to hide in the sparse cover.

Early the next morning, we found more elk a good distance away. We cut across country and waited, hoping they would feed our way. When some cow elk fed within easy range, I got excited about the prospects of the bulls following, but when it looked like the bulls were going to feed the other way, the guys tried some cow talk. A couple of bulls squealed a little but had no intention of coming our way. We quietly watched as the herd fed over the distant horizon. Alex mentioned a big draw the elk were headed for. He said it was fairly deep and had some shade in the bottom. The intense heat minimized chances that the elk would stop there, but we all decided it was worth a try.

The hike across the grainfield was quite a contrast with the normal hike across a huge canyon in the Rocky Mountains to get to elk. When we reached the crest of the hill, Alex eased over the top and peeked into the draw. He immediately dropped his head and crawled backward. I knew the elk must be right there. There were six bulls, and I was hoping one was bedded within range.

Alex said there were elk everywhere, cows and bulls bedded as well as up and feeding. He eased back up and found the bull he thought was the biggest and tried to explain where he was. We made a plan to slip ahead a little farther in the grass: first me, then Joe with the camera, and finally Alex with the rangefinder. I would nock an arrow with the bow lying flat on the ground; Alex would rise up and range the bull. I would draw on my knees and then rise up to shoot with Joe right behind me.

Alex slowly rose and then quickly got back down. The rangefinder wasn't working. He tried it again, with no result. He passed the rangefinder to me. I opened the small cover with my pocketknife and scraped the battery posts, then put the cover back and screwed it down. By the time that project was over I wondered if the elk were still there. This time it registered a range—seventy-seven yards. Alex encouraged me to hurry: One elk had stood and was looking our way.

I rolled over, pulled my knees up under me, drew, and slowly rose. Much to my surprise, three bulls lay fairly close together and two of them looked bigger to me than the one Alex had told me to shoot. I was confused for what seemed like a full minute. When the other elk began standing up, I came to my senses and lowered the sight pin onto the bull I was supposed to take. I used the sixty-meter pin, given that the shot was at an extreme downhill angle. I held as steady as I could, squeezed the release, and heard Alex mumble. It is always amazing to see the arrow start out so high above the critter—to the point that others wonder what you're shooting at. But, true to form, gravity brought the arrow back to earth and to the target. The arrow

*Author (left) at entrance to ranch and Carnaza Hunting Club, San Luis Obispo, California, August 1997.*

hit higher than I had planned, though. The bull immediately tried to get up, but I'd broken his spine. He struggled a bit and fell over backward off a four-foot bank. The other elk scrambled out of the draw and stood on the hillside watching for a few moments. We immediately jumped up and ran forward. There was no need for a second arrow, but I put another one into the heart and lung area to make sure the bull died quickly.

Although he wasn't as big as I had hoped, just getting a tule elk on this trip was a godsend. This nice 6x6 was definitely something to be proud of, especially considering the terrain we'd been up against. The bull exceeded the Pope and Young minimum for Yellowstone elk, so they let me enter him in the club's records. SCI, of course, accepted him as a California tule elk. I had a California tule elk and was proud of it.

Chapter 16

# Buffalo of the Arctic—Muskox

After my polar bear hunt, I had always been interested in another Arctic adventure. When Archie Nesbit related his story of taking a huge muskox with Adventure Northwest LTD's outfitter Bill Tait, I couldn't help myself and immediately booked a hunt for 5 through 14 April 1991.

When Bill informed me who my Inuit guide would be, I placed a call and asked about the details. After a good conversation, I asked what I could bring to make his life in the Arctic a little easier. He told me he had always wanted an ice auger with an extension capable of drilling through at least eight feet of ice. It was no easy undertaking, but I had one put together.

For the most part, I've always tried to develop a friendship in advance of my hunts, to get to know my outfitter and the guide I would be sharing camp with. Doing something nice for people who work hard to help me is just good manners in my book. Besides that, the Inuit people have a hard life.

I had read several books on the Arctic prior to my polar bear hunt, and I read a couple more before this muskox hunt. The most informative of all was called *The Arctic Grail: The Quest for the Northwest Passage and the North Pole 1818–1909* by Pierre Berton. It explained in detail the exploration of the Arctic, and I found it interesting how many places I would be seeing that were named after or by Arctic explorers. *The Arctic Grail* also contained a lot on the history and culture of the people.

The Inuit people, I learned, have a history that dates back four thousand years. According to archaeological records, the modern-day Inuit is derived from the Thule culture, which originated in Alaska and spread east as far as the western coast of Greenland. Traits of the culture that have been carried forward to modern times include strong instincts in hunting, such as the

*The airport terminal was the last stop in civilization before hunting camp, Gjoa Haven, NWT, Canada, April 1991.*

ability to understand and determine the migrating patterns of animals and birds. The records also indicate close kinship relationships among the Inuit communities, a strong language bond, and the sharing of possessions, food, and the land with related social groups. Especially notable was their ability to adapt to one of the severest climates on earth and maintain a generally pleasant, easy-going attitude.

The Inuit, as Eskimos prefer to be called, refer to the muskox as *omingmak*, the animal with skin like a beard. It is not an ox and has no musk. The name probably derives from the fact that the bulls emit a pungent odor similar to that of a bull elk in rut. A more appropriate name for the muskox would have been Arctic buffalo.

Muskoxen live in herds of less than a dozen in summer and band together into larger groups that may exceed sixty in winter. A muskox herd is a loosely organized social grouping, continuously changing in size as it splits from or joins with other herds. Herds usually include bulls and cows as well as subadults of different ages. Within each herd there is a social order based on age-sex classes. Adult cows dominate subadult males at feeding sites. There is also a dominance hierarchy within a class. One adult male, the lead bull, is dominant over all. Muskoxen are continuously on the move. During feeding periods, constant movement prevents overgrazing. Herds travel about thirty miles (fifty kilometers) during a month's wanderings.

Muskoxen are famous for a special defense formation. When confronted with danger from wolves, low-flying aircraft, or hunters, muskoxen use this characteristic formation. The herd members line up side by side facing their attackers. Their rumps are pressed tightly together, the calves wedged safely between the adults. If surrounded, they form a solid ring from which the adults break out to charge the enemy. Muskoxen are known to be easy to kill, but finding them on the Arctic landscape and then stalking within bow range proved a lot more difficult than I'd expected.

Although I had taken a compound bow on my previous Arctic hunt, I decided to take a custom-built (take-down) Big Horn recurve by Fred Asbell. It drew 55 pounds at 26 inches. I practiced a lot for this trip and was determined to shoot the muskox with the recurve. I was shooting 31-inch Easton 2117 arrows with 125-grain Thunderheads and feathers. (My draw length was 29 inches.) I felt I was shooting pretty well with it, but I also threw in the old compound (a Bear Whitetail II), just in case the distances necessary were beyond my capability with the recurve.

The trip to Gjoa Haven was a long and arduous one, as are all trips to the Arctic or the Northwest Territories. I went via Chicago, Edmonton, and Yellowknife. I stayed at a hotel in Gjoa Haven called the Kekertak Co-op. It is amazing how much it cost to stay in a hotel there, even back in those days. In 1991 the price was $110 a night. Of course, everything there is expensive because all of it is hauled in from various parts of Canada via airplane. The Inuit people put on the hunts and then contract with an outfitter, which added to the cost of the hunt as well.

Our mode of transportation was snowmobiles pulling large sleds. We were able to cover more country with the snow machines than with dog sleds, as I'd done on the polar bear hunt. Also, the machines were a lot faster and more convenient for finding the nomadic muskox bulls. Some of the sleds had plywood boxes built over the front end to break the wind. The covered part of the sled is where the hunter would ride, along with the necessary

*Samuel Takkiruq, our Inuit guide, cooking bread in our snow house, Gjoa Haven, NWT, Canada, April 1991.*

gear. My guide's sled, however, didn't have much of a windbreak—although it was adequate if I lay semiflat toward the front of the sled.

The clothing necessary to survive Arctic temperatures has to be extreme, to say the least. I took several different types of clothing with me, to make sure that I had the right stuff. That included my seal- and caribou-skin suit, which had been handmade for me by the Inuit on the polar bear hunt. An interesting note here is that the seal- and caribou-skin suit had been stored in a freezer for two years prior to this hunt. The Inuit women tan the seal and caribou hides in the native way, and the skins will deteriorate at normal temperatures.

I also brought with me a down suit purchased from Cabela's and the heaviest wool suit made by King of the Mountain. Among these three, I figured to stay warm and have extra changes of outerwear if necessary. My sleeping bag was rated to forty below and weighed twenty-two pounds. My boots were Cabela's Minus Forty pacs with double-insulated felt liners. I also had boot blankets over my boots. However, no matter what I did, my feet were always cold.

We packed the sleds the next morning and headed for an area along the ocean called Sherman Basin. This jaunt was to be around 140 miles on snowmobiles and rough-riding sleds. Mike Warner, a doctor from Rock Springs, Wyoming, would share our camp and hunt with one of the other guides, an Inuit named Andy, who made part of his living as an interpreter. Andy was very knowledgeable, well spoken, and well read. He knew a lot about the history and customs of the Inuit people. I had noticed on the polar bear hunt, and observed on this hunt as well, that the younger generations seemed to have very little interest in the old ways. Andy was interesting to visit with and pleasant to be around.

My guide's name was Samuel Takkiruq. Sam knew some history, too, but he wasn't as well versed as Andy. He hadn't guided all that much, although he had taken many muskoxen for his village. I was confident in his ability to find a good muskox bull.

We traveled all day but didn't reach our destination; we had to set up camp and spend the night. Snow blocks were cut for a tent base, and the canvas tent was put over them. Some snow blocks were also stacked outside around the windward side of the tent to break the wind. On the inside, caribou skins were put down and foam rubber went on top of the hides. Our

*This igloo with a double-wall canvas tent over top was our home away from home, Gjoa Haven, NWT, April 1991.*

sleeping bags were laid on top of the foam. The tents were tight for room but comfortable, being head and shoulders above the tents we'd used on the polar bear hunt. The temperature was at least ten degrees warmer on this hunt than during the bear hunt. It was a month later, too, making quite a difference in temperature ranges. During this hunt, temperatures stayed between minus 20 and minus 30 degrees.

After reaching our destination the next day, we spent most of that day setting up the camp. Come the following morning, we ranged from the camp a short way and saw only a few muskoxen. We tried a couple of stalks, but the bulls were a lot wilder than I thought they would be. As soon as they saw our sled, they took off running down into small basins or valleys and hid the best they could. They didn't bunch up and face us as I'd expected. This was definitely going to be a bigger challenge than I'd planned for.

That evening, back at camp, some folks from the Boone and Crockett Club stopped by on their way through. They were looking to take a new world-record muskox in the area. They had taken two muskoxen for meat and intended to give it to their guides' village. They also had a wolf. While out tracking a lone muskox bull, their guide found that the bull had a wolf harassing him. Tracks in the snow told the guide that the wolf had circled the bull several times, contemplating how to take him down. "One wolf is not enough to take a healthy muskox bull," commented the Inuit.

When the guide caught up to the pair, they were face to face. The guide shot the wolf first and then the muskox. The bull was meat for his family, and the wolf would provide fur for his family's parkas. The B&C group departed after some good conversation and a tea break.

The next day Samuel and I went in one direction to hunt, and Andy and Mike took a different direction. Samuel and I were making a lot of miles with very little luck. During our tea stops we talked about how hard it is to judge a muskox bull. The hair between the bosses (where the bases of the horns come together on the skull) is key in making a decision between a good and a mediocre bull. The difference can be only fractions of an inch. The closer the bosses, the better the bull. Length of horn, of course, plays a huge part, too.

We went a lot farther that day than we had before. Our gas and food supply seemed a bit short to me for a long trip, but we hadn't seen many muskox and just kept going. We finally found a small group of bulls in the afternoon. Samuel shut down the snowmobile, and I tried to stalk within range. I got to about forty yards, but before I could get off a shot the bulls moved out of range. While I was making a second attempt, they spooked and went over a ridge.

We went back to the snowmobile and circled to find them again. They hadn't gone far, so I stalked again. It is important to make your stalks short. If you break a sweat trying to get into position, you will pay for it. Any moisture freezes immediately when you cool down, so you have to pace yourself and pick your stalks carefully.

This time I crawled on hands and knees to within forty yards. The four bulls knew I was there and kept a watchful eye, but they weren't spooked. I acted like I was just some Arctic critter. I didn't focus on them specifically; I just wandered this way and that, as if I were looking for food, but inching ever closer. I've had good success with that technique on many species. Man's upright position has a tendency to spook animals.

Once I reached forty yards, it didn't seem I should press it any farther. About that time the bulls started moving. I nocked a 31-inch Easton 2117, tipped with a Thunderhead 125 broadhead. The recurve creaked in the cold as I drew. I had deerskin gloves on, but it was darn cold. I concentrated on the vitals of the oldest bull as the group moved by. When I released, the arrow hit the mark but the penetration was poor. It went in only about ten inches. The bull ran a few yards and then stood with his head down. He was obviously sick, but I felt I'd better get another arrow into him. I crawled around a small hump and down into a swale, and put another arrow in his lungs, just behind the other one. He ran hard for fifty yards and went down.

I was elated to have a muskox down, but the cold had taken a toll on me. The cold continuously tries to burn you and break you down. It's a battle to stay warm and out of the grasp of frostbite. And the clothing necessary to accomplish that is an impediment to your ability to move—and to shoot your bow. Shooting with that many clothes on was a struggle all by itself. (By the way, it became obvious that I hadn't practiced enough at home with all those clothes on, including my deerskin shooting gloves. A word to the wise.) Constantly looking for a big bull and traveling long distances in the sled was tough. Each time you take your mittens off to glass, your fingertips begin to freeze. If you take your facemask off, frostbite sets in. There weren't many times when some part of my body wasn't struggling against the cold.

It is amazing how beaten down you get and what you are willing to shoot compared with your standards at home. This bull wasn't the biggest in the Arctic, but he was mine. I was ecstatic to have my second Arctic species—and to have survived. Having shed my mittens and heavy outerwear to stalk and make the shot, I finally snapped back to reality when I realized that I was freezing, literally. We still had to gut and load this heavy beast, and then get back to camp alive. I hadn't survived yet.

Once we'd loaded the bull, we began the long trek back. Samuel followed the snowmobile and sled tracks we had put down earlier in the day. Unfortunately, we had made several big circles looking for muskox. At one place there were a lot of snow-machine tracks, and the way back to camp became confusing. Since there are virtually no landmarks in this area—and in the Arctic in general—it has always amazed me how the Inuits find their way in winter. After four hours of snowmobiling, however, Samuel shook his head and admitted that he didn't know where we were. We continued to try different directions, but to no avail. Samuel stopped about every fifteen minutes, shut the machine off, and listened for other snow machines. We even tried backtracking to the muskox kill to get back onto the right trail.

After several attempts to find our way, it started getting dark. Samuel stopped to check the fuel level and then shut the machine off. My heart sank to the bottom of my boots. Let me tell you, once the darkness creeps in and the air turns black, a human mind—at least this human mind—begins to feed an already growing fear. My head raced through all the terrifying possibilities. We were completely out of food and water, and the darker it got, the colder it got.

We listened in the darkness for two hours. It's hard to describe the feeling. The closest I can come is this: The earth stood there, surrounding us in all directions, with its back turned. I couldn't see it, but I felt it. And Mother Nature opened the valve on the deathly cold.

"We warned you," I'm sure the fates would say. "You two are nothing in the scheme of millions of years. Add 'em to the tally." I had mused earlier about surviving another Arctic adventure. I began to shiver.

Somewhere around midnight Samuel heard the faint hum of a snow machine. Soon I heard it, too. It was a long way off. We sat in the darkness for a long, long time, listening to the whisper of a second chance. But the sliver of hope was dashed by the thought of the machine's possibly being on another trail—not the one we had left. A prayer came from my mouth aloud before I realized I'd said anything. The whisper slowly became a noise. The noise got closer and closer, steadier and steadier.

But the chances of their seeing us out here in the dark Arctic terrain, even if we turned a light on, were minimal. Every now and then we could see the weak flicker of a light beaming up into the blackness a good distance away. As the machines continued in our direction, we realized they were on the same trail we were.

When they got within a quarter-mile, Samuel started our snow machine and the headlight came on. Just as quickly, the machine sputtered and died. Samuel frantically tried to restart the motor, but the machines coming our way began flashing their lights. The feeling was unbelievable. They had seen us!

*Success comes hard when the temperature is minus 10 degrees. Gary shot his first Arctic muskox with a recurve bow, Gjoa Haven, NWT, April 1991.*

Soon figures jumped from their machines and embraced us both. They quickly fixed hot tea and handed us each a chocolate bar. As soon as I'd drunk two cups of tea and eaten the candy bar, however, I began to get woozy and nauseated. By that time I had the shakes pretty bad. Our rescuers quickly gassed the snow machines, and we followed them to camp. It was the longest trip of my life. In fact, we stopped and gassed the machines one more time before reaching camp. By the time I got there I was shaking uncontrollably, scared out of my head, and disoriented. They helped me to the tent, and I crawled to my sleeping bag. The Wyoming doctor, Mike Warner, took one look at me and said, "Hypothermia." He quickly had the guides bring more hot tea and started trying to warm me up. At last I got into my bag, wrapped up, and continued trying to get warm.

I slept well into the next day and didn't emerge from our tent until afternoon. I continued to feel unsteady for quite a while. But after some soup and other nourishment I started coming around. Later Mike and I helped with the butchering and getting the muskox ready for the trip to Gjoa

Haven. We were expecting the other hunters to come back that night and then all leave for civilization the next morning.

Nobody showed up except a grandfather and grandson who came from Gjoa Haven with another load of fuel for the trip back. Of course, the whole camp then began to get worried. When we awoke the next morning, the others were still not back.

Our trip back to Gjoa Haven would be delayed until the others showed up. Since one of the snow-machine tracks was broken, our guides couldn't go looking. In addition, our big wooden sled runners needed repair. All the rocks sticking out of the snow made it extra hard on equipment.

After noon one of the guides from the lost group, by the name of John, showed up. He said they had killed a muskox but had run out of gas in both snow machines. They'd built an igloo and spent the night. The next morning John walked to where he knew some aviation fuel was buried and brought some back. By mixing the av-gas with some oil he got his machine running. The others were still out there and needed more gas to get back. The guides loaded up and went after them.

The following morning the whole group helped break camp, and our caravan of sleds and snow machines headed for Gjoa Haven. It was a fourteen-hour trip, and everyone was ready for a hot meal—and a safe and secure hotel room.

The hunt was successful, and I was thankful to walk away with my life. I now know this much about the Arctic: It is a place of wonder and beauty. The people are fascinating and live like true pioneers each day. The birds and animals there are the hardiest on earth. I would love to go back and hunt there again one day. But I know for sure that I don't have the endurance or the mindset to live like the Inuit in the Arctic. It simply isn't in me.

Chapter 17

# Alaska-Yukon Moose

My first Alaska-Yukon moose trip was scheduled to be with outfitter Richard Guthier. Rob Holt had introduced me to Richard at a convention in March of 1995. I booked a hunt for moose with a chance to take a caribou if I booked the first hunt of the year. Richard took around eight moose a year and averaged bulls with antler spreads of 58 to 62 inches. I was looking forward to the hunt because Richard had a good reputation for a great camp and a 100 percent success rate on moose.

However, I received a call in early summer that dashed my hopes. Richard had been doing some early scouting and found dead moose everywhere. He called the Game and Fish, and they determined that the moose herd in the area had contracted a disease. After doing some research, they closed the season entirely. Richard sent my deposit back, apologized, and hoped we could do business in the future. Thus ended my first attempt at an Alaska-Yukon moose.

My second attempt was with Sam Fejes's outfit, about forty-five minutes down Alaska's north coast and slightly inland from his main camp, Tsiu Lodge, which was established in 1981. It is located near Bering Glacier, one of Alaska's largest glaciers.

We hunted for several days in some of the worst weather Alaska could dish out. I hunted with one of Sam's guides, Frenchy. We located a monster bull moose, one of the largest the guides and I had ever seen. We spent two rain-soaked, foggy days trying to get him, but he was too cagey and heavily brushed up. I told Sam that he should bring a rifle hunter over from one of the other camps and get him. They did just that. I forget what the bull scored, but it was tremendous. If I remember right, the hunter's name was Terry Portement from Andalusia, Alabama.

*How Sam made it in, we will never know . . . remote ocean shoreline, Alaska, September 1998.*

My third attempt came after accomplishing one of the most exciting, hair-raising, and humbling hunting experiences of my life. Alaskan brown bear had given me the most trouble of any species. But a brown bear hunt with Sam Fejes proved to be the ticket to success. Oh, but believe me, not without difficulty. This book's brown bear chapter is one you don't want to miss.

The Alaska-Yukon variety is the largest of all moose. The largest bulls stand 6½ to 7½ feet at the top of the hump and have been estimated to weigh as much as 1,800 pounds. Their antlers are also the largest of all moose species. Alaska Yukon moose are found primarily in Alaska, the Yukon, and the Mackenzie Mountains in the far western areas of the Northwest Territories.

The date was the fall of 1998. Sam had just helped me get a good brown bear, and since the trip was booked as a combination bear and moose hunt, we flew from bear camp directly to Sam's Tsiu River camp. There we took a long-overdue shower and had a hot meal. My bow, which had been lost by the airlines, finally showed up. Man, was I glad to see it. I had just been hunting a brown bear with a borrowed bow—as you will read.

We repacked our gear and loaded one by one into two Super Cubs. It took four trips, each about twenty-five minutes, to get everybody in. Sam set me up with two guides. Chuck Denault was my cameraman. We quickly set up two dome tents and a couple of tent flies between some trees. The flies were used to cover equipment and keep gear out of the rain. One of the guides climbed a tree near camp and glassed for moose until dark. He didn't see anything that evening.

The following morning a guide by the name of Doug Powers climbed a tree near camp and glassed for a while. One of the other guides hiked away from camp a good distance and climbed another tree. The trees these guys were climbing were at least eighty feet tall. Some had the top sawed off to make a seat from which to sit and watch for moose. These guys were far more gritty than I—especially when the wind rocked the huge pines back and forth. Doug didn't find anything, but the other guide hurried back into camp with good news. He had found two bulls. I didn't know it at first, but Doug Powers, for a young man, was one of the most woods-savvy guys I had ever run into. His instincts were almost like those of an animal. His skill at calling was amazing, too.

*Sam's main camp on the Tsiu River, Alaska, September 1998.*

*Spike moose camp on the Tsiu River plain, Alaska, September 1998.*

We sneaked into the area where the bulls had been spotted. Both were big but one was a whopper, according to the other guide. Doug called for a while without an answer, so we moved up another hundred yards and called again. Doug used a set of shoulder-blade bones for rubbing on trees and clacking on brush. They imitated the sound of a bull moose rubbing its antlers and challenging other bulls. This time we heard a bull grunt out in the swamp. Before long we could see a huge set of antlers coming through the willows. He grunted again as he moved slowly in our direction. It is quite a sight to see a massive animal like a moose taking slow, deliberate steps, his antlers and head swaying to and fro. They posture that way to display for a fight and to woo a cow in heat.

The bull hung up in some thicker cover seventy-five yards or so ahead. Doug said that we needed to put some pressure on him. He whispered to follow directly behind. He put the shoulder blades on his head, simulating the paddles of a small bull, and we advanced.

The moose responded with a series of grunts and began coming in our direction again. I got behind some small trees, and Doug backed off (the paddles still on his head) and got in some cover well behind and to my right. The idea was to get the bull to go directly to him and pass me broadside. When the moose got within thirty yards of me, it stopped and raked some willows. It's hard to keep from getting excited with a bull moose that close. I was watching the bull's body language closely to make sure it wasn't zeroing in on me. I remember thinking, *I ain't fast enough anymore to outrun a mad moose, and these trees here are too small to climb. I'll have to shoot my way out.*

Doug raked the willows from his position, coaxing the bull to come on in. This bull had shown up to fight. He was definitely in a trance. After beating up the willows for a few minutes, he headed for Doug's position and passed me at thirty yards, perfectly broadside. I waited for him to get by and be quartering away slightly before I drew. He caught my movement and hesitated for a moment. My 80-pound-pull Hoyt Tenacity barked, and the ACC 371, tipped with a Thunderhead 125, buried itself up to the fletch behind the moose's shoulder. He ran a short distance and went down.

The whole calling sequence and setup had been perfect. We couldn't have written a script any better. Doug's calling skills were a pleasure to watch, and his instincts and ability to read a situation like this were unbelievable. As we were shaking hands and congratulating each other, Doug shook his head and pointed out into the swamp. A hundred yards away the granddaddy of them all, the Godzilla among Alaska-Yukon moose, stared us down. This old moose had let the other bull see what all the excitement was about, and it had saved his life. I wasn't disappointed, though, because I had a darn nice moose. It sure made me want to come back the next year.

Sam flew over us as we were quartering the moose. He was back shortly with more help, and we got the moose out quick before a big brown bear might decide to claim him. This entire hunt had been unbelievable. In three days I had put years of frustration and misadventure behind me in the quest for a brown bear with a bow. In another two, I had taken the last moose species needed for the North American Slam. I had only a short way to go to finish the North American Twenty-Eight.

I don't want anybody to think that it is normal to get a brown bear and a Yukon moose in five days because that is just about unheard of. I think that because of all the hardships my many guides, crews, and I had faced

*This hard-earned Yukon-Alaska moose was shot near the Tsiu River, Alaska, September 1998.*

on all the other hunts, the powers above had cut us some slack. However, I was feeling pretty good about having it all behind me. Sam was feeling good, too. In fact, he suggested that we load up, since we still had four more days left in the hunt, and fly to an area where there was a wealth of black bears—so many, according to Sam, I would be done in a day. So we hopped aboard the planes and headed into the bush.

Well, Mother Nature humbled us for our cocksure attitude. It fogged and rained us in our tents for three days solid. On the fourth day the weather broke just a crack. But the old girl made sure that the weather didn't improve more than a crack. She did not want us to get any ideas. Sam got us all out of there by the skin of our teeth. I've learned this lesson a jillion times: The moment you think you are finally in control is when you find out you're not.

Chapter 18

# The Elusive Dream—Desert Bighorn Sheep

My desert bighorn quest started back in 1986. I took my first desert ram with a rifle in the southern Baja of Mexico. I also completed my first sheep slam with a rifle in that same year. In 1990 I started drawing annually for another desert bighorn permit, to attempt to take a ram with a bow.

Mexico was the least expensive route to take for hunting desert bighorn. The permits for sale and auction in the United States were out of reach as far as I was concerned, and the chances of drawing a license were nil. Carlos Hermosillo, an outfitter in Mexico specializing in big-game hunting, bird hunting, and assisting in the acquisition of limited government permits and governor's tags, helped me to acquire another sheep permit.

Permits to hunt desert sheep are either drawn for or purchased in the form of a governor's tag. If you draw a permit or buy a special tag, another drawing takes place for the area and time of year. The sheep drawings are run by the government, and hunts are contracted with an outfit called the Consejo Nacional de la Fauna. Once the dates and areas are set, they are set in stone. The hunts are scheduled for seven days, although you can buy extra days at $250 each if necessary. Another interesting thing about hunting in Mexico is that a medical certificate must be produced to show that you are healthy enough to survive the hunt, as well as a document from the U.S. police to prove you are an upstanding citizen.

Desert bighorn sheep are one of the toughest species to get. The terrain, the temperatures, and the language barrier make this hunt a real challenge. The deserts of Mexico are harsh, unforgiving places, where temperatures can soar above 100-degree mark even in January, February, and March, the months in which the hunts are conducted. In addition, if you don't speak Spanish, communicating is tough.

*The island in the background is home to a herd of wild desert bighorn sheep and a national park, another conservation success.*

There is another worry, too, one that plagues your mind during any trip out of the country these days, no matter how hard you try to forget it: a fear based on stories of Mexican bandits and murderers in the desert. That is, an American goes to Mexico and never comes home.

It is not the people you know that are worrisome. It is the new helpers in camp, people you don't know: packers, spotters, cooks, and so forth, whom you've just met. These people live hard lives, and an American hunter gets a few sideways glances when he begins to pull out up-to-date equipment and talk about life in the United States. Once the interpreter has relayed what you've said, you get more funny looks. Those looks and disconcerting stares were fierce enough at times to be alarming. I learned to keep my mouth shut about certain things. I also considered it just good manners. I didn't want the guys helping me to feel that I thought I was superior to them, because I'm not. I put my pants on one leg at a time, too. Besides that, they were far more talented than I in this part of the world. A hunter, alone or otherwise, is at the mercy of the guides and people who know the desert. Good relationships are imperative.

In 1991 I was lucky enough to draw a permit for the 1992 season. The outfitter for the Consejo was Ivan Romo Pavlovich, Big Game Outfitters Hermosillo. He had obtained the permit for his area. The hunt was scheduled for 21 January through 1 February. A bowhunting friend of mine, Jimmy Ryan, had hunted sheep with these people and highly recommended their operation. Ivan also conducted a lot of sheep hunts in Sonora for the government.

I flew into Tucson, Arizona, from Grand Rapids and then took AeroMexico to Hermosillo. From there we drove into the desert for what was supposed to be a three-hour trip to camp. Instead, we drove around in the desert, in the dark, for seven hours. According to the driver, they had moved the camp. Talk about getting nervous! I was more than a little concerned, and I thought I might have to shoot my way out of this mess. I don't recollect the driver's name, but he turned out to be a great guy. He was just mixed up about the location. We arrived in camp around 1:30 A.M., making for a short night's sleep.

The next morning we got up early and had some breakfast. The camp was nicely set up, with my own tent and all my gear in one spot. We had all the basics, including lots of water and coolers with ice. The camp stayed clean, and the food was excellent.

The terrain is mountainous, but not particularly rough. It was more a high-plains landscape, yet in the desert. There were a lot of rock outcrops, high ridges, and hills—and, of course, miles of flat desert. The land was covered with all sorts of sparse plants, most of which had thorns or were poisonous. The rest of the vegetation was cactus of various sorts, including cylindrical saguaro, which tower above the rest. When you glass across the desert, those tall cacti look like sentries keeping a watchful eye.

The ground was hard, dry sand with lots of volcanic rocks and gravel. Apart from the outcrops, the rocks were loose and hard to walk on, and noise was hard to contain without going very slow. There were lots of washes and old creekbeds where water ran in the rainy season. They call the rainy season the monsoons. Because the ground is so hard and rocky, the rains run off the hillsides with a vengeance, cutting waterways; very little water is absorbed into the ground. Those washes and old creekbeds made great avenues for stalking the open country. There were very few springs, and the animals have to depend for water mostly on cactus and the early-morning dew.

*Guide Quirino Sandoval holds the skull and horns of a desert bighorn sheep that had been shot by poachers. We found it in a dry creek bed, Sonora, Mexico, 1992.*

The very first day I got a good education on what to watch for in the way of stickers and thorns. There were some cactus thorns lying on the ground. Dried and dead from the previous season, they were camouflaged just enough to catch a person off-guard. When I stepped on or brushed a boot against one, they would completely penetrate my boots. They were sharp enough, and toxic enough, that I immediately stopped and removed them. You didn't dare brush against any plant, or it would likely penetrate your clothes. Flat tires on the trucks were common because of the cactus. There was one willowlike plant in particular that the guides told me to avoid and not to let the leaves touch my bare skin. If I did, I would break out in a rash. There were other things to watch out for, too, including rattlesnakes, poisonous spiders, and scorpions. With all the distractions, it's challenging to get around in the desert and keep your mind on your goal.

The first morning was cold, with ice in the water buckets. We climbed and glassed the cliffs along the sea the first day. I hadn't hunted sheep along the sea in the desert before. I'd hunted alongside the sea in the Northwest Territories, Canada, and Alaska, but this was quite different—the desert scenery juxtaposed with the aquamarine sea has a beauty of its own.

I always had two main guides, two or three spotters, and a biologist with me when out in the desert. It was really quite a crew. The two guides were brothers named Quirino and Ramon Sandoval. They were both great guys and took very good care of me. Although they didn't say much, especially in English, they made sure things went right.

The group drove Dodge pickups around on rutted roads—two tracks so faint that at times we could hardly see them; they had been made for the most part by old prospectors and poachers. We would stop a mile or two away from good sheep country, and everyone would take a position: in the bed of the truck, on the hood or roof, or in the shade of a big cactus. They concentrated their glassing on the slopes, hillsides, and rock outcrops, looking mainly for sheep bedded in the shade. These guys could easily spot sheep two miles away. How they did it with the low-quality optics they had, I don't know. Half the time I couldn't see the sheep, even when they told me where to look and even with my fancy binocular. Their eyesight was incredible.

That first day was a little sparse. We saw only ewes and lambs. On the second day, though, we spotted a couple of small rams in the morning, bedded in the rocks on a hillside. We could also hear two other rams butting

*Lunch break on the desert floor with spotting scopes close at hand, Sonora, Mexico.*

heads in the same drainage. We waited for an hour or two before we got a look at the combatants. They were both good, legal rams in the 160-class. We made our way around the mountainside to get the wind in our favor and peeked over the top. The rams, however, were already on the move. The wind had swirled several times during our stalk, and we were sure they'd winded us. With the loose rock and gravelly footing, they'd probably heard us coming, too. But in any case these rams were extremely nervous and spooky. The guide explained that there was a lot of poaching going on in the area. The poachers would sneak up on the rams and shoot them in the head with a .22 magnum rifle. The .22's report didn't carry far in the desert and would not alert the federal boys or area ranchers. Then they would sell the horns on the black market and either eat or sell the meat.

The rams moved out over the top and disappeared. Back at the truck, we ate our lunch and made a plan to drive around the mountain to find the rams again. On the way, we had our first flat tire. Cactus was the culprit, as it would be half a dozen more times during the ten-day trip. Ten- or twelve-ply tires were not an option for these guys, so we had a lot of flats. Another hour and a half of glassing found the rams bedded in a shady basin. They were a long way off, and the remaining daylight wouldn't permit enough time for a stalk. So we went back to camp and figured to try them again in the morning.

The third morning we were posted and waiting to glass the four rams at daylight. We had two more spotters that morning, hoping to cut down on the time we'd spend finding the sheep. We spotted only one old ewe where the rams had been the night before, but one of the spotters found a single ram on another ridge in the opposite direction. They studied and figured him to be the legal minimum of 155, at the most. We decided not to take after him because he was just borderline.

Quirino sent two of the spotters up into the country where the four rams had last been seen. It took quite a while for the men to get into glassing position. When they did, the signal was that they had found five rams not far from our position. Quirino and I sneaked around the edge of a small knob and into some outcropping rocks to get a position on the sheep. When my guide peeked over the edge, they were bedded fifteen yards below, staring up at him. It sounded like a herd of buffalo running through the rocks when they busted.

The rams scattered across the desert floor on the dead run. Two went one way and three another. We watched the two biggest rams cross the flat and head for another ridge. One was a bruiser in the mid-170 class. We found that ram later, but there was no chance for a stalk. He was acting nervously, and the guide said we should leave him and come back in a few days. We figured to save him for a rifle kill toward the end of the trip, if necessary—if we could find him, that is, because the desert just seems to swallow them up.

The trip was filled with both excitement and disappointment as the rams continued to elude my bow. On the eighth day, though, I had a chance. We found a bedded ram and made a long stalk. When we got where the ram was supposed to be, he was gone. We moved up the ridge a bit farther to look over the other side. Quirino stopped dead in his tracks and pointed to the ram. I couldn't see him at all. Quirino kept pointing at the ram and saying, "Shoot him."

For the life of me, I couldn't find him. When the ram finally busted, he was only twenty yards away, bedded in some heavy brush. Talk about being disgusted with myself.

*My main guides and friends for life, brothers Quirino and Ramon Sandoval, Sonora, Mexico.*

The ram ran around the edge of the ridge we were on but had to come back our way to get out of the basin. We backtracked and made a run to cut him off. He ran right into us and stopped at twenty yards. Unfortunately, my guide was caught between the ram and me. Besides that, I could see only the sheep's head and neck. I wasn't going to take an irresponsible shot.

On the ninth day I decided to take my rifle and find the big 170-class ram we had left alone. As luck would have it, we couldn't find him, or any rams at all, the whole day. My stomach was in a knot most of the night. The thought of not getting a ram with a bow was disappointing enough, but to go home without a desert bighorn at all—that possibility really had me down. Not to mention the fact that this was a very costly hunt.

On the tenth and last day we went back and hunted near the sea. We were sitting and glassing when a ram came out of nowhere and stood about seventy yards away. He wasn't a legal ram, and, being young, he was very curious. He stood around and stared for quite a while. I was hoping he had company and a legal ram would show up. No such luck. We took several photos of him.

Later that morning we spotted another bedded ram and went after him. When we got to where we needed to be, he had completely disappeared. Around midday the guys found yet another ram, smaller but legal. I decided to take my bow, just in case we could get close. When we surveyed the situation, though, there was no way to get within bow range. We went back to the truck and got my rifle.

Quirino and I stalked to within 250 yards and waited for the ram to get up. He was lying on a rock ledge and took his time. When he finally rose, I couldn't get a steady rest because a bunch of cactus was in the way. I had to shoot lying down, but raised up enough to see over the cactus and rocks in front of us. I just couldn't hold still. The ram was getting nervous, so I pulled the trigger as the cross hairs steadied on his chest cavity. I shot him three times to get the job done. I wasn't proud of the shooting, but we had a sheep, a good, legal desert bighorn. Just by feeling the condition of the horn, Quirino told me he thought the ram was old. There was also some gray hair on its head. As it turned out, the animal was very old. I was glad he was on the downhill side of life and that I hadn't killed a young ram that might someday have turned into a real trophy.

The guides and Ivan encouraged me to come back and try again with a bow. They thought that we could pull it off the next time—after all, we did sometimes get close. It just didn't work out that year, however.

As soon as I arrived home, I started work on getting another permit and ended up buying a president's permit for the 1993 season. The hunt was scheduled for January. I went down to Mexico early and spent some time vacationing and looking at real estate—before discovering that my hunt had been canceled. There was some trouble in the Mexican government, and they were talking about canceling the season. Finally, however, things got worked out, and a redraw for dates and areas was to take place. Once the redrawing had been held, the date was changed to February and the new area, according to Ivan, was not as good as the previous one. My schedule was full in February, including a visit from some hunting guides and friends from Russia. I didn't see any possible way to change my schedule.

I sent a letter to that effect and received a letter back. The Mexican government said, in no uncertain terms, that I either go in the allotted time frame and to the assigned area or sacrifice the permit. I had no choice.

*Author shot this sheep on the afternoon of the last day of a ten-day hunt, Sonora, Mexico.*

My hunt began on 19 February 1993 and was to run through 5 March. Ivan assured me that this time we would take extra days if needed. Again I flew from Grand Rapids to Chicago, on to Tucson, and then AeroMexico to Hermosillo. I stayed one night at the Holiday Inn in Hermosillo. Ivan came and got me the next day, and we stayed at his home for a couple days. I had a chance to meet his family and parents. I felt welcome. These people were salt-of-the-earth kind of folks.

Once again camp was set up in fine fashion, and we had a good reunion with several of the guys from previous hunts. This was my third hunt with Ivan and several of the others. I had hunted desert sheep, a desert mule deer, and now another sheep. I picked up some beer, pop, and tequila for the crew. Although a person doesn't want to get too wild with the booze, a cold beer or a glass of tequila at night tastes pretty good. The crew really appreciated it.

The first few days we saw several sheep, but nothing stalkable. We used pickups again following two tracks and glassed large mountains, ridges, and basins. One morning the guys spotted two huge rams that they figured would push the 180-class. The mountain was one of the largest in the area, and below the crest of a saddle was a shady basin, wide and deep. The rams were bedded in that basin. The guides' eyes never ceased to amaze me. These sheep were at least a mile away. It took me quite a while to pick the rams out among the rocks.

We went back the way we had come and got on the backside of the mountain. We tried to hurry so that the sheep wouldn't move before we got there, but the terrain was difficult and noisy. When we eased through the saddle, we quickly found the pickups and spotters, but it took us quite a while to find the sheep. They were both huge desert bighorns. Unfortunately, they were bedded two hundred yards below the saddle under two good-size trees and in a position we didn't have a prayer of getting close to.

We lay on our bellies and watched for about two hours. The shade the rams were lying in grew longer, so we had no hope that the sun would make them move. Quirino decided to crawl around so that he could motion for the others to ease into the basin on foot, hoping that the rams would move toward the saddle. It was a long shot, but about the only option we had. Quirino and I sneaked to a position in front of two big boulders next to the saddle.

The sheep got nervous right away when they saw men walking in the desert. They stood and stared for a minute or two and then started up our way. When those two huge rams headed in my direction my heart pounded like a sledgehammer. The bigger ram went to the right of our position farther than expected, but he presented a slightly quartering broadside shot at sixty yards. I drew my 70-pound ProVantage FastFlite bow, put the pin on him, and released. The shot looked perfect. In midflight the arrow hit a cactus limb and zinged across the desert basin. The ram jumped and disappeared, all in one move.

These particular cacti are like bamboo, with long, thin limbs. Each plant holds a dozen or so hard-to-see limbs, ten to twenty feet long. I just couldn't believe it. The guide was dejected, too, and insisted on finding the arrow immediately. Although a very sharp hunter, he had forgotten about the other ram. The language barrier played a huge part in our befuddled thinking. He spoke no English, so I had a hard time convincing him that we should be getting ready for the other sheep. After many English and Spanish exchanges, as well as hasty hand signals, he understood.

We'd no sooner started to hide than the 170-class ram topped out at twenty-five yards. We weren't ready! He'd caught us in the open, and, what's more, I didn't have an arrow nocked. I felt like a complete idiot—a

*Cooking dinner in the desert. There was lots of food, and it was all very tasty.*

naked one at that, with my bow in one hand and binocular in the other. What a helpless feeling! It was a once-in-a-lifetime experience even to see two sheep like this, let alone to have them within bow range. The big ram took three or four jumps down the mountain and disappeared. It was a long and disappointing hike back down that mountain.

On the third day we found the larger of the two rams again. He again was in a position where a stalk was impossible. I thought about shooting him with a rifle, he was so huge, but I gritted my teeth and passed. The next few days we saw very few sheep. Quirino split the spotters up and sent them to different areas to find any legal sheep. Four more days passed, and we didn't find any stalkable rams. We also went to the far edge of our area, where there were supposed to be more sheep, and found none.

We decided to go back to the foothills along the sea. Quirino, Ramon, and I found two legal sheep late in the afternoon. The three of us watched them until dark and then sneaked out with flashlights and went back to camp.

I stared into the fire that night and wondered what the following day would bring. It was hard to be optimistic about getting the job done with a bow. I left the ironwood fire and gazed up into the darkness. There were millions of stars. The heavens seemed closer than usual, so I took the opportunity to visit with God.

I thanked him for the good fortune he'd allowed me, and for the blessings he'd bestowed on me along the way. But I also asked, humbly, why my tests were so hard. Why the frustration of always taking things to the wire. Was I missing something he needed me to see? Was I doing something wrong in my life? In closing, I prayed for the guidance to understand, and I asked him to take over. I was too weary to control things any further.

A weather front woke me in the middle of the night. It rained hard. Thunder and lightning crashed all around. Normally, I would have fretted that the sheep would move out of the country with that much commotion in the hills. But again I turned things over to a power greater than I and drifted to sleep. I slept more soundly than I had in months.

The next morning we started out with flashlights and then held up short of the area where we had last seen the sheep. We would carefully slip into position without the lights.

We spotted the rams feeding where we'd left them the night before. We kept track of them for quite a while, waiting for an opportunity. They were very interested in watching a thunder and lightning storm that was moving in from the sea. They would look up each time the lightning flashed and the thunder rumbled, some five miles away, as if being entertained.

When the rams walked slowly out of sight, Quirino and I made our move. Ramon stayed back and gave us hand signals. It was a tense situation, trying to come over the rim with the sheep just under us. The light rain and heavy thunder covered our noisy approach—I truly felt the storm was God-sent.

When we peeked over the ridge, the biggest ram was forty-one yards away, feeding broadside. I ducked back down and drew. When I raised up and settled the pin on his vitals, he was quartering perfectly. As soon as I anchored, the arrow was gone, and it hit the ram square in the boiler room. He ran a short distance and went down. When he fell, he immediately disappeared. We ran over to see if he'd gone off a cliff or something, but there he lay in a small wash. Talk about excited! We were jumping around like school kids and hurrahing. Ramon joined us, and we all marveled at the accomplishment. We had a good, mature ram, a great representative of the desert species of sheep.

I can't say enough for the crews we had on these hunts. They were dedicated right to the very end. They made huge efforts to help me reach this goal. And once I'd gotten to know the Mexican people associated with Ivan, I made friendships to be proud of, friendships that would last a lifetime. These were good people!

There is something unique about the desert. To me it is the most forbidding and yet some of the most beautiful country I've hunted. Nowhere else on earth are the terrain and plant life so fascinating and mysterious. The ways in which the plants and animals survive are miracles within themselves. Most plants, mammals, rodents, reptiles, and arachnids there were very "serious"—they all had a definite attitude when we crawled into their space, stalking sheep. It is because life in the desert is so serious. There is no room for mistakes. You are either prey or predator. There is so little in the way of food and water that plants and animals, as a matter of survival, need to take advantage of every small opportunity: Either strike or flee.

I wondered about that same serious attitude I saw in many of the Mexican people. Most Americans are fortunate and take for granted the ability to survive with ease. In Mexico you had better pay attention and maximize every opportunity to get food and water, provide for your family, and protect what is yours. You could see it etched in the faces of the sheep-hunting crew.

It was good for me to hunt Mexico again, good to renew friendships and make new acquaintances with solid, down-to-earth people. I'd forgotten, again, about the less fortunate, forgotten how lucky I am for all the opportunities and freedoms we enjoy in the United States.

There are not enough words to express my sincerest appreciation for Ivan Romo Pavlovich and his family. I truly felt like I was a part of them all, and I truly regret not having time to spend with them. Thank you, Ivan, and God bless!

Chapter 19

# Doubled Up— Rocky Mountain Bighorn Sheep

In my quest for the North American Twenty-Eight with a bow, sheep were giving me a lot of trouble. I had been on three Dall sheep hunts without taking a ram. Having had a rifle along on two of those hunts allowed me to bring home a couple good rams, but getting a shot with a bow had proved impossible for me. I decided to try for another species of sheep. Rocky Mountain bighorns are tough to get, but hunting them during the rut would improve my chances considerably. One of many potential problems would be the weather during the month of November!

In 1991 I booked my first Rocky Mountain bighorn bowhunt outside of Kananaskis, Alberta, Canada, in the Canmore, W.M.U. 410, bow zone. I signed with Rick Guinn Outfitters, Ltd., and the hunt dates were 4 through 30 November. Rick had become a good friend through our association in the North American Big Game Club and the Foundation for North American Wild Sheep. He also owned and operated the Boundary Ranch in Kananaskis Country.

The Canmore bow zone offered only eight nonresident permits for the entire area. Each outfitter licensed to hunt the area was allowed two permits. The area was walk-in only. The drainage we planned to hunt, Exshaw Creek, required a ten-mile hike into the backcountry and a three-thousand-foot elevation change. However, supplies were flown into camp via helicopter. There was no way we could pack enough supplies on our backs for the planned twenty-six-day hunt. The chopper pilots had to be not only topnotch but also a bit crazy. I was amazed at their ability to get the supplies in, given the treacherous winds and wind shear along the mountainsides.

This particular spot was a winter range for a large number of sheep. They had already made the trek out of the extremely high, remote country

*Rick Guinn and the pilot lash the gear to the helicopter, Canmore, Alberta, Canada, November 1991.*

and were in full rut at this time of the year. Rick told me to expect very cold conditions and snow depths from nothing to three feet. We would hunt the head of a big drainage and a pass where sheep regularly traveled. Many rams, looking for ewes in heat, used this pass.

The country was absolutely vertical except for the valley bottom where we hiked toward camp. There were two camps, one low and one high. There was another hunter on this trip, and he and his guide dropped off at the lower camp. It was an additional two-hour climb to the high camp, and let me tell you, it was a widow-maker. We pitched our tent on the top of a small mountain ridge in some stunted spruce trees over a hundred years old. The next two weeks brought me the toughest sheep hunt I had ever been on. The footing was slick and dangerous. We bucked snow waist-deep and worked our bodies until by nightfall we were about to drop. But no matter how hard we tried, nothing we did provided a shot at a bighorn. By the end of the hunt, and after we had walked out, I thought, *I must be snake-bit on sheep! There's got to be an easier way!*

My second bighorn hunt was in Colorado. I drew a tag in the Colorado bow zone and contacted friend and outfitter Tom Tietz. Tom was a bowhunter who had already taken the North American Sheep Slam with a bow. Everything was arranged, and we were both optimistic about our chances. Unfortunately, a dark period moved into my business life just then. I was having some very serious problems with a new real-estate development, and when the hunting date arrived, there was no way I could leave the project without great risk of having it stall and possibly fail. I called Tom and explained the terrible situation, and he was most understanding. He told me that if I could get away for just a few days anytime during the season, he would make himself available. With a quick phone call, I slipped away and flew to Denver to hunt the last two days of the season. I hadn't practiced as much as I would have liked, but I felt confident that I could get the job done if I had a reasonable opportunity. Tom picked me up at the airport and immediately drove us to the hunting area.

For two days we hunted in light rain and then heavy, wet snow, with flakes the size of half-dollars. We stalked several sheep to distances just out of my range in the steep, timbered hillsides. All we needed was a few more yards on several good rams. I tried one shot, but it was a clean miss. The break from business felt good, but in the back of my mind lurked a nagging

*Guide and outfitter Rick Guinn taking a cold nap at Exshaw Creek, Alberta, Canada, November 1991.*

and serious matter that I had to get completed at home. We said good-bye, and Tom made a pact with me that he would keep putting my name in for the annual sheep draw. If I got lucky and drew another permit, we would hunt again. Unfortunately, I never drew another sheep tag. A special thanks to Tom Tietz, anyway.

I didn't try for another bighorn ram until the fall of 1998. In the meanwhile, I had finally, after many attempts, been successful in arrowing all the other sheep I needed to complete a Grand Slam: the Dall, the desert, and the Stone. I had just gotten back from the successful Stone sheep hunt in August of the same year. Now I needed only the Rocky Mountain bighorn to have the sheep slam.

I booked another hunt with Rick Guinn for the dates of 9 through 23 November. Another hunter, Jim Scull, was already in camp. Jim and his guide walked to camp a couple of days ahead of Rick and me. The snow wasn't as deep when we walked in, but it was mighty cold. It began to snow heavily once we reached camp. Jim was from North Dakota and on his first sheep hunt with a bow. He was a pleasure to share camp with, and we became good friends right away. We both stayed in the upper camp. It was a little snug but adequate.

We all worked together on this hunt by trading who was going to hunt high and who would hunt low. We also traded days in a blind that Rick and his crew had built near the pass. We took turns scouting for each other, too. It was a good thing that the hikes we had to take were reasonably short because the deep snow and treacherously slick conditions were punishing. We used crampons on the bottom of our boots in many instances to stay on the hillsides.

We spotted several sheep on the first day, but they were mainly young rams and ewes. The second day I was sitting in a natural juniper blind watching the pass when a good ram came over the ridge. He was by himself and obviously looking for ewes. He worked slowly in my direction. Jim was in a blind about three hundred yards above the ram. The ram appeared to be a mature sheep, in my estimation in the 175-class. It wasn't long before he proceeded down the slope to within ninety yards and began paralleling my position. I had practiced a lot at that distance, but I hadn't shot much at such a steep upward angle, having come from the flatlands of Michigan. I nocked an arrow, and when the ram stopped I released. I couldn't tell whether I'd missed him high or low, but the ram simply jumped forward, turned, and ran in Jim's direction—but unfortunately, not within Jim's range. The ram simply proceeded on his way. Rick, on his way up with some food, had seen what happened, but he couldn't tell what had happened to my arrow.

I was shooting an 80-pound Hoyt, modified to be longer than normal. The arrows were ACC 360s tipped with a fixed three-bladed Thunderhead 100 weighing 390 grains. It was a good setup for sheep because it was flat-shooting. The bow was also smooth-drawing and worked well in the cold. My camouflage was a white coverall with brown blotches that blended well with the snow and other surroundings. Felt-lined packs were required to keep our feet warm.

Rick guided me for a few days but had to leave because of some other obligations. Peter Whitlow, a guide with whom I had shared a successful Stone sheep hunt, took over. Peter was a good guide and mountain man. Kent Maxwell was Jim Scull's guide.

The next morning was Sunday. Since there is no hunting on Sunday in Canada, we slept late, got our gear ready for the next day, and dried a

*Author, his new hunting friend, Jim Skull, and the two rams they shot with bows only hours apart, Exshaw Creek, Alberta, Canada, November 1991.*

few clothes. We also glassed the slopes and the pass to see if any sheep or new sheep tracks were present. Thanks to the deep snow, any sheep tracks showed up well on the open hillside around the pass. Once a band of sheep came over the pass, they were in our territory. Whenever a new group of ewes showed up, it wouldn't be long before a ram or two would follow.

The tent was nestled into the same thick patch of spruce trees as on the previous hunt. (Those trees were more than a hundred years old.) It was hidden under the lip of a bald ridge, just below where we were hunting. In fact, there was a good sheep trail twenty yards from the tent. We were careful in the mornings to peek out of the tent before exiting because a ram could be standing within range. It was a great spot because we could see over the ridge, just behind the tent, and glass all kinds of sheep country.

We were taking it easy that Sunday evening, right around twilight, when we spotted some ewes within a hundred yards of camp. Peter and I took the video camera and stalked closer. The ewes and lambs worked their way up the slope and over a windswept, grassy knob toward our position. Suddenly a legal ram showed up. They were now within fifty yards of the tent, and eventually fed to within thirty yards. I had never been that close to a ram in my life. The ram knew I was there, and we both just stared at each other. I think he knew I couldn't do anything. The whole group hung around for ten minutes. Wouldn't you know? It had to be Sunday.

The next morning we found the group of sheep again, just below camp. They were on the edge of a small ravine where a stalk was not feasible. The ram was the lowest sheep in the bunch and the farthest away. There were several young sickle-horned rams in the group and a couple of half-curls, but nothing else legal. The ram finally moved into a position where I decided to attempt a shot. It was on the outer limits of my range. It just wasn't likely I would get another opportunity. Unfortunately, I misjudged the steep downward angle and overshot. The group hardly even spooked, then drifted down the ravine into the timber. We strolled back to camp, got some breakfast, and made a new plan. We needed to get closer, based on my performance so far.

Jim Scull had decided to sit on a barren slope above camp within a quarter-mile of the pass. We had cut out a makeshift blind in a small clump of scrub spruce, and he sat there most of the day, enduring several snow squalls and high winds. Just before dark a good ram came over the pass and walked within Jim's effective range. Jim drew and shot the ram but hit him a little far back. The ram ran uphill a short distance and lay down. Since it was getting dark and there was no way to stalk the ram, Jim and his guide, being smart, sneaked from the blind and headed back down the mountain to the camp, leaving the ram until the following morning. That night there was plenty of discussion about the ram and his whereabouts. We all hoped for no more snow, too.

At daylight Jim and his guide headed up the mountain, hoping that the ram would be lying where they'd left him the previous evening, or somewhere close. Peter and I went about two hundred yards from the tent and found a place along the edge of a spruce thicket to sit and watch—in case Jim's sheep made a run for it. We also kept an eye out for other sheep coming over the pass. There was a good trail through the thicket, but many times in the previous days, while we'd been watching, the sheep had run through the timber there instead of walking. They seemed to be nervous about what might ambush them in the trees. We decided to sit below the timber and on the edge, where it was a bit more open.

*Our cozy camp was nestled under a ridgeline out of the wind and in a small stand of spruce at the head of a drainage, November 1991.*

We hadn't sat long when a ram came over the pass and worked its way down the slope in our direction. As he proceeded downhill, we noticed that he kept watching something beyond and behind us. When we got a chance to look, we saw that the bunch of sheep we'd stalked the day before had emerged from the timber. They were on the slope where I'd taken the shot at the ram, but that ram was nowhere now to be seen. The ram we were watching kept eyeing the ewes and lambs. There was no question that he was interested, and we hoped he would approach. This ram was a bit larger than the one I had shot at the day before.

We were pinned down until he decided to come off the top. He had three ways he could possibly go: along the mountainside and around to the ewes, down the trail we guarded in the spruce thicket, or down the ridge and into the chute below us. He stood and stared for a long time before he started off down the ridge and into the chute.

When he dropped into the chute and went out of sight, we jumped up and sprinted through the thigh-deep snow toward the edge. It was a reasonably short run, roughly 150 yards, but it seemed like a long way in the deep snow. We hoped that he would stay in the chute and we could cut him off. When we broke into a small opening on the hillside within thirty yards of the deep cut, there stood the ram on the edge of the chute, staring at us. I thought, *That ram must have run as fast as he could go to get there!*

Although winded from the run, I flung my mittens off and nocked an arrow. I looked at Peter to make sure he was legal. The ram threw his head downhill and in one jump was out of sight. We ran to the edge hoping for a shot, but he'd already gone too far down the chute and had passed us. Peter did say he was legal, and that made me feel even worse.

We were both disappointed and muttering to ourselves when Peter suddenly said, "It's not the same ram." In fact, the ram looked a lot like the one I'd shot at the day before. When I turned around and looked up the chute, there, standing behind two small spruce trees, was the ram we had seen coming off the pass. He stood less than thirty yards away. I continued my turn uphill toward my right and whispered, "Uphill, Peter, uphill! Is he legal?"

The ram was looking directly at us, making it hard for Peter to tell. When the ram looked from side to side, as if making a decision which way to go, Peter immediately said that he was legal. In two jumps he could have been out of sight to his left. Moving to his right would take him across the ravine to a trail down the mountain toward the ewes. He took the ravine.

As he lunged in the deep snow, I drew. On what I believe was his third lunge, and with my sight picture filled with a sheep, I released the arrow from approximately twenty-five yards away. The shot passed through the animal, but the angle was not what I'd hoped for. The ram was quartering toward us more than I'd thought. Although the shot would be lethal, I feared I'd taken out only one lung. I needed to get another arrow in him, anywhere. I nocked another shaft as fast as I've ever nocked one. When he hit the crest of the chute at thirty-five yards, I dead-centered an arrow on his rump, hoping for a perfect "Texas heart shot."

We quickly waded the deep snow in the ravine. I was certain we would get the ram, but how far would he go? We heard a crash just after he went over the top and assumed it was the ram falling—or was he just kicking it into high gear down the other side? All the doubts a man can muster flooded my mind as we eased over the crest. An arrow was on the string and our eyes avidly searched the snow ahead, but the sheep was nowhere in sight. I was praying we would find him quickly. If the ram had gone down for keeps, I'd have completed the Grand Slam. Could it be? Had I finally done it?

The ram had to be right there somewhere. The blood trail in the snow was wide and strong. Another fifteen yards on the crimson path revealed the sheep in a small group of scrub spruce. He had pile-driven himself among the trees to the point of being completely out of sight. We both gave a shout of joy. I looked skyward and said a heartfelt thank you!

We immediately began hearing more shouting and hoorays from above us. It was Jim and his guide. As it turned out, they had found Jim's ram and were on their way down with him. When they saw my ram come over the pass, they realized that we would probably be stalking. They actually had seen us on our run to the edge of the chute and had stayed put until they heard us holler.

We wrestled my sheep out of the spruce trees while Jim and his guide slid his sheep down the steep mountain. They had quite a struggle, even though it was all downhill. They finally got Jim's sheep into the same chute where we were. We all congratulated each other whole-heartedly. We were beside ourselves, hugging each other and marveling at our luck. I could hardly believe it had really happened. I felt this was a very special blessing given to both of us.

The next trick was to figure out how to get these sheep off the mountain. We had to decide whether to take the sheep back up through the deep snow to the tent, or go to the lower tent camp a half-mile below. The lower camp this year was where we had been keeping extra supplies. The decision was made to head there. We helped the guides quarter and cape the sheep and then stashed the trophies on the spot. We hiked back up to the upper camp to get the bare necessities for the trek to the lower camp; we would need enough gear not only to spend the night in the lower camp but also to get us through the long hike to the highway the following day. We had to leave enough room in our backpacks for meat, horns, and capes, too.

It was quite a puzzle to figure out what to take and what to leave. How much would we need if a storm blew in on the way out? The helicopter would get the rest of our gear later, but how much later? We had to take our bows, even though we were done with them. It's a Canadian law that you must carry your bow out with you. By the time we got our stuff together and had hiked back to the rams, packed up the meat and horns, and arrived at the lower camp, it was very dark and very late and we were exhausted.

What's more, everything in camp was frozen because no one had been there for a week or so. But we started a fire and began to thaw things out. It wasn't long before we had some supper going. There is nothing like backing up against a woodstove in a canvas tent, especially with your ram down. It does your weary mind and bones good.

To our surprise the guides had hidden two bottles of wine among the supplies. We cracked them open and clinked our plastic glasses in celebration. Before long the day's arduous trip had faded and things seemed a lot cheerier. About that time a couple of local men, headed up the mountain to hunt sheep, saw the light of our tent and came in for shelter. Unbelievably, I knew one of them. He was a well-known bowhunter and friend from Calgary, Alberta by the name of Archie Nesbitt.

You know, it's funny . . . the true realization of what I'd accomplished didn't start setting in until I began thawing out and a little wine had hit my bloodstream. It is amazing how tuned a person stays on a hunt like this. The intensity level one maintains every day until the hunt is over is extraordinary. It's flat out entrancing to begin to relax. I had finally reached one of my hardest fought goals: the Grand Slam of North American Wild Sheep with a bow. It was almost overwhelming—I was now the eleventh person ever to have accomplished this feat. It was an incredible feeling to share my adventure with some true friends. If I had melted into the stove at that moment, never to hunt or be heard from again, it would have suited me just fine.

A special thanks to my good friend Rick Guinn and his family.

Chapter 20

# High and Hot—Shiras Moose

My successful Shiras moose experience took quite a while to materialize. The permitting process for moose anywhere in the United States is a tough proposition. For several years I tried to draw permits in Wyoming and Montana without any luck. I also tried bidding on several governor's and commissioner's licenses in the two states but was unsuccessful. Archie Nesbitt, a friend of mine, hunted with an outfitter by the name of George Daum in Utah. Archie killed a great moose that year and saw an even bigger moose they didn't get a chance at. He returned the next year but was unable to find the big bull. Archie recommended I give George a call to see if George had a landowner permit available.

Also, Mark Condit, the outfitter who had squired me on a successful mountain lion hunt, wanted me to buy a governor's tag in Wyoming. He had some big moose spotted in his hunting area. I was never successful in bidding there, either. Finally, I decided to purchase one of the few landowner tags available on the ranch that Archie Nesbitt had hunted in Utah with George Daum. The place was known as the Morgan Durst P.H.U. area. So my first moose hunt was near Wendover, Utah. George Daum was the outfitter and had permission to hunt the C. R. Tippen and Sons Ranch. It was a huge place, and we were to be the only hunters there.

I flew from Grand Rapids, Michigan, to Chicago, then to Denver and on to Salt Lake City. George met me at the airport, and when we went to the baggage claim, my bow case wasn't there. Baggage personnel didn't know where it had gone. It goes without saying, I suppose, but that's every bowhunter's nightmare. I was supposed to start the hunt the following morning and had no weapon. Since camp was a couple of hours away, there was no use going anywhere until I got my hands on my bow. We

*Winter moose range in Utah, November 1992.*

rented a motel room and waited to see if they could find it before the hunt was half over.

Luckily, they tracked the bow case and had it flown to the airport by midmorning the next day. Believe it or not, everything was still in one piece. We happily hit the road for camp.

When we got into the high country, we found that Old Man Winter was there. It was snowing hard and piling up fast. We had a little trouble getting George's camp trailer pulled in because of the deep snow. His trailer was more like a sheep wagon—small but well insulated and with a woodstove. It made a great camp and was very comfortable. George also had horses up there, so we could get back into some remote areas.

We were supposed to be the only ones hunting the ranch. However, first thing the following morning we ran into some muzzleloader guys hunting for moose, too. It turned out that the ranch was for sale. The realtor had some clients, to whom he was showing the ranch, and whom he was guiding on a moose hunt. It was George's understanding that they weren't to be there for another week. George was a bit upset, and so was I.

We spotted a few moose over the next two days, but nothing worth going after. On the third morning we saw a good bull with a few cows while riding horseback down a ridge. They were quite a distance off, so we had a long way to go around to get the wind right for a stalk. When we got to where we needed to be, here came three guys on horseback riding up through the draw. They were hunting moose, too. So much for having the place to ourselves.

George stayed and talked to the hunters, and I headed down the ridge on foot through deep snow after the bull. I worked in above the moose through a patch of aspens and sneaked in as close as I could. The snow had a little crust and was noisier than I'd hoped. The moose were about sixty yards out and milling around in the bottom of a draw. For some reason they were getting noticeably nervous. When I listened carefully I could hear George and the hunters talking. I grumbled to myself and refocused on the moose.

The bull was working some cows and began to come in my direction. I drew three times but my peep sight was not lining up right. It was turned slightly out of position. On the fourth pull I got a partial view through the peep. Having had this happen before in cold conditions, I reminded myself to replace the setup with a hose type or an automatic peep setup.

As the moose continued my way I remember thinking, *Maybe this will work after all.* But at the last second some turned and went in a different direction. When the bull got to an opening some fifty yards away, he stopped and turned broadside. It was going to be a steep downhill shot, but I was sure I could make it, so I drew and let an arrow go. The arrow nicked a pine bough and, I thought, went over his back. Of course, the moose left the country.

I went down to find my arrow and, surprisingly, found a few drops of blood. I couldn't believe I'd hit anything. But I continued on the bull's tracks for a quarter-mile or so and found a drop of blood here and there. I even jumped the bull once in the timber but could not see a wound. About that time George caught up with me and said that he had seen the bull cross a draw and go up a steep slope not far from him. He'd had a good look at the hulking animal and had noticed a graze with some shaved hair on the top of the shoulders. He said the bull wasn't hurt and not to worry about it. By that time, the moose was hellbent for the tall timber.

*Bill Townsend, my guide, reading on the porch of our cabin. It was hot and dry in Jackson Hole, Wyoming, in September 1994!*

It was upsetting to both George and me that there were people hunting here with us. We hunted for a couple more days and decided to give it up. The snow was getting deeper each day, anyway. I was supposed to come back later in the year, but it didn't work out and I ate the permit.

The Shiras moose, also known as Wyoming moose, is the smallest of North America's moose; however, it is still quite large. Shiras moose are found in Wyoming, Montana, Idaho, British Columbia, and in isolated areas of Utah, Colorado, and Washington. The Shiras has smaller antlers than the Canada moose. A bull's antlers can span five feet and weigh more than fifty pounds. Its body color is a rusty-brown to black, with a pale-brownish saddle, and its legs are gray to white. Moose of both sexes have a "bell" or "dewlap," which is the flap of skin and long hair that hangs from the throat. The Shiras cow moose is slightly smaller than the male and does not have antlers. The bulls can grow to seven feet at the shoulder and can reach ten feet in length. Mature Shiras moose weigh six hundred to fourteen hundred pounds.

Moose habitat varies with the season. In spring and summer they can be found in marshy areas and meadows as well as higher elevations.

During winter moose prefer forested areas but can often be found in valley bottoms eating willows. Moose are browsers and feed on leaves, twigs, bark, and buds of trees and shrubs. In the summer they feed heavily on aquatic plants and can often be found with their head under water eating from the bottom of ponds.

Breeding occurs from mid-September through mid-October. Females attract males with both calls and scent. A mature bull will stay with a cow only long enough to breed. Bulls engage in fights with other males to breed cows, and bull behavior during mating season includes rubbing and scraping trees with their antlers and breaking off shrubs and trees to display dominance. They will also create wallows by digging in the ground and urinating in the dug-out area, then rolling in it. Moose generally avoid human contact, although during the rut bulls are unpredictable and may charge. Cow moose are also aggressive when they have a calf. Moose in Canada and many other areas are considered one of the most dangerous animals in the woods. They are responsible for human deaths every year.

Wes Vining of Trophy Connection set up my next moose hunt, in August of 1994. I bought a governor's permit offered by the Hap Dumont World Series Little League organization in Wyoming. The licensing division of the Wyoming Game and Fish handled the silent auction. It was up to the hunter to choose an area within thirty days of the issuance of the permit. Some areas were closed to the governor's permit holders, and Game and Fish made sure we knew about those.

We took a look at a couple of outfitters and settled on Paul Gilroy. Paul operated out of Jackson Hole, Wyoming. He originally came from Chicago, but as soon as he graduated college he came to Jackson and never went back. He had several areas he recommended and could guide in. Because of other hunts I had booked, we decided the area right around his ranch would be best for an early hunt.

When I flew into Jackson Hole that year, I saw smoke covering the entire high country around the airport. Paul was waiting to pick me up and said that a huge grass and forest fire was burning out of control. The country was so dry that the fire was burning up residences, homesteads, cattle, and a huge amount of countryside. Many of the areas had been closed to any kind of traffic. This was my first experience with a western forest fire.

*Shiras moose in dark timber high in the mountains above Jackson Hole, Wyoming, September 1994.*

Paul ran the largest horse operation in the valley. He rented horses to dude ranches, outfitters, and hunters. He had two hundred horses in his operation and kept busy transporting and delivering to whoever needed good mountain pack and saddle horses. He also provided driving teams.

Bill Townsend was my guide. He worked in construction around the valley and guided in the fall. He also took snowmobile tours through Yellowstone National Park in the winter. The weather was hot and dry when I arrived, and the moose were mainly in the timber, according to Paul and Bill. They had scouted quite a little and had noted that the bulls weren't coming out until late evening, just before dark, and were going back to the timber at daylight. The foliage was dry and would make stalking almost impossible. The guys said that the hunting would be very tough, but we would do the best we could.

The idea was to load the horse trailer in the dark of a morning and travel to the cooler high country, where the moose were feeding. Then we would jump the horses out and ride in the dark to a vantage point where we could see a lot of country. We hoped to catch the moose out in the meadows and get ahead of them while they headed for the dark and cool timber to lie down for the day.

Paul's outfit was very well equipped. All the tack, equipment, and horses were in great shape. I had brought along a good bow scabbard and a hip quiver for my arrows. I'd found over the years that this was the safest way to carry a bow and arrows on a horse. In the mountains on horseback you want both hands free.

There was lots of game around, and it surprised me to see elk, deer, and the occasional moose in and around the houses in that mountain country. There was a lot of construction around the area, too. Bill got a big kick when I asked, "Which hotel is building in this area?" We had just passed a huge complex under construction. He laughed and said it was someone's house. I couldn't believe it. Bill told me that the entire area was being bought up by wealthy individuals from around the world. A local working guy couldn't afford to buy anything around here anymore. Many of the locals now live thirty to sixty minutes away and drive back into the area to work.

I was impressed by how well Bill knew the area and where the moose hung out. We saw fifteen bulls over five days. The weather was so dry that stalks weren't really an option, and we couldn't still-hunt in the timber, either, because moose are more wary than you might think. On the third day at dark we saw several bulls feeding on a steep hillside. We decided to be back the next morning at daylight and ambush them when they headed for the timber. It was a good plan, but it didn't work. The bulls were way ahead of us and got to the timber before we could cut them off.

We rode back to the truck for lunch and saw another bull feeding just below the truck. We took after him, but he heard us coming and sneaked into the dark timber.

On the fourth day we were back in the same area at daylight and spotted the same bulls feeding in thick timber with small breaks. We hiked around the mountain to get the wind right and cut them off. When we finally got there and found the bulls again, we watched two of them slip into the timber and disappear. The other two bulls were sneaking into a basin below us and were on the move. We hurried around in front of them and almost bumped into them as they worked up the slope toward us as we were coming down. The bulls were feeding right to us.

My heart started pounding, and I began to shake—as usual. I had to concentrate to keep myself together. One of the bulls paused at fifteen yards, but there was too much brush for a shot. He eased past us and continued up the hill, browsing along slowly toward an opening thirty yards away. I was drawn and waiting when he stepped into the lane. When the arrow went through him, the bull turned and ran in my direction. At first I was sure he was going to run me over, but then he veered and ran right by me. It was like a freight train passing. It didn't scare me . . . much!

We could hear the bull crashing downhill through the timber. There was one last, huge crash before the woods went quiet. The blood trail was wide and heavy. We found the bull in no time beside a big tree he had run into, head-on. He was a good-size Shiras. The moose were still in velvet at that time of year, and the antlers were beautiful.

By the time we had dressed the moose, hiked back to the truck, and made the long trip to the ranch, there wasn't enough time to get the bull out before dark. The next morning we went back at daylight with some big packhorses and some helpers. We took more pictures and quartered the bull and loaded it onto the horses. It was a good thing we had some big horses and lots of help. I always forget how big a bull moose is.

It was a great hunt, given the conditions, and a great adventure. I met some fine people there. I've always appreciated the expertise of Paul Gilroy and Bill Townsend in making my moose hunt a success. I also appreciated all the local folks who keep Bill advised if they see a good bull moose.

I want to thank Paul and also Bill (who is no longer with us, but in a much better place). Paul Gilroy is not only an outstanding person and outfitter but also a great horseman and wildlife conservationist. Paul's hunting area had great numbers of elk, moose, deer, and some sheep. Since that time, however, the increasing number of grizzlies and the reintroduction of wolves have greatly reduced the number of game animals there. The hunting has become poor, and probably sooner than later hunting will be a thing of the past in the area. It is a tragedy. Where is common sense in all of this? I thank you, Paul, for your hard work in trying to save wildlife and in trying to preserve the traditions of hunting and outfitting. I know all the people who knew Bill will remember him kindly.

Chapter 21

# Newfoundland Monarch—Woodland Caribou

The woodland subspecies is one of the five caribou necessary to accomplish the North American Twenty-Eight. I had taken the Quebec-Labrador caribou in 1993, but it was time to start working on the rest of them. I had never hunted or even seen a woodland caribou in the wild. In Canada, woodland caribou have been divided into five distinct populations, depending on where and how they live: boreal, northern mountain, southern mountain, Atlantic-Gaspesie, and Newfoundland. Newfoundland was the area I concentrated on because of the number of caribou reported there.

After doing quite a bit of research and after reading many ads in the hope of finding someone who specialized in taking bowhunters, I gave up and turned to my old standby, Wes Vining of Trophy Connection. Wes said he knew of a guy, Joe Peddle, whose operation had been in business for thirty-five years and sported one of the few 100-percent success rates at that time. Peddle Outfitting took a limited number of hunters, but he did take bowhunters. A majority of the hunts offered in Newfoundland were moose and caribou combinations. Joe had sold a big part of his hunting area, but he kept a piece of premium country to keep himself busy. He had an opening and welcomed the opportunity to take a bowhunter for caribou.

I took cameramen Chuck Denault with me on this trip to record the hunt. We traveled from Michigan to Halifax, Newfoundland, stayed overnight there, and then flew to camp the next morning in a turbo Beaver. The plane was a million-dollar modification of an old Beaver with a turbine engine. This former airline pilot found this plane a cherry. With the power it possessed, you could load it down with everything including the kitchen sink and take off just about anywhere.

*The old monarch gathering his cows during the rut, October 1996.*

We flew into a large, long lake with few inhabitants. A couple of cabins at the far end, owned by some local residents of Halifax, were about all I could see. They also had to fly in. There was a four-wheeler trail you could ride in on, but it was a long, long way and not very practical. It started raining and spitting snow that night, and the wind howled.

The first morning, we hiked to the top of a plateau above the lake. Groups of ptarmigan we saw along the way were starting to take on their winter white plumage, and the white plus the summer color of rusty brown made them more beautiful than usual.

When we reached the top we could see that the landscape was riddled with caribou trails, trails these animals had traveled for eons. They zigzagged in and out of the timber patches, scrub bushes, and stunted spruce. The country was either wide open or heavily timbered. It looked like a stalk would be very difficult here, although in some places the trails went through timber so thick that it appeared a person could hide well enough to get a caribou with a spear.

Woodland caribou generally prefer mature or old-growth coniferous forests associated with lakes and rivers. Those forests offer high concentrations of ground and tree lichens. In the winter woodland caribou tend to favor uplands, bogs, and south-facing slopes where the snow is not too deep. Their winter diet consists of up to 80 percent ground and tree lichens. In summer they prefer areas with forest edges, marshes, and meadows that provide the fresh green growth of flowering plants and grasses. At one time there were woodland caribou in Michigan, and that fact endears the species to me.

We tried stalking a good bull late that evening but couldn't get close enough for a shot. The caribou were in rut and chasing back and forth quite a lot. Even though I couldn't get a shot, we gathered some excellent videotape and were hopeful based on what we were seeing. We had to wear our rain gear most of that cold and blustery day, and the weather couldn't seem to make up its mind. It would be sunny for a while and then rain. The low clouds spit some heavy, wet snow, too. A thick fog moved in later in the day, and it would have been nice to go back to the cabin and play cards and drink coffee. But if we truly wanted a bull, we had to stay out there no matter what.

The following morning before daylight we were on the move to where we had left the bull and cows the night before. The weather had deteriorated overnight, and the fog had not lifted. The wind was strong and cold. Try as we might, we could not find the herd. My guide, Carl Snooks, decided that we should take a long walk and look into another basin. By now snow covered the ground, and some ornery squalls made sure that we didn't get a chance to dry out. We walked a good distance, topped out, and crawled to a row of scrub spruce on the edge of the basin.

There was a good-size group of caribou in the bottom. The two bulls in the group looked good. One was a bit larger and obviously the dominant male. The cows were feeding their way up the mountainside toward some scrub trees, and Carl thought we should hustle around and get ahead of them, then try to ambush them using the brush and scrub timber along the trail for cover. While we made our move, the fog began to break.

We made our way around in front of the group and crawled into position. We stayed low because the cover was sparser than it had looked. The big bull was continuously running the smaller bull out of the group. He finally decided to chase his rival completely off, and the younger bull took a route near our position. I decided to take him if he got within range. The foul

*Gary and his woodland caribou bull at Alex Pond, Newfoundland, October 1996.*

weather had a lot to do with my decision, as did wanting to get the woodland caribou for the North American Slam.

The smaller bull walked within fifteen yards of us, stopped for a moment, and stared at us as we tried to hide in the junipers. Rain and sleet were still coming down, and his coat was wet, sleek, and handsome. I was about to draw on him when out of the corner of my eye I noticed that the big bull was following. He would soon be in range, too. I let the first bull go and focused on the elder. When I rose from a crouched position to my knees, the big bull pegged me. He stared for quite a while, then shook his head, grunted, and proceeded after the younger bull. He looked over at me one more time when I drew, but more out of annoyance than concern. He was so intent on getting rid of the other bull that I'm sure he was thinking, *First things first. After I get this one gone, I'll come back and run that other little runt out of the country, too.*

The big bull continued his deliberate walk and was quartering away when I came to a full draw and settled the Hoyt's twenty-yard pin behind his front shoulder and released. Because of his steady walk, the Easton ACC 360 tipped with a 100-grain Thunderhead hit him a little farther back than

*Alex Pond hunting camp staffers Linton Gilbert, the cook, and Carl Snooks, the guide, stand in fresh snow, October 1986.*

I intended. But with the angle of the shot, it exited just in back of the off shoulder. The bull walked a short distance and immediately lay down.

The other bull quickly saw there was something wrong with the old monarch and cautiously came over to see. He seemed to know instinctively that the old bull was finished because he immediately began herding the cows and displaying his dominance. A change of leadership was taking place right in front of me. I wondered how often anyone gets to see the change of guard in the wild this way. It is one of the few times I have felt strange about what I've just done. I even lifted my eyes to heaven in hope of a sign that it was OK.

The herd spent no time in mourning. A whole new chapter in their heritage had begun—in the blink of an eye. The old bull's reign was over. He had bred his last cow. Although his genetic inheritance would continue on for many years, his presence obviously would not be missed. This has been the way of the wild since the world began.

When one of their members dies, animals have no choice but to return immediately to their survival instincts, without reflection or remorse. The human is left dominant, having dealt death to another living being. But here one difference between humanity and the animal kingdom is revealed: In spite of his dominance, a good man or woman, a true hunter and conservationist, feels empathy for the fallen king and expresses sympathy for his loss. And he shows humble respect for the gift that, in death, the fallen elder represents. The proper human response in this day and age? It is use of the meat, admiration for the animal, and the management of the species in perpetuity.

I stood there in the wind and sleet and stared as the other caribou went on their way. Moisture welled in the corner of my eyes, and it wasn't from the sleet. The harshness of God's cathedral is tough to swallow at times. But it is the way it must be. We made some tea and properly acknowledged our respect for the monarch. Then it was time to prepare the bull for the long journey back to the States. I was very grateful for an excellent trophy and a very special experience. Thank you, Joe and all!

Chapter 22

# Grandfather's Blessing—Central Barren-Ground Caribou

Some believe that the word "caribou" was derived from the Micmac *xalibu*, which means "the pawer." Inuvialuit people and Inuit people call the caribou *tuktu* or *tuktuk;* Chipewyan Indians say *et-then;* Dogrib people refer to them as *ek-wo;* the Gwich'in say *vadzaih;* and to the Slavey Indians the caribou are *ekwe*.

Four subspecies of caribou are found in the Northwest Territories. Barren-ground caribou have the widest distribution range over the taiga forests and tundra of the mainland. They are the most abundant subspecies in the Northwest Territories and have the greatest cultural and economic importance.

Woodland caribou are divided into two populations in the NWT: boreal and northern mountain. Northern mountain caribou herds can number in the thousands during late summer to late spring. They have distinct seasonal migrations and live in the Mackenzie Mountains. Boreal caribou live in the eastern parts of the Mackenzie Mountains, tend to gather in small groups, prefer to stay with the forest most of the year, and do not migrate.

Peary caribou range throughout the Arctic Archipelago. Grant caribou, the last but not least of the subspecies, are found mainly in Alaska and the Yukon. The caribou of the Porcupine herd winter in the northwestern corner of the Northwest Territories.

Wes Vining of Trophy Connection had sent one of his clients to a place in the Northwest Territories called Camp Ekwo. The gentleman came home with the No. 1 Boone and Crockett rifle kill. Of course, Wes recommended this hunt to all of his clients from that point forward.

Because of scheduling difficulties I arranged a hunt in the month of November 1996. It was hard to get away during the normal caribou season,

*A barren-ground caribou takes a swim in Humpy Lake, NWT, August 1997.*

August and September, with all the other hunts I'd planned. November is late for hunting caribou, but the outfitter said that we could probably get the job done. The last herds of the winter would be migrating through and could provide an opportunity at some of the largest bulls of the year.

I flew to Calgary and then to Yellowknife, where I caught a charter flight to camp. They had a nice camp set up on the tundra. The weather was cold and the tundra treacherous. An early snow had insulated the ground and kept it from freezing solid, and there were a lot of soft spots under the snow that made traveling on snow machines tricky. The top layer of snow was frozen just enough to hold the caribou up. To add to the trouble, many of the caribou bulls had started dropping their antlers early that year. We stalked, we waited along migration trails, and we set up in the rock piles at water crossings. Nothing was working. We spent three tough days hunting caribou and digging out snowmobiles. We tried every trick in the book to get a shot at a caribou. Finally we gave it up, and the outfitter offered me another hunt, at a reduced price, for the following year.

The next year I returned with cameraman Chuck Denault in the month of August, and we were the first group of the year. Chuck came into

Calgary, Alberta, from Toronto, and I flew in from Grand Rapids, Michigan. We stayed overnight and then flew on to Yellowknife. We were supposed to load onto a twin Otter and head for camp immediately, but the weather had other ideas. We waited half the day for the weather to lift and then flew in to Camp Ekwo.

Ekwo, on Humpy Lake, was a great caribou operation well run by Moise and Joyce Rabesca. They provided some of the best camps and caribou hunting anywhere. Three world-record bulls—bow, rifle, and muzzleloader—were killed out of this camp. Camp Ekwo is north of the Arctic Circle. Moise is a Dogrib, a tribe rich in native heritage, values, and culture. His ancestors had hunted this part of the world for hundreds of years.

The country there is different from any part of the earth you'll ever see. It is far enough north that timber stops growing. There are a few stunted alpine trees, but mostly what you see are brush, rocks, rivers, lakes, and rolling tundra. There is just about as much water as land, and of all things, diamonds have been found in great quantity because of all the volcanic pipe in the area.

Late August brings the first frost and turns the foliage into brilliant reds, yellows, and oranges. The moss on the tundra turns a beautiful red and orange, too. The water was crystal clear, the air the freshest ever to circulate in these lungs. There was and still is a purity to this land, a solace. It is a place virtually untouched by man, and I could feel it.

Hoyt USA, my bow sponsor, had decided to send along two 35mm photographers from California for an advertising program they had on their planning board. One of the two was Neal Bellefeirelle of Bull Dog Drummond. The two missed their connections and had to be flown in via special charter the next day on an old, beat-up Beaver. These guys had never been in the woods or Far North before. They had hiking clothes but no camouflage, and hardly enough gear if the weather went sour. Their job was to take all kinds of still photos in black and white of every aspect of the caribou hunt.

The first morning out we had to take two boats because the photographers wanted shots of us running up the lake. The boat ride lasted around thirty minutes. We got out on a big ridge and found two good caribou working in our direction. To say the least, the whole stalk was a joke. With my video cameraman, the two 35mm guys, two guides, and myself, we looked like a

*The author's central barren-ground caribou near Grandfather's Rock and Humpy Lake, NWT, August 1997.*

prison-camp exodus. The two photographers knew nothing about hunting and were trying to get photos of me and the caribou in the same frame. You can imagine how that turned out.

The photographers then decided that they needed some pictures of only the caribou. They were sure they could catch up with a bunch of caribou that had passed our position and get some good photos. We tried to convince them that there was no way they could match the speed of traveling caribou. Of course, like most of us on our first caribou trip, they figured they could catch a "slow-moving" caribou. We watched them for several miles—they didn't even get close and were worn to a nub when they returned.

Caribou travel twice as fast as they appear to, even at a walk. A man at a full jog would have trouble keeping up. Moreover, the tundra is so tough that it slows you down considerably. You simply cannot catch up with them from behind. A hunter either has to intercept them or wait for them on well-traveled migration trails.

We sat out of the wind on the ridge for the rest of the day and waited for migrating caribou. A wolverine approached our position almost within bow range. I contemplated a stalk, aware that the wolverine was headed for a caribou kill not far from our position. I had a license, too. But, if you have ever seen a wolverine and their nervous mannerisms, you understand that a stalk would be very difficult in such open terrain. A second wolverine happened by a little later. Toward evening we tried a few more stalks on approaching caribou but had a hard time getting close to anything with the parade of bodies following us.

Once back in camp, the still photographers, who were from the city, wanted to know what the deal was with the electric fence around camp. The tall-strand electric fence was there to keep out barren-ground grizzlies drawn to the cookhouse aromas and the scents from the meat house. The outfitter has shot a few persistent bears over the years, for the safety of the camp. The fence was now mandated by the Fish and Game Department to prevent bear-human confrontations. The city boys didn't care for that idea much at all.

There was a ridge behind camp in the shape of an L. At what I would call the tip of the bottom of the L there was a high point called Grandfather's Rock. That is where Moise's father and grandfather had sat with other villagers during many caribou migrations. Over a multitude of years they had shot many caribou and dried enough meat for the entire village's winter stores. Back in those days any caribou within range of their weapons would be shot—cows, calves, and bulls alike. They used to cross miles of country on foot to reach this hunting destination. How they got the dried meat, hides, and such back to the village I haven't a clue. It had to be back-breaking work.

As his father got older, he couldn't get to the rock on his own anymore, so Moise would help him walk out there. That was a sacred place to his father and the whole family. Their village survived many winters because of the bounty of caribou there. Moise's father would take his lunch, as he had in his younger years, and sit there all day. Even in his later years he shot a few caribou for the village, but he would mostly sit, reminisce, and watch the land, water, and caribou. Moise's father lived well into his nineties, and until just a few years before his death, the family helped him get to the rock every fall.

The long end of the L was a ridge alongside the ocean where caribou would come from afar through water and over miles of tundra. They would

*Our ride back to civilization from Humpy Lake to Yellowknife, NWT, August 1997.*

climb the ridge and then be skylined, and their silhouettes could be seen from camp about eight hundred yards away. Once they hit the top of the ridge, we would try to intercept them. But we just couldn't get the job done with all those people following us. It just wasn't going to work with such an entourage. On the third day the two photographers had to leave. They were decent guys, but we were glad to see them go. We needed to get some real hunting done.

Caribou hunting is a different sort of experience for the average whitetail hunter. Finding a trophy is difficult when you see a herd of bulls coming your way. Your first impression when a sea of antlers is flowing in your direction is to think, *There are several huge bulls in that bunch!* If you saw antlers like that in the whitetail woods, you would faint dead away.

It is important, as you quickly find out, to look closely at each bull and observe all his qualities before making a judgment on which one to shoot. Trophy bulls have several qualities you must look for: double shovels, big bez with several points, and, if you're lucky, two backscratchers and large tops with a lot of points. Close examination reveals that few bulls have all these qualities. With experience, most hunters learn that if the bull has big

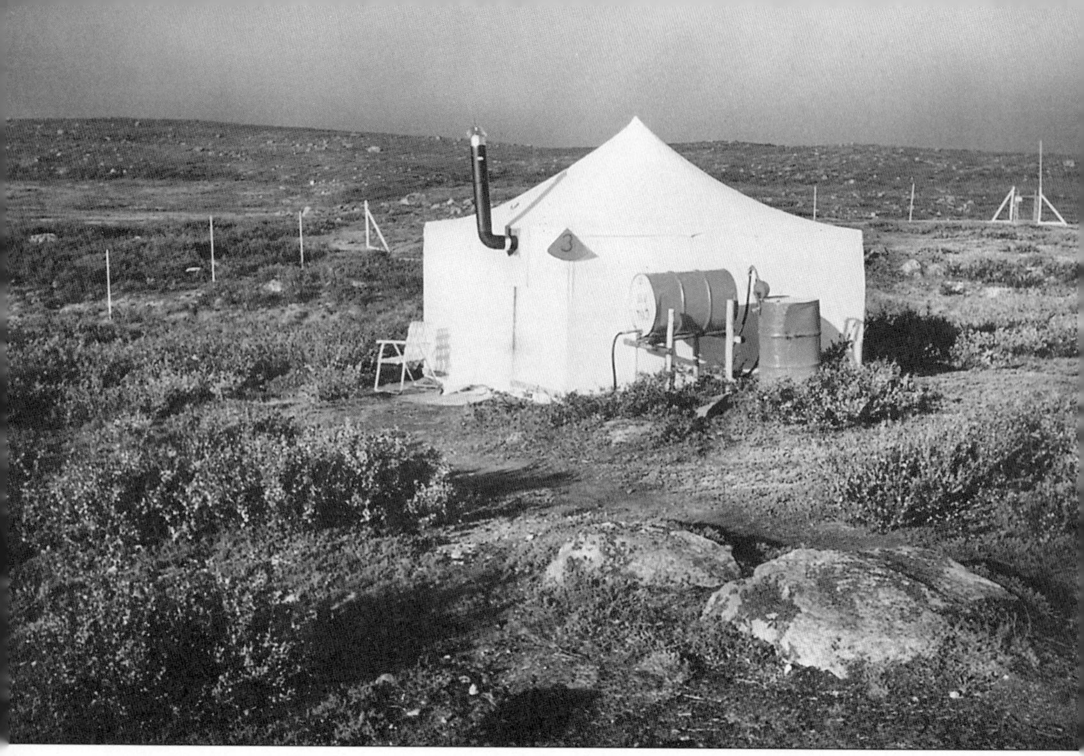

*Note the electric fence. It was an attempt to keep out the grizzlies, which didn't always work! There were lots of bears at Humpy Lake, NWT, August 1997.*

bez and good points there, it is likely to have only one shovel and no tops. Or if it has good tops with lots of points, it has poor bez and little or no shovels. A lot of double-shovel bulls are weak in antler growth somewhere along the line, too. Finding the bull with everything is tough. If you get excited about seeing all those antlers mixed together—you will probably make a mistake.

On the third day we sat on Grandfather's Rock. There was an aura about the place. I felt honored to have permission to sit there. I pondered the granite and the small patches of moss in its crags as we waited. For how many thousands of years has this rock been exposed to the elements? For how many hundreds of years has this moss-covered granite hosted the vigilant and determined eyes of a Dogrib hunter perched on this very spot? I felt small in the overall scheme of things.

I also felt a presence. And, I felt something else, though I don't really know how to explain it other than this: Even though I was trespassing on sacred ground, the presence was calm and nonjudgmental. Although it seemed to wait to see what I was made of, I felt stronger instead of diminished as it watched. Some of the greatest hunters that had ever lived surrounded me. Did they approve, I wondered? If only I could see them. I would bow to their wisdom and thank them humbly for the chance to experience what they had lived every day.

Moise's voice, like a distant echo, penetrated my trance. He pointed across the tundra. There was a group of caribou bulls headed in our direction. They were quite a distance off, but he was pretty sure he knew where they were headed. We ducked behind the rock and got ahead of them.

The caribou came through in a different place than anticipated but suddenly turned and ran in our direction for no apparent reason. They ran as if they had been spooked and were flat-out packing the mail (like a Pony Express rider). One of the bulls was good. If he stopped within range, I would take the shot. As if by magic they swung around in front of us and ground to a halt. The big bull turned broadside and was looking back where they had run from. It was a fairly long shot, but I drew and settled my fifty-yard pin on his vitals. The arrow passed completely through the bull before he could react. He ran a short distance and piled up.

I looked back the way the caribou had come to see what had spooked them. There was nothing there—at least nothing we could see. Tears welled in my eyes. I knew then . . . the ancients had approved. Thank you, Moise, for sharing your stories and this special place with me. I will never forget.

Chapter 23

# Wintry Canada Moose

My quest for a Canada moose started in 1974. I booked a hunt in British Columbia with Swift River Outfitters. Merd McCullen was the outfitter. Dr. Joe Verschueren, a large-animal veterinarian and friend of mine, actually put me onto this hunt. It didn't take much arm-twisting to get me to go, but I'd never spent so much money on a hunt—or any family vacation, for that matter. We drove my brand-new 1974 Pontiac station wagon all the way to British Columbia. Swift River, BC, is on the southern border of the Yukon and was a sizable trip from Michigan. The Alcan Highway wore the paint off the wheel wells on my new car.

We took a meat box large enough to bring back two Canada moose and two mountain caribou, if we were that lucky. We didn't know any better. We had no doubt that we were going to get them all. Well, we were surprisingly right. But it was not without considerable difficulty and outfitter trouble.

I didn't take my bow on this trip because I was spending a small fortune and I wanted to maximize my chances. Also, my partner wasn't a bowhunter. I wasn't going to spend all that money and get nothing—at least that's how my thinking went. It is amazing how we think in our younger years. Experience is the only teacher.

My second trip for moose was a thirty-day combination Stone sheep, Canada moose, and mountain caribou hunt in 1988. I booked it with Stone Mountain Outfitters in Toad River, British Columbia. Dave Weins was the outfitter and Barry Clark my guide. Again, I didn't take my bow and shot the various species with a rifle. Moose was not my priority on that trip, but Stone sheep was. The guides convinced me, however, that the meat on a moose was best at that time of year. Besides that, the carcass would make excellent grizzly bait. I had a grizzly tag, too. A huge bear was working

*This giant western Canada moose was shot on Kawdy Plateau, Linda Lake, British Columbia, October 1996.*

that part of the country, and we hoped to lure him in. I didn't get the grizzly but was fortunate enough to take a moose, mountain caribou, and Stone ram. The ram held the No. 12 spot over all for many years. I was pretty proud of that ram.

In September of 1990 I booked my third moose hunt with Skyline Outfitters. Bill Moynihan was the outfitter. The outfit also had another division called Northwest Ranching and Guiding. The owner of both was an outfitter by the name of Jack Racarion. I'd been grizzly hunting with those two the previous spring with no luck, but I'd met another guide named Ken Contrail. Ken was an old prospector, fisherman guide, and hermit. He was a contrary old guy, and the natives didn't like him much. Almost every time he went to town (which was once a year or so) he got into a fistfight or some other sort of altercation. But for some strange reason I got along with him well. I think he liked the idea that I hunted with a bow. Ken told me about Mess Lake, a small lake north of Telegraph Creek that he called home. He called that area the stockyard because the moose were so thick. "There will be so many moose we'll probably get run over," he said. So I booked.

We were to fly into Wrangell, Alaska, take a charter to Telegraph Creek, BC, and then fly twenty minutes north to Mess Lake. Ken had a small flat-bottomed boat and motor that would be our transportation upriver. Well, the summer had been very dry, and the river was at its lowest point in years. We spent the next day and a half dragging the boat upriver by hand. We gave up on getting to where Ken had wanted to hunt and went back downriver to the lake and his cabin. The next two weeks were spent trying to find a decent moose. We couldn't find a bull worth shooting, though, and it seemed to me that the moose were a bit thin in the area around Ken's cabin. Maybe they were all in his freezer. In my opinion a man has a right to hang some meat once in a while, living this far out in the sticks with no electricity or running water—a tough way to go 360 days a year, in my opinion. I did, however, kill a huge black bear and a wolf with Ken's rifle. It was a good trip—but no Canada moose.

My fourth trip was to the Kawdy Plateau with outfitters Stan and Linda Lancaster in September of 1996. Their sons, Bart and Cam, were also guiding for the family operation, Kawdy Outfitters. Their specialties were big Canada moose, mountain caribou, Stone sheep, and grizzlies.

Stan didn't care much for bowhunting, but his sons hunted with bows and welcomed the challenge. The boys had teamed up with Bob Fontana, a bowhunting guide I'd chased bighorn sheep and elk with. Bob and the Lancasters had bought Nahanni Butte Outfitters from Greg Williams (another outfitter I knew well), noted for taking bowhunters. Bart Lancaster agreed to guide take me on this trip. We were going to concentrate on mountain caribou and Canada moose.

My friend and cameraman Chuck Denault and I flew into Vancouver, then from Vancouver to Watson Lake in the Yukon. From there we chartered a plane to the main lodge, which was on a lake back in British Columbia. We then hopped another plane and flew to one of their camps on Linda Lake. The word was that if tiny Linda Lake froze, we would have to ride horses ten to twelve hours back to the base camp when it came time to leave: No airplane could land on the ice up there. If the base camp lake also froze, we would have to make another very long jog to the Alaskan Highway. And the weather forecast didn't look all that good.

*Packing out! It was two days by horseback to the road or less than two hours by plane to the airport, Kawdy Plateau, British Columbia, October 1996.*

On our flights up we had had a short layover in a town called Smithers. While there, I realized I had forgotten my sleeping bag. It was by the door in my house . . . back in Michigan. I quickly went to a general store and bought the best sleeping bag they had. I couldn't figure out why it was so inexpensive since it was rated to zero degrees. Once I arrived in camp, I realized that it said zero degrees *Celsius*. It makes you wonder: Why so intelligent at times, so foolish at others? Man, I paid for it, too, because it turned very, very cold.

That first evening in camp a snowstorm blew in. The next morning the little lake had a half-inch of ice on it, and the temperature was close to zero. Everybody would definitely be riding horseback down to the base camp when the time came to leave. Each day from that point forward the ice got thicker and the snow deeper. The nighttime temperatures were zero and below. I slept in my clothes every night and shivered like a dog passing peach seeds. The sleeping bag was worthless. There is nothing worse than being bone-cold at night and trying to sleep.

We pursued caribou first. There were quite a few mountain caribou around and a few Pope and Young bulls, but there just wasn't anything Bart wanted me to take. He was hoping I would get a big bull and that their outfit would get a little press from the deal. They were accustomed to taking large bulls out of the area, but we couldn't find one. In retrospect, I should have tried to shoot one of the smaller bulls. The way it turned out, I had to make two more trips to Canada for mountain caribou to get the job done.

After three days of chasing and glassing caribou we decided to go after a moose. The first day, Bart called in a bull right off the bat. I could hear him coming, breaking sticks and grunting. I was struggling to stay calm and concentrate on the shot. When you see one of these huge beasts at fifteen yards, your heart jumps up to your throat. The bull turned out to be a small paddle-horned two-year-old. He was determined to find the cow calling to him. He circled our position and finally got our wind. Even though he was small, it sure got the blood flowing. Close encounters like that, regardless of the animal's trophy quality, are what bowhunters live for.

The snowstorm was relentless. It piled up, making the going tough on horses and men alike. We spent as much time walking and leading the horses as we did riding. Those icy, rocky trails are treacherous, and more than one hunter has broken a leg, or worse. The snow hung heavy on the vegetation and trees and, no matter how hard I tried to cover up, inevitably ended up down my neck, in my lap while riding, in the tops of my boots, and in my gloves. We were wet constantly.

Times like those are when you have to reach for more fortitude. After shivering all night in the cabin, though, the last thing I wanted to do was find more fortitude and spend another miserable day. Most of our clothes were still wet in places the next day. Our boots were still damp inside. I wondered how the horses tolerated the frozen saddle blankets and stiff leather each morning. They are so incredibly tough it's unbelievable, standing outside all night and then loaded down with all sorts of cold horse garb. The garb weighs at least 75 pounds, and then some lopsided dude climbs on their back adding at least another 180 by the time you count all the clothes and equipment. By God, if they have to do all that in the name of my hunt, the least I could do was get my tired old carcass out of bed and get moving. Sometimes that thought was all that motivated me.

Once I'd shuffled over to the stove and warmed up a bit, I would also think of the hard work the guides and cook were doing in my behalf. Even

*The author's black bear that he shot with his guide's .30-06 at the headwaters of Mess Lake, British Columbia, September 1990.*

though the trip was tougher than expected, it was time to get a hold of more grit—from somewhere.

At most good-looking moose pockets and swamps we stopped, tied the horses, and set up for a calling sequence. Sometimes we could hear a bull grunting out in the distance, but the storm was keeping the moose in heavy cover. Many times, fresh tracks told us the moose were close, but they wouldn't come in. They were rutting, all right, but deep in the woods.

One afternoon we heard a bull grunt quite a ways above our position. We cow-called and pleaded with him to come down to us, but nothing was happening. The bull would call back, rake a tree, but stay put. Bart decided we had better go to him.

We stalked as best we could up through the willows and underbrush. The heavy snow and big flakes made the visibility poor, and the snow-laden branches and slick conditions made the going difficult. The bull grunted a few more times and then went silent. We eased up the slope in quiet search, but found only his tracks and the scrub pine he had been rubbing.

Bart gave a light cow call again, to see if we could locate him. The bull unbelievably had passed us on our way up, and he grunted from somewhere below, where we had started calling.

We agreed to go after him again. We were about halfway back to our starting position when Bart spotted the bull working his way back up the slope. We quickly set up and waited. Bart cow-called one more time, and the bull responded. He wasn't far. I heard a small twig snap and saw his huge antlers first. Then his big, black form lumbered slowly through the willows and spruce trees. He was in full display at fifteen yards, looking for a cow in heat.

As he went behind a small spruce I drew my 80-pound Hoyt Alphatech and anchored. I had to concentrate on picking a spot. He was so big that I was tempted to hurry the shot at that range. They look like you could never miss. I repeated in my mind, *Pick a spot, pick a spot,* and settled the pin on his vitals. His shoulder blade was back just a bit, partially covering his vitals. At that range, though, I was confident I could put the arrow in the perfect spot. The Easton 2413 XX75, tipped with a 100-grain Thunderhead payload, streaked to the mark. Just as I released, the bull's front leg moved forward a fraction, ensuring the vitals were wide open. The arrow penetrated all the way through but hung on the vanes on the far side. When he turned to run, the broadhead caught some brush and the arrow fell to the ground.

We could hear the bull crashing down the steep mountainside and through the brush on the dead run. It was extremely loud, and we looked at each other in surprise. Suddenly the noise stopped. We listened carefully for a moment or two, questioning what had happened. A second later there was a big crash. I gave Bart a hug for a job well done, and we patted each other on the back.

We were sure the animal was dead but gave him fifteen minutes before taking up the trail. The arrow showed good blood, and the blood trail was easy to follow. The 1,600-pound bull had freight-trained a couple of four-inch trees on his death run, snapping them off almost at the ground. When he finally tipped over, he sheared another good-size tree. That much weight hurtling blindly through the brush is a scary thought. He was a great Canada moose, well matured and with a great crown of horns. He was everything a hunter could hope for, and he was mine. Plus, we had it all on film.

*The author's wolf, shot with his guide's .30-06 on the last night of the hunt and less than 100 yards from the bear kill, Mess Lake, British Columbia, September 1990.*

Now, the real work began. If you ain't never packed out a moose, you ain't never had no fun! It is all two men can do just to get the guts out and do the quartering. Once again the horses were worth their weight in gold.

I wondered, as always, what predators this big bull had fought off during his lifetime. How many miles had he traveled finding food and looking for cow moose during the rut? Given his age, I'm sure that his progeny will live healthy, long lives.

We left the bull there for the night and came back early the next morning to pack him out. The horses slipped and slid with all the ice on the trail. We led them most of the way there and back because of the treacherous conditions.

We went out the next day and hunted mountain caribou, but to no avail. The weather was getting worse. The following day Bart's brother showed up with a large string of horses and said that we needed to move camp out of the mountains before the big snows arrived. If we didn't get out soon, we would be there all winter. It took considerable time to get the camp packed up and hit the trail. The packstring was pretty impressive—

we could hardly see from one end to the other. It was a long, hard trek to the main camp, where we hoped an airplane could get to us and fly us out. If it snowed too much for the airplane to get to the main camp, however, it would have been another two-day ride to the next landing strip, which was the highway. This had been a good trip, but I was as ready as I had ever been for a hot shower and a warm bed.

Bart's efforts to make this a successful moose adventure were second to none. It was a pleasure to send him a number of clients for their first moose hunt. Thanks again, Bart.

*(Author's note: Something I discovered the hard way during this winter's hunting adventure was to be very careful with a mechanical release aid. A little melted snow around your hand followed by a refreeze is disaster in the making. The trigger will freeze at the most inopportune time.)*

Chapter 24

# Now You See Them, Now You Don't—Alaska Barren-Ground Caribou

With only three species left in the quest for the North American Twenty-Eight, I was beginning to feel the pressure. Only four others had accomplished the task with bow in hand.

I had been on one hunt for Alaska barren-ground caribou. It was a combination brown bear, moose, and caribou hunt with an outfitter by the name of Kelly Vrem. The brown bear hunt was full of excitement, but that is another story. We were concentrating on a brown bear, so we really didn't spend too much time looking for caribou. There weren't many around, anyway. I think we spent three days trying to stalk some of the local caribou but without any luck. The last night of the trip there was a foot of snow, and I tried with no success to stalk some caribou that had come into camp. The next morning we had to stomp out two tracks on which the Super Cub could land. A good friend of mine and business partner, Dr. Gordon Heller, had come along on that trip and had been sent to a different camp. He was lucky enough to get all three species: brown bear, Alaska barren-ground caribou, and moose.

My second trip was on 12 October 1997. Dave Kidder, a booking agent in Grand Rapids, Michigan, set up this trip for me. Outfitter Mel Gillis of Sandy River Outfitting in Alaska had a brown bear, caribou, and fishing camp that was one of the best for steelhead fishing in that part of the world. This trip was to be for barren-ground caribou only.

There were not a lot of caribou in the area, compared with other parts of Alaska. But Mel thought we could find a good one, even though the Fish and Game Department had cut the season back quite a few days because of declining numbers. Herds elsewhere in the area were experiencing a population explosion. Once we arrived, it wasn't long before we could see

*This Alaska barren-ground caribou was shot at Taylor Mountain, Alaska, August 1999.*

that the migration hadn't yet begun. We used a Honda four-wheeler with a trailer behind (where I sat) to travel the country. It was one of the roughest rides I've had to endure. We covered a lot of territory, but the caribou were just not there. Mel was a professional and a complete gentleman, and he offered me a refund.

One day we were quite a distance back in the bush, scouting. Some local residents hunting for meat in the area were killing caribou of every description. We saw evidence of cows, calves, and bulls they had killed. Evidently, they took whatever they could. It appeared to us that they had hit a caribou they didn't know they'd hit. It went down out of their sight, we imagined, and we found the carcass.

A huge brown bear was camped on the dead caribou. When he saw us coming he lay down, completely covering the caribou. He was going to make a stand on his meal, no matter what. Mel drove the four-wheeler within fifty yards of the monster, but we quickly figured that we'd better move on. He lay there and didn't move, but we could imagine the wheels turning in his head and see the look in his eye. Of course, I didn't have a permit. That may have been a good thing, for I truly believe that if we had dismounted the four-wheeler, that bear would have been on us in a flash.

I hung around for a few more days without any luck and decided to hook a ride out with a pilot who came though two days before my trip was over. That was my first hunt focused primarily on barren-ground caribou.

My third caribou hunt began 21 August 1999 in the Taylor Mountains of Alaska. Carl Brent, a good friend, outfitter, and fellow bowhunter, helped me book it. Carl also was an excellent Super Cub pilot. He flew for many outfitters in Alaska but mainly for Wayne Woods Outfitting. Wayne, who hunted in western Alaska for caribou, moose, and grizzly, had been a registered guide for fourteen years and had a great reputation. Carl was also the Alaska Bow Hunters Association president, and he invited me back the following year as a speaker and to present new bows to every young new member. There were more than twenty of them.

We flew from Seattle to Anchorage then up to base camp. Ryan Cornish was my cameraman and would record all the action. Carl flew us to base camp and would be our supply pilot, too. Getting there we had to fly through a pass where winds are always terrible. As we went through the turbulent pass, we could see some planes that hadn't made it through and lay smashed against the rocks below. Sights like those sometimes make me question my reason for putting myself in these situations.

We couldn't get from base camp to spike camp that day because of bad weather. Wayne decided that we would go ahead and hunt around base until the weather straightened out. Even though caribou trails were everywhere and the sign was reasonably fresh, the report from Carl wasn't encouraging. He had flown a seventy-five-mile radius around base camp the day before our arrival and had found very few caribou. That is the way caribou hunting can be. Waves of caribou come through, and overnight they can disappear into the tundra. At the time of this hunt the Mulchatna western Alaska herd numbered nearly two hundred thousand and was rapidly expanding.

The first day we awoke to a steady rain. The river by camp was running high and muddy, but we took a four-wheeler across it and went up the mountainside as far as we could. We climbed out on a ridge above camp and glassed the vast expanse of tundra. A few caribou were visible, but a good distance away. The country was mostly wide open but had thick

*Carl Brent and son with Super Cub at base camp on Taylor Mountain, Alaska, August 1999.*

patches of alder brush in the bottoms and various low brush. We hiked all day and saw very few caribou.

The weather broke the next day, and we put together our gear for spike camp. A spike camp is a fairly meager existence, but it is adequate if rigged up right, usually consisting of a sleeping tent and a rain fly strung between trees for a cooking area. A minimum of gear is a must because of weight considerations in the Super Cub. It is always hard to figure out what to take and what to leave, but bare necessities are the rule of thumb. One thing to take for sure is the best rain gear you can buy. You will have to endure a lot of wet conditions in this part of the world.

It was reassuring to have Carl flying us in to the spike camp. His experience and wisdom gave me a lot of confidence that we would get there in one piece. Flying over the area we planned to hunt, we noticed that the caribou were thick. While setting up camp, we saw caribou running by. In Alaska, however, you can't hunt the same day you fly. You have to wait until the next day. When we finished setting up camp, I put my arrows and broadheads together and fired my bow. The bow had made the trip well and was shooting where it should.

The next morning, as soon as we could see, we climbed a small ridge above camp and went to glassing. To our astonishment, there wasn't a caribou to be found. The wave of animals we had seen the day before had already moved through.

Wayne thought the caribou might be in another drainage, a place in which, he felt, they would slow down to feed for a few days. Getting there required a long, tough hike. Some caribou were there, but not enough to make the hike worth it every day. We decided we might have to move camp closer.

The next day we were getting ready to move camp when Carl flew in supplies. Wayne and Carl decided to try to find a bigger concentration of caribou by airplane. After a few hours they returned looking solemn. They couldn't find enough caribou to justify moving camp. There was no place to go. We would have to wait for another wave to come through.

The next day was slow until late afternoon, when we found a group of bulls on a ridge across from camp. They seemed to be spending a lot of time feeding and milling in one particular spot. When the caribou went behind some cover, we made a mad dash across the valley and up the ridge. The caribou trail leading to the top of the ridge petered out right in the middle of an alder thicket, and we had no choice but to push through the tangled mess. The caribou heard us coming, of course, and disappeared just as we broke out. They headed back the way they had come, over the ridge.

It was getting dark and there was no sense in chasing them any farther. It was very disappointing—not to mention hard on an old man—to have run all that way and spooked the caribou out of the country. But we decided they might be back tomorrow. The words no sooner left our lips than the bulls came running back over the hill, right at us. We crouched down and waited as they closed the distance. They knew we were there, so drawing would be risky. They turned broadside at forty yards, and I drew. The motion spooked the lead bull, and the whole herd broke into a dead run. Disappointed isn't the word. I hate it when I get teased like that. But there are always lessons to learn, and I guess I was getting a bit too impatient or something.

Things just didn't work out over the next few days. The caribou stopped coming through with any predictability, and we were having a hard time finding any. We would sit on the ridge above camp for a few hours and then go back to camp for tea and a snack. Wayne just wouldn't give up, though,

*Spike camp for Alaska barren-ground caribou, Taylor Mountain, Alaska, August 1999.*

and he took one more trip up the ridge to glass until dark one evening. He had just crested the ridge when he saw a good bunch of caribou on the opposite mountain, headed our way. He ran as hard as he could back to camp and convinced me that we had enough time for a stalk before the day ended.

I grabbed my gear, and we headed across the tundra. When we got to where we needed to be, we had to make a decision which valley crossing they would use. About that time we saw the top of a set of caribou antlers going up the high trail—back the way they had come. We all made a run to the last bit of cover to cut them off and waited. The biggest bull in the bunch was in the lead, and he finally came out a good distance away. Having made the run to get into position, I was completely out of breath. But when the bull hung up just a bit, I drew and put the seventy-yard pin on his vitals. I held my breath and turned an arrow loose.

The 85-pound Hoyt Striker sent the Easton 2413 arrow, tipped with an NAP Shock Wave, seventy yards in a white streak. But the bull took a couple steps forward before the arrow arrived, and it struck him in the hind leg. My heart sank when I saw the arrow sticking out of his hip. Suddenly I realized that I should have used the next yardage pin, but how could I have predicted that he was going to move? He was ten yards farther off by the time the arrow got there, but I'd gotten caught up in the moment and wasn't thinking fast enough.

The bull went about twenty yards and stood still. I looked through my binocular and noticed that the arrow had struck the femoral artery in the rear thigh. The bull staggered and went down in less than a minute. I wasn't proud of the shot, but I had my Alaska barren-ground bull. Sometimes things don't turn out the way you'd hoped. In fact, sometimes they aren't pretty at all. I thank God, though, that the bull didn't suffer and went down fast. That night we went to bed pretty happy. I finally relaxed and slept well.

When I got up the next morning, Wayne was already gone. It wasn't long before he came running back with news of more caribou coming, including a good bull. We grabbed our stuff and took off again. Nonresidents can take two caribou in some parts of Alaska because the herds' exploding population is threatening to endanger their habitat.

Wayne stopped before we got too close to the caribou, and we talked about which crossing to guard. A quick decision took us to where the majority of the caribou had been going past. We hurried to the first alder patch, but the caribou were closing in faster than expected. The cover was low, and we weren't quite where we wanted to be. A cow caribou was leading the group right to us. We crawled slowly around a small clump of low brush, but another cow spotted us and turned the herd, leading them around to the other side of the brush we were hiding behind.

We crawled on our hands and knees like crazy back to the other side, hoping to get a shot before they left. The bull I had my eyes on turned broadside, and it was now or never. I raised up and drew. The entire herd pegged me—but not before the arrow was on its way. It struck home, and the bull went down fifty yards away. I had just taken two barren-ground bulls in a twenty-four-hour period—although it took forty-five years to get it done.

I was now just two species away from the North American Twenty-Eight, the Super Slam of North American animals with a bow. I could feel the pressure. The two species left, mountain caribou and Coues white-tailed deer, were two of the toughest customers to land. Could I get it done? I'd already been on three Coues deer hunts and two mountain caribou hunts. My internal clock was ticking, and pressure continued to build inwardly as I pondered the future.

Chapter 25

# Tough Customer in the Yukon Winter—Mountain Caribou

Mountain caribou had given me a bit of trouble in the past. I had been to Fox Lake, British Columbia, in 1998 and had just returned from a fruitless hunt in Norman Wells, Northwest Territories. As soon as I got home, I started combing my files for an outfitter for another mountain caribou hunt. After I'd made four or five calls, Dave Coleman said he had a cancellation I could fill.

Mountain caribou are a variety of woodland caribou native to the mountainous inland temperate rain forest region. They are distinguished from other caribou by their dependence on hair lichens such as old-man's beard and horse hair which accumulate in the branches of high-elevation old-growth forests for winter food. The animals move upslope in late winter to find these lichens after heavy snows bury ground-based foods in lower-elevation cedar and hemlock forests. By January, as the snow gets deeper and solidifies, mountain caribou move into upper slopes and ridges where subalpine fir parkland habitat dominates. Their large feet act as snowshoes, enabling them to walk on top of the snow and feed. In summer, mountain caribou move back to mid- and upper-elevation slopes and valleys dominated by old subalpine fir and spruce forests; there they feed on herbs, shrubs, grasses, sedges, and mushrooms. All of the world's mountain caribou live in the mountains of British Columbia, the Yukon, and the Northwest Territories.

My cameraman, Ryan Cornish, a good friend at Wolf Creek Productions, and I flew to the Yukon and arrived at Whitehorse. Dave's wife picked us up and drove us over to the air charter service, where they would fly us in to camp. The flight was to be just under an hour in a Cessna 206. However, the fog and snow were so thick that we had trouble seeing camp.

*Gary and his trusty riding mule at base camp in Yukon, Canada.*

The pilot made a couple of passes and told us to watch for a small lake with a creek feeding it. Camp should be right there, somewhere. We couldn't see it because of the weather, so we had to fly to the little town of Farrell. We waited there for two and a half hours for the weather to break. When it did, we landed near camp.

We were there by 2:00 P.M., which allowed enough time to ride a half-mile from camp and do some glassing. We didn't see anything, but we got a feel for the horses we would be riding and how the equipment would work.

The next morning we took a long ride to the top of a mountain and glassed the surrounding countryside, peering over the edges and looking into the basins below. We spent all day glassing but saw only three head of moose. There weren't any caribou or caribou tracks in the snow. It had been a long, cold, and windy day by the time we unsaddled our horses back in camp. My eyes were bloodshot from all the glassing, and my face was windburned.

We had a good hot supper and hit the sack, planning to head up the trail by daylight the next morning. Mother Nature, though, had other ideas. We awoke to a snowstorm and fog. Our second day was spent in camp drinking tea, eating a bit, and telling tall tales. Even though a man should relax and be patient at times like these, the pressure of the quest kept nagging.

By midafternoon blue sky was showing through a few "sucker holes," as I call them from my flying days. One of the other hunters, a young man with whom we had shared camp the previous day, and his guide came riding into camp late in the afternoon. They had ridden out the day before with a packstring toward an upper mountain camp. The young man's father and another guide also had made the trip to hunt caribou for a few days higher on the slope. When they arrived there, they found the camp torn to pieces. For the third time that season a grizzly had destroyed a camp. It tore two sheets of plywood completely off the cabin and ransacked the entire contents. The floor was covered with molasses, and the bear had eaten all the food, including forty-five pounds of oats for the horses. The cabin was filled with snow. They spent a miserable night there.

The next morning, however, they slipped up on a bunch of caribou they'd seen the day before, and the son shot a good one. They packed him up and came out. The father and the other guide were going to hunt their way down and be in later. I took some good photos of the boy with his caribou and congratulated him. Lowell Davis, who was to be my guide, and I both hoped we would get our opportunity tomorrow.

On the third day we rode halfway up to the grizzly-riddled, high-mountain camp. We saw one single bull, high on the mountain. He was young and traveling steadily, looking for other caribou. We spotted a group of fourteen caribou farther up the valley. There was one decent bull in the bunch, so we crossed the valley to start our stalk. The wind was good, but the minute we started to climb it switched. When we broke over the crest of the basin to take a peek, the caribou were going over the top. Obviously, they'd gotten a good whiff of our scent and had "sold out." They were an exceptionally spooky bunch, and we wondered if the old grizzly had been harassing them. It was a long ride back down.

To top things off, the weather turned ugly again, and it began to snow hard. You couldn't see a hundred yards at times, and we got good and wet. Once we broke off the top, however, it seemed like a different world.

*Gary and his wintry mountain caribou, Yukon, Canada, October 1999.*

It was a moderate day in the lower country near camp, but we knew bad weather loomed just above us and might sock in later.

The next morning we woke up to at least four inches of new snow topped with fog. By midday we had some scattered blue sky, but the wind had picked up. The high country where we needed to be was still shrouded in clouds. From the looks of the clouds and the rate at which they were moving, the winds had to be whistling up there. We spent the fourth day in camp, drying clothes and preparing for the following day.

We hoped there would be enough of a break in the weather that we could load two packhorses and go to the high camp, the one the grizzly had destroyed. We decided to clean up the mess and try to hunt there at least three days. It was just too hard on the animals, and the hunters, to ride four or five hours daily to get to where the hunting was—let alone get back to camp at a reasonable time in the evening. It didn't leave much time for hunting, either.

On our fifth morning the sun broke over the ridge, shining brightly. It had been chilly in the sleeping bag the night before. The temperature overnight had gone from around twenty degrees above to minus twenty-five. According to the radio forecast, there was only a 30 percent chance of snow, and the temperature would climb to twenty or so during the next few days. The high plateau was an eight-hour ride—if everything went well. That would be our last attempt to get a caribou; any day at this time of year the weather could snow us in—until spring!

It was noon by the time we could get everything together and leave camp. Climbing out of the valley, we found the conditions tough. We spent most of our time leading the horses, which isn't easy when you are bundled up in heavy clothing. The trail was steep and very slippery for us on foot. A slight stumble or fall, and your horse would be on top of you. Now, that could ruin your hunt!

Dressing for the wind and cold temperatures is easy, but then try to walk or get on and off a horse—let alone ride for long distances. Also, your bow is strapped to the horse in a big leather scabbard and your arrows are in a hip quiver or backpack. How did those Native Americans do this? We finally made it up under the first plateau and on the side of the first mountain. While resting we spotted thirty or so caribou, including five very good bulls. They were high in the shale on the face of a slide, where it was impossible to stalk. We were only three hours from camp, so if there had been a chance, we would have waited them out.

A couple more hours up the trail we spotted another group of caribou, with three nice bulls. It was good to see all these caribou. We pushed hard to the camp and got there at dark. We worked hard and fast getting it cleaned out and repaired. That bear had certainly made a mess. It must have been a huge grizzly because he popped both the bear-proof drums like they were tin cans. It was even tough to get a good fire going because the balsam wood up there wouldn't burn well, but we settled in for the night and made the most of it. I slept restlessly, wondering about the grizzly—and when he would return.

The next morning, while it was still dark and we were saddling horses, I caught a movement out of the corner of my eye. *Grizzly!* I thought, and I froze. My heart skipped a beat or three. It turned out, though, to be a 45-inch bull moose walking smack through camp among the horses. He caused a bit of a ruckus but then disappeared into the darkness. Now it's funny, but for a long second it was panic time.

*There were no caribou that year during the author's second unsuccessful hunt in the high northern beauty of Canada—base camp, Norman Wells, NWT, September 1999.*

We rode down the valley and glassed the slopes where we had seen caribou the day before. It wasn't long before a squall blew in and snow began piling up. The fog made it tough to see anything. It was as disappointing as anything gets to know that the caribou were there but we couldn't see them.

The caribou were probably timbered up now, anyway, so we forged our way toward the end of the valley. We decided to lead the horses up a ridge we had seen caribou on before. The fog now began to thin, and we could see quite a ways from time to time. Toward the top of the ridge, Lowell spotted a bull coming over the mountaintop. All we saw were the antlers, and it was so far away the bull looked more like an ant.

He had spotted our horses sky-lined on a small ridge, so we quickly hid behind them and stayed hidden for at least ten minutes. The bull probably thought our horses were caribou because he started down the mountain. That's just how hunting works: days of hardship and toil, and all of a sudden an opportunity. Once the bull had disappeared into a ravine on the mountainside, we started to run for cover.

But a smaller bull came over the top and pinned us down again. When he followed the older bull, we dropped our horses' reins and ran the eighty or ninety yards to a big juniper. I hoped that the horses wouldn't leave because it would be a long, cold walk in either direction. About then I remembered that I'd better get my release on and my mittens off.

The bigger bull reappeared a third of the way down the mountain. He kept staring at our horses and working his way down. The smaller bull had joined him and was headed our way, too. Soon they were across a big draw 125 yards away. They walked along its edge looking for a place to cross. The bigger bull was acting like a typical bull in rut, snorting and challenging the horses. Lowell encouraged him by mimicking the snorting sounds from behind the juniper. The horses, scraping the snow and looking for feed, were behind us a hundred yards or so. When the bulls finally dropped into the deep wash, we ran like mad to where we figured they would come up on our side. We were huffing and puffing and excited about the possibilities of at least getting a shot at the bull down in the ravine. To our surprise, the smaller bull came up and out of the draw first. He stopped and looked right at us. I started to draw but stopped as Lowell whispered a range. Out of the corner of my eye I could see the antlers of the bigger bull coming up out of the draw.

The big bull passed the young one and presented a perfect shot. Having just heard the range of the first bull, I pulled the Hoyt to the stops and anchored. I centered the fifty-yard pin on Mr. Big's vitals and released, watching the orange-and-white fletch of the Easton 2413 streak forward. We heard the typical *thunk* of an arrow hitting home, but neither of us saw it. The bull leaped forward and started running hard. Lowell spotted blood on the bull's side and hollered, "You got him!"

The regal animal went over the crown of a hill forty yards away, and when he reappeared, he turned a quick circle and went down. It was an exciting moment. Finally, the fifth North American caribou. Lowell knew how important this species was to my goal. He ran, yelled, and jumped with excitement. He had used all the skills he possessed, and it had paid off. I had only one species left to complete the North American Twenty-Eight.

I ran to Lowell and the caribou, kneeled down in the snow, and reflected on the whole experience. We then took a good look at a magnificent, mature mountain caribou. We wondered about his age, what other perils

*Gary prepares for the trip back to base camp, Yukon, Canada, October 1999.*

he might have faced in his lifetime, and how much country he would have seen in his yearly migration.

I looked around to get a good picture in my mind of the rising white mountains, the valleys, and the deep snow. I wondered how I would describe this huge, desolate area. I also wondered if anyone else had gotten a caribou here. The local inhabitants of the area, perhaps? This was a great bull and sported a magnificent set of antlers—more than I had hoped for. I looked up and gratefully thanked the man upstairs.

We caped the bull and then boned all the meat, including the ribs, and laid it out neatly in the snow to cool. We left some bags covered with human scent in the midst of the meat, to keep the bears and wolves away, and then started the long ride back to our spike camp. We arrived late but fixed and ate a big meal of fried ham and macaroni and cheese, drank hot tea, and discussed the successful day.

The next morning we were up early, pulled camp, and were on our way to get the caribou. Lowell decided that we should keep our eyes out for a bull moose on our way back up. We did see one 45-inch bull, maybe the one that had run through camp, but passed on it because our minimum was a 55-inch spread. Upon reaching the area where the caribou was laid out, we sneaked to a spot where we could glass him. It wouldn't be good to surprise a grizzly or a pack of wolves. A few birds are all we found.

We loaded the meat, cape, and antlers and started the long journey for the lower camp. The horses were loaded heavily, and the trail was slick. Leading the horses all the way down to the valley was the only option. Several hours later we finally mounted up on the valley floor and made the short ride to camp. The entire team in camp was ecstatic about the mountain caribou. They all knew how important this trip had been and were glad to have been a part of it. I had reached the end of another quest, having harvested all of the North American caribou.

After a big dinner that night I became very ill. Mother Nature wasn't done with me yet. I've learned the hard way: Never speak too soon about the end of any quest. Nature and God will teach you another lesson if you do. The next day I felt rough, was running a pretty good fever, and had a bad headache and abdominal cramps—bad water, maybe, or food poisoning. Regardless, I was down for the count. It didn't matter much. We were socked in by fog and another blinding snowstorm. Airplanes, according to the radio, had been grounded for three days.

When we finally did reach Whitehorse, we met Todd Brady and his father, from Louisiana, who had been hunting moose with Dave Coleman's outfit. We found out that we had a lot in common and had trod the same turf while hunting whitetails on the King Ranch in Texas. It is a small world in the hunting circles.

I want to thank Dave Coleman and Lowell Davis for making the short-notice arrangement, and for the special efforts that produced success. Thank you!

Chapter 26

# Double Toil and Trouble—Alaska Brown Bear and Sitka Blacktail

After the passing of many, many years, I consider myself fortunate to have seen most of North America. I have been blessed, too, in having hunted the majority of its species. My travels and adventures have taken me as far as Russia, Asia, Africa, and the South Pacific. Among all the species, pursuing the bears of the world has offered my biggest challenges, greatest thrills, and most serious lessons. I had been on four unsuccessful Alaska brown bear hunts and was still pursuing that colossal carnivore.

Without exception, even of the polar bear, the Alaska brown bear is the largest land-dwelling carnivore in the world. It is considerably larger than its relative the grizzly. The brown bears of Europe and Asia are also smaller. The great size of the Alaska brown bear is the result of a protein-rich diet of salmon and the mild climate in which the bears live. Their thick coat is usually brown in color, though individual bears vary from blond to almost black.

The Alaska brown bear is one of the top trophies of the North American continent. The hunting conditions will test your grit: Wearing hip boots and rain gear while carrying a heavy pack and rifle or bow separates the men from the boys. The hunter must be in excellent condition to wade rivers and negotiate mucky swamps, alder thickets, heavy snow, and steep mountainsides. Should the hunter find a good bear after long hours of glassing, he must get within range quickly. These bears seldom remain in one place for long. A person's shooting skills need to be sharp under pressure, too. A wounded brown bear is a serious matter—especially with archery equipment.

A hunter can spend endless hours or days seeking good outfitters with excellent hunting areas. Past experience has shown me that it is hard to beat

*This was the shortest landing strip I had ever seen, Tsiu River area, September 1998.*

the assistance of a knowledgeable hunting consultant. This service generally comes at no additional cost to the hunter. On this occasion I turned once again to Wes Vining of Trophy Connection in Cody, Wyoming.

Finding an outfitter willing to take a bowhunter for brown bear isn't easy. Finding one where I wanted to hunt this time, Kodiak Island, was even tougher. Wes did some research and talked with many of the leading Island outfits. Some said, "Hell no," and others said not without a rifle backup. After extensive research and some serious discussion, we decided on Rob Holt. I also decided that a rifle backup made a lot of sense for my and the crew's longevity—if something went dreadfully wrong.

Rob was raised on Kodiak Island. He spent a number of years working for a successful bear hunting operation before going out on his own. I also liked the fact that Rob had done some bowhunting himself. He understood some of the needs and limitations. Rob was running his own small hunting operation on Kodiak, as well as on the mainland, currently taking only three spring and fall bear hunters. His area encompassed some excellent native lands near the village of Old Harbor. Rob advised that he had previously guided only one other bowhunter, who, after several days of frustration, opted to shoot his bear with a rifle. I assured him that wouldn't happen with me.

I booked a spring hunt in 1994. The licenses were on a drawing basis, and I was lucky enough to get one. The results of any spring bear hunt are unpredictable. Success depends heavily on the weather. Also, even though one sees a lot more bears at this time of year, few are stalkable. The bears are constantly on the move, looking for food and a breeding partner. The cover is minimal at that time of year, too.

We spent fourteen days in some of the worst weather Rob and I had ever seen. Although we managed to get out every day, the bears were staying in heavy cover because of the weather. What few bears we saw were in poor positions to stalk. But the trip wasn't a total loss. It was one of the most interesting and challenging adventures I'd been on. Kodiak Island has some interesting history. Plus, I made quite a few new friends.

Shortly after returning home I received a surprise call from Rob offering me a special deal for a return fall hunt. He encouraged me to come back then and was eager to help me get my bear. My hunt would be for fifteen days and would start the last week of October. The advantage of hunting in the fall for a bowhunter is that the bears are preoccupied with constant eating, stoking up frantically for the winter hibernation. The cover is better, and stalking opportunities are more abundant on distracted bears. I immediately booked the hunt and practiced shooting the rest of the summer.

Here's what appears in my 1994 journal entries:

Arrived in Old Harbor, October. Met Rob and packer Rocky Christianseal. Had their hunting clothes and hip boots on. Said high tide was in. Needed to get upriver, now. Changed to wool and hip boots, from cottons and loafers.

Eight miles by boat. Took three hours. Unloaded boat twice, log jam and sand bar. Tide starting out. Arrived base camp around dark. Unloaded fast, starting to rain. Base camp set on riverbank. Great fishing hole fifty feet from door.

Morning winds, cold and gusty, spitting rain. Made way to lookout point. Important to stay up high to avoid spreading scent throughout valley. Glassed upper valley and river. Saw several bears, including some in river busy fishing. Wind gusting downriver. Thought: *Let's get down there. Perfect for stalk.*

Quarter-mile from river. Several hundred feet above bottom. Bottom and steep slopes choked with alders, cottonwood, tall grass, swamps, and

*This hunt brought the author's long quest for a brown bear to an end, Tsiu River, Alaska, September 1998.*

creeks. Stalk too difficult from here, according to Rob. 11:00 A.M.: Bears had enough fish. Left river for a nap.

All eyes on huge bear that fished downstream all morning. Headed upslope toward us. I made way down to cut him off. A spooky and tedious wait. Bear turned out of range and parallel to thick alders. No chance in thick stuff. Backed off.

Later, bears return to river. Same huge boar on upper end, fishing downstream again. Coming downwind. The chance we waited for. Rocky stayed as lookout. Rob and I slipped into valley, back to river crossing. Struggled getting there. Thick alders. Timing important. Bend in river—bear's favorite fishing hole.

Tried to hurry. Tough going. Being sneaky, almost comical. Pulse racing. Heart pounding. Catch breath, calm down. Starting to shake.

Moving again. Concentrating on quiet. Steady move toward bend. Watching for other bears. Winds steady downstream. Cover growing thin. Exposed to far bank. Last one hundred yards seemed like a mile.

Stalking along riverbed. Loose rock and gravel noisy. Air hard to come by. Heart thundering in ears.

Suddenly, bear on far bank. Ducked down, froze on ground. Not the one. Big bear, though. He stepped from alders and surveyed area. Stepped into river to fish. How could he not see us?

I'm completely exposed. Seconds ticked like minutes. Concentrated to slow my breathing. Bear not in range yet. Pinned down. Awaiting next move.

Bear flinched and tested air. Stood upright. Gazed upriver. Quick, fluid leap put him on the bank. Disappeared in alders. Rob looked at me. Mental telepathy said, "Boss man coming downriver."

We broke toward deadfall fifteen yards away. Didn't make it. Too open to get there. Huge bear coming around bend. By then on hands and knees. Worried he'd think we were a bear in his fishing hole. Felt like an ant taking on anteater. No doubt he'd spot us. Rob chambered a round.

Colossal bear fished downstream, stopped, and stared. *Pegged us,* I thought. *We're in trouble*. He's staring at fish swimming upstream. Still hadn't seen us. Amazing. In the wide open, forty yards away.

Bear staring downstream, broadside. Bow in my hands felt like marshmallow roasting stick. Thought about David when he laid eyes on Goliath.

*Rob Holt shot this huge brown bear after Gary's arrow fell off the rest and struck the bear through the midsection, Kodiak Island, Alaska, November 1994.*

Mouthed words "Thirty plus" to Rob. He nodded. Now or never. Bear moved forward. Quartering toward. Bad deal. Shaking hard. Hoyt ProVantage to full draw. Bear stopped. Brain faltered. Bear started coming, quartering toward. Picked a spot. Other basics flew from brain. Thousand pounds of muscle coming to visit. Nerves took over. Arrow fell from rest. Landed between riser and rest. Didn't register in mind. Released string. Shot went way right. Arrow flashed through his guts. Lodged in offside rear leg. Muttered aloud, "Oh, no!"

Monster bear exploded with rage. Biting his side. I stared in bewilderment. I nocked another arrow without looking, faster than I ever had, but the mighty roar of Rob's rifle rang in my ears. The giant collapsed in the river. Second and third shots rang and silenced his thrashing. Heart in my feet. Lungs empty of air. We both stood in shock.

I'd choked. Choked worse than ever had. For a moment, river stopped flowing. Could hear a pin drop. I was human, like it or not.

Rob probably saved our lives. Kept bear from suffering, too. Hard lesson for me. A lesson needed, I guessed. Lowest point in my hunting career. Failed in a clutch situation. Confidence shaken considerably.

*******

The Alaska brown bear squared 10 feet, 4 inches and scored $28\frac{10}{16}$. He would have been a formidable new Pope and Young or SCI world record. It wasn't meant to be.

The next few days we fleshed and took care of the bear hide. The subject of the blunder was brought up very little. Both Rob and I were disappointed that it turned out the way it had, but thankful that the bear didn't suffer and that we had walked away with our lives. Rob convinced me that we should go and look for a Sitka black-tailed buck and put the bear behind us. Although it was hard to get excited about that, I agreed.

The Sitka black-tailed deer is a native to the wet coastal rain forests of Southeast Alaska and north-coastal British Columbia. Its range has been expanded by transplants, and established populations now also exist near Yakutat in Prince William Sound, and on Kodiak and Afognak islands.

The Sitka black-tailed deer is smaller, stockier, and has a shorter face than other members of the black-tailed group. The average October live weight

*Bears had killed this moose and were working over the remains, Tsiu River, Alaska, September 1998.*

of adults is about 80 pounds for does and 120 pounds for bucks, although dressed weight of more than 200 pounds have been reported for bucks. The summer coat of reddish brown is replaced by dark brownish gray in winter. Antlers are dark brown, with typical black-tailed branching. Normal adult antler development is three points (including the eye-guard) on each side. Antlers are relatively small, with very few scoring more than 110 points by the Boone and Crockett system. A Sitka's average lifespan is about ten years, but a few are known to have attained an age of at least fifteen.

Summer and winter home-range areas vary from thirty to twelve hundred acres and average about two hundred acres. During summer, deer generally feed on herbaceous vegetation and the green leaves of shrubs. During winter, they are restricted to evergreen forbs and woody browse. When snow is not a problem, evergreen forbs such as bunchberry and trailing bramble are preferred.

Throughout much of the range of the Sitka black-tailed deer, normal dispersed hunting pressure has little influence on deer numbers. Bag limits vary from complete closures to six deer of either sex, depending on populations. Early-season hunting is concentrated in the alpine and subalpine areas. The largest portion of the harvest is taken in November, during the rut, when both sexes respond to a call resembling the bleat of a fawn. During late November and December, heavy snow sometimes concentrates deer at low elevations, making possible high harvest levels when local weather conditions are favorable.

Sitka black-tailed deer inhabit a good part of Kodiak Island. The area we were going to hunt was near Three Saints Bay, where the first Russian Orthodox Church settlement was founded in 1784. Hunting Sitka blacktails is a spot-and-stalk proposition. We proceeded downriver and glassed the slopes for feeding or bedded deer. The blacktails also come down to the beach to eat kelp and lick salt. Our first morning out, we spotted a buck and a few does feeding up in an open meadow above the thick brush. We beached the boat and began a stalk through the tangled alders. Bear trails and tiny deer trails were the only way to get through the thick vegetation.

When we broke out of the alders, we slipped around on the various open knobs and hogbacks in an effort to stay high enough to spot the deer and stay out of the noisy alders. We slowly peeked over each rise until we spotted the buck and does feeding in an open area. Rob directed me to get into position on the edge of the alders saying that he would make a half-circle behind the deer and attempt to push them in my direction. I could hear Rob coming slowly through the alders before I saw the black-tailed buck sneaking out ahead of him and coming directly to me.

Thirty yards away the blacktail turned broadside and looked back toward Rob. I drew the Hoyt and anchored solidly. Then, with confidence, I picked a spot and put an arrow through his vitals. As he crashed through the alders on a death run, I wondered why the bear hunt couldn't have gone that smoothly. I wondered why some hunts just seem to be given to a man, and some are so extremely difficult. I dismissed the worry and felt a bit better, having a black-tailed deer down. He wasn't a huge buck, but he put me one step closer to getting a personal goal accomplished.

We took a few minutes to reflect on the deer's life in these mountains and on the other challenges he may have faced. He would be good eating, and I was thankful we weren't far from the boat so that the bears wouldn't have an opportunity to eat him before I did.

It took a while to build my confidence back, but I wasn't going to give up. After so many brown bear hunts, it was difficult to decide where to

*Even clad in all this rain gear, we were soaked to the bone, Tsiu River, Alaska, September 1998.*

go next. I had met Sam Fejes, a well-known outfitter, in 1980. Sam had a good reputation for moose, brown bear, and several other species in Alaska. I saw Sam at a show and thought, *Why haven't I booked with Sam before this?* He was one of the best outfitters around. He had shot many species with a bow, including brown bear, and he truly knew what he was doing. He had an opening, so I booked a combination brown bear and moose hunt for the fall of 1997.

The coastal weather was horrible that year. It rained for two weeks solid and kept the streams riled and devoid of bears. We tried to hunt moose for a few days but were rained out there, too. I began to think that the gods just didn't want me to have a brown bear. Sam was disappointed, too, but he wanted me to book again for the following year. He was going to spend as much time as possible to help me reach my goal. He truly wanted me to be successful and get the brown bear jinx behind me.

The fall of 1998 couldn't come fast enough. When I arrived in Cordova, Sam was there to pick me up. As we waited for the baggage I had a bad feeling. Sure enough, my bow didn't make it. I knew at that point I was again going to be tested to the max. Maybe I really wasn't supposed to have a brown bear.

It didn't look like my bow was going to be found anytime soon, so Sam said I could borrow his. I agreed, but since Sam's bow had an overdraw (a touchy setup, and short for me), I needed to come up with another idea. Luckily, I had a friend, John Wilson, who lived in Cordova. I'd sent him a Hoyt Tenacity, identical to mine, a year earlier. I contacted him at work, and he went home to get all the equipment. We had Sam's bow back at camp to use as a spare if needed.

John and I had met in Hawaii. Our wives had been talking on the elevator in our hotel during the SCI convention and found that each had a hunter for a husband. They introduced John and me, and a great friendship developed. We hunted together after that first meeting, including a successful brown bear hunt in Russia.

We loaded up and flew into Sam's TSIU River camp. Once we got things organized in camp, I took John's bow out to practice and quickly realized that he had given me the wrong arrows. These arrows were for another bow he had, one with an overdraw, and were four inches too short for this bow. I felt sick. It was more than an hour back to Cordova by plane if I couldn't find any other arrows that would work. I had some old, extra arrows I always carried in a plastic tube, just in case of total disaster. It appeared I might be able make them work. I put some together with NAP 100-grain broadheads and went out to see what would happen. To make things more difficult, John's draw length was 2½ inches longer than mine, and there was no way to make an adjustment. I was anchoring behind my ear and in open air—not the most stable situation. The arrows I'd brought were an inch short, and if drawn fully the broadhead would hit the rest and pull the arrow off the string. Anchoring on the backside of the "valley" of John's long draw length was all I could do: guesswork at best.

I finally adjusted two pins to a place where I could at least hit the target reasonably well. I hit where I was aiming a half-dozen times. Sam watched and said, "No problem—you got it, and I know you can do it."

I reminded him that we were going brown bear hunting with a bow I'd never shot before. He laughed and said that everything would be fine. I was hoping he knew something I didn't.

That evening we flew his Super Cub into a spike camp he had set up. The runway was the shortest I had ever seen in the history of my piloting and beat anything I'd seen on a hunt, anywhere. Sam is an excellent pilot. We anchored the plane to some willow trees and unloaded. I'd brought cameraman Chuck Denault with me to record the action. He had never been to Alaska and was amazed by the scenery and the vast wilderness.

The next morning it was raining, and the wind was blowing hard. But we got our gear on and headed into the darkness. When we reached some tall trees, Sam climbed a hundred-foot spruce and glassed a moose kill he'd found on a scouting trip. The kill was just a quarter-mile mile from camp. Now I understood why Sam had wanted us to be quiet around camp. He'd said that the moose kill was close to camp, but I had no idea it was that close. He stayed in the tree quite a while, looking things over. When he came back down he had a funny look on his face. I asked what the matter was, and he said, "We've got problems."

I thought, *I've already got problems with a bow I have very little confidence in. I don't need more problems!*

Sam said, "There's not just one bear on the moose; there are five. One of them is a sow with two cubs. A big boar is keeping the rest of the bears away." The others were around the perimeter in the bleachers, waiting for their chance to feed.

When bears are on or near a kill, they become unpredictable—more so than normal. They are very possessive and always acutely aware of their surroundings while feeding, even the bears that are just waiting their turn. They have no problem running off intruders or fighting to protect their food, sometimes to the death. This was a dangerous situation. We were going to sneak into the middle of a gang of brown bears and try to run a sharp stick through one of them.

At times like these a sane man thinks of all the critters he's helped to manage—killed for the meat and to keep the wildlife at a manageable level in proportion to its habitat. He also thinks of animals killed for the thrill of the hunt in younger years. He thinks of all the trips he's made to enjoy and experience all that God and Nature have created. He ponders the need that all humans have to walk the edge of life and death. He thinks, too, *What if? What if it's time for the score to be evened? Is this the position the powers that be have been working me toward, to balance the scale? An eye for an eye, tooth for a tooth?*

You never think about those things when you are young. Youth is strong-headed and invincible. You just charge in and damn the torpedoes. Age and experience ask different questions. Thoughts enter your brain that never had a chance before. I call it seasoning.

After wading in water for a good distance we came to a thick stand of timber that we had to get through to see the kill. We called it the "enchanted forest." It was an eerie little patch of timber where trees loomed high above, creating a canopy. Moss hung from them like the scraggly hair of a sleeping giant. A carpet of lichen and moss covered the ground. It was just the kind of place where spooky fairy tales originate. What dangers lay within a few yards of our path, cloaked in a hypnotizing fog? Enchanted? You could say that. You could also say electrified with apprehension and perhaps ill-fated courage. We eased forward into the vapor.

"He's standing on the dead moose," whispered Sam.

The colossal creature turned and stared in our direction. Breathing ceased. Bone-chilling moments later, the big boar went back to feeding. It was barely daylight, and the sound of a low-flying airplane caught the bear's attention. He looked up as the plane passed. Then the bear got

*After his brown-bear encounter, Gary shot this black-tailed deer on Kodiak Island, Alaska, November 1994.*

nervous and wandered into the woods. As he was walking off, he again looked in our direction.

When he had disappeared, we quickly placed our cameraman behind a bush and said, "Don't move!"

We closed the distance to within thirty yards of the dead moose. To do so we had to be completely in the open. Within half a minute the big Alaska brown bear returned. He stepped out of the woods, stopped, and stared in our direction. We froze in place. I awaited a chance to draw. But the bear saw something, and his posture changed for the worse. He walked over and began circling the moose in a slow, foreboding manner. Halfway around, he averted his eyes and tilted his head. What happened next was paralyzing: A thousand-pound killing machine came charging on the dead run!

As the monster closed the distance, Sam instantly sprang to his feet and began screaming at the bear. He had his rifle up, ready to fire, and I was at full draw with my makeshift equipment (as if that could stop him). The enormous carnivore stormed by so close that I could have stuck him with an arrow by hand. The mad bear veered off at the last second and disappeared into the bush. If Sam hadn't risked his life, there is a good chance I would not be here to tell the story.

It was a long walk back to camp in the drizzle and fog. Emotionally spent, we spoke very little. We ate lunch and then talked about the incident. Sam commended me for not taking a sloppy shot out of fear, and wounding the bear. He also said that the bear was mainly bluffing, or he would have taken us out. We took a long rest and then regrouped for another stalk on the moose kill that evening.

What is it that makes a person go back into the lion's den? In my world, if you fear and do not conquer it, self-esteem suffers. At that point in my life it was important to play this thing to the end. I'd been blessed so many times throughout life with great and triumphant adventures. If it was in the Master Plan for me to be snuffed out here, so be it. I had to prove to myself I had what it takes to face death head on, or be vanquished to worthlessness. A person's self-esteem, however vain, defines a soul. I am so thankful to those who lead me to these ends, risking their lives at times. I hope these challenges may have helped them define their own spirit and soul along the way, too.

We sneaked back through the enchanted forest, one or two steps at a time, aware that it was getting darker. Sam caught something out of the corner of his eye to our left. A sow and two cubs were standing in the nearby bush, staring. Sam quickly made some racket, hoping to spook her off. It worked. As soon as she had left, a big boar came out of the bush, ambled over to the kill, and began to eat. He kept a constant vigil as he ate, and once in a while stared in our direction.

We crept forward each time he tore at the dead moose. We finally reached the thirty-five-yard minimum I needed, according to Sam's rangefinder, but the bear saw us take that last step and immediately started in our direction. Sam and I both thought, *Here we go again.* He turned broadside, quartering toward us, trying to decide whether to charge. Sam said, "Take him."

I quickly drew, centered the pin, and let fly. I missed completely, and low to boot. The bear bolted for the brush.

Come to find out there was a small limb hanging from a tree in front of the bear that Sam's rangefinder had locked in on. Sam had ranged it twice and hit the limb twice. What are the odds of that happening? That accounted for the low shot, but I also overextended and pulled the shot left.

*Longtime friend John Wilson, a resident of Cordova, Alaska, saved the trip by loaning the author his Hoyt bow and arrows.*

Man, I was low. While we were standing there shaking our heads, the big sow and her cubs came out of nowhere and began feeding. She knew we were there and didn't care. We stood and watched for a while before heading back to camp.

I was fading fast, both emotionally and physically. I flat-out wasn't meant to kill an Alaska brown bear—that was becoming obvious. Sam kept encouraging me, though, and we never gave up.

The following morning we ate nothing and were out the minute we could see our way. After making our way through the enchanted forest, we spotted a different boar lying on the moose kill. He was sleeping, for the most part, but looked up once in a while to make sure he was alone. We again placed the cameraman behind a bush and started our approach. This bear appeared to be about a nine-footer. I've been on a lot of stalks in my day, but this was the most demanding I'd ever experienced. There was absolutely no cover for thirty yards, and we were threatening a food source of the largest carnivore in the world. I felt utterly naked.

When we got to our thirty-five-yard mark, Sam threw a live rifle round into the bushes to our left. The bear heard it but didn't get up. Sam threw another shell directly at the bear, and this time he was up and looking right at us. The bear took a few steps forward, and Sam said, "Take the shot."

It was strange. I had just been thinking, *I hope he tells me to pass.* I was so mentally drained I didn't want the pressure of having to make the shot. But instinct took over. I smoothly drew the Hoyt Tenacity (being careful not to overdraw the ill-fitting bow), picked the spot, and released the string, sending the NAP broadhead right where it needed to be. The big brown bear groaned and bolted for the woods.

Ever so slowly we backed up to the enchanted forest, never taking our eyes off the bear's route. Reaching the woods, we took deep breaths and embraced with a big hug. Was it real? Had we really done it? *Thanks, God, for this opportunity,* I thought. *And thanks, Sam.*

After some time—it seemed like hours—we took up the trail. The shot had looked good, but who knew? We slowly and quietly stalked over to where the bear had disappeared. Sam was ready on his rifle. I was ready in case there was a chance for another arrow. And we were only too aware that four other bears were close by. We hadn't gone twenty yards into the bush when we found my bear, dead as a stone.

What an unbelievable experience this had been, and what a finale to a long and extremely difficulty quest for an Alaska brown bear. This species had given me more trouble than any other and had tested me to my last ounce of courage and resolve. Yes, I'd salvaged my vanity. But at the moment that seemed a lot less important than bringing this hard-fought struggle to an end without costing my friends their lives.

My hat will be eternally off to all the guides and friends who endured my numerous brown bear follies. I owe each one respect and admiration as modern-day pioneers. Many of us hunters put ourselves in your presence not only to reach our goals but also to live for a short time right alongside men and women who have achieved our secret dream—the dream to hunt, fish, and live in the outdoors every day. Some of the greatest and most down-to-earth folks in this world are guides, outfitters, their help, and families.

Chapter 27

# The End of a Forty-Six-Year Quest—Coues Deer

My first Coues deer hunt was in Mexico in 1997 at the Sierra Madre Hunting Resort. Juan Raynal was the outfitter and ranch owner. His two sons helped him, but no one there was experienced in taking bowhunters. Once again Wes Vining of Trophy Connection introduced these folks to me. I was a little concerned that nobody had any experience with bowhunting, but the people were so very accommodating. They wanted me not only to be their first bowhunter but also to help them understand how to handle bowhunters. Bowhunting in that area was a novelty. Everyone was fascinated by the thought of being able to get a Coues deer, or any deer for that matter, with a bow. The local newspaper even came out and did a story on my hunt. It appeared on the front page of the sports section.

Juan and the boys were trying to figure out ways to make ends meet on the ranch and felt that hunting would help. They picked my brain considerably on the subject of bowhunting. When I arrived they asked me to stay in their home for a night until the trip to the ranch the next day. They were great people. Juan's two brothers were priests in the area. The ranch was about a five-hour trip from Chihuahua City. Ranches in Mexico are generally very large, and this one was no exception at twenty-five thousand acres.

The country was very open, with rolling hills and a few pine trees. There wasn't much good stalking country around, so the hunting was tough. The deer were extremely nervous, too. I attributed a big part of that to the huge number of coyotes. I saw more coyotes there than in any other place I've ever visited. They had to be very hard on the mature deer as well as the fawn crops. I advised Juan and the boys to put a predator-control policy in place as soon as possible and take whatever

*With this Coues deer came the end of the author's quest for the North American 28, Blue Mountains, Arizona, January 2000.*

other steps were necessary to get the situation under control, or there wouldn't be a deer left.

We tried everything I could think of to get close, but there was no way to make it work. I even climbed a tree near water and waited on bare limbs. A couple of small bucks went by, but I couldn't get a shot. We finally gave it up. I advised Juan to build some blinds by water and maybe a few tree stands if they wanted bowhunters to have any chance at all. I thanked them for all their hard work and for their friendship. What a special Christian family.

I didn't get back to the Coues deer until December of 1999, by which time the species was the last of the North American Twenty-Eight I needed. I'd talked to a lot of guys who had tried to get a Coues with their bows and heard some discouraging tales. But according to an article written by Doyle Moss, fellow bowhunter Jimmie Ryan had taken a new Pope and Young Club world-record Coues deer. He'd shot the deer on a ranch in Mexico I had never heard of. The following year Chuck Adams took another new world-record deer there.

Hoyt received a letter from a U.S. agent, Manuel J. Chee, MD, inviting a few of us on the Hoyt pro staff down to hunt Coues deer on the same ranch that Jimmie and Chuck had hunted. Peter Cimmellaro, a Coues deer expert and outfitter in Mexico, was the contact I had to call for advice. Peter said that he was no longer associated with the people who owned the ranch, but that it would be a good place to go. He also said it wouldn't be easy.

The ranch was owned by Sergio and Fernando Gonzales and hadn't been hunted for eighteen years until Jimmie Ryan visited the year before. There were some great bucks, but the deer were extremely nervous, and we just couldn't get them to cooperate. We again tried everything we could, including hunting the water holes. We built a homemade blind and had spotters signaling when deer were coming. The deer just wouldn't come in to the right spot. They didn't like our blind setup, either. I had to commend Jimmie Ryan and Chuck Adams for their accomplishment of taking world-record deer. We didn't have the luxury of the rut, as they had, but they still did very well just to get one. I was extremely disappointed in the hunt because I figured that if I were ever going to get a Coues deer with a bow, it would be there.

I was getting pretty frantic to acquire the "ghost of the desert" and finish the longest quest I'd ever undertaken. Part of my goal was to be in the top

*Packing a Coues deer out on horseback is not much of a problem, Blue Mountains, Arizona, January 2000.*

five bowhunters to ever get the job done. Given that I started when I was twelve years old and now am pushing the "golden years," I now find it odd that in the beginning the quest wasn't a part of the reason I hunted. But the closer I got to achieving it, the more the intensity level increased—not just because others were trying the same thing but because it gets into your blood and becomes a driving force. Of all the feats we can accomplish in our lives as men, few affect us like hunting feats. Hunting defines a man as being similar to the founders of this country who had to use their wits and brawn to survive all sorts of perils. It is just part of our makeup deep down, and it doesn't matter whether you do it with a rifle or a recurve. It's a steep mountain to climb and a great feeling of personal accomplishment.

Fellow bowhunter, guide, and hunting partner Jim Van Norman killed a record-book Coues buck in Arizona sometime in 1998. He took his buck from a tree stand and had a cameraman with him. I got on the horn as soon as I got home. Jim put me onto a guide by the name of Bill Bishop. Bill's home is in Lakeside, Arizona, but he hunted an area he had trapped for many years before the antihunters shut trapping down in Arizona. It was a different type of Coues deer habitat than I had ever seen. The elevation was around eight thousand feet, and the terrain was more like elk and mule deer country. In fact, there were elk all over, as well as wolves, mountain lions, and bears. There was huge, heavy timber as well as juniper and scrub oak. Some of the old pines and junipers were a hundred years old or more.

Jim had seen an article in the NRA magazine *American Hunter,* telling how a couple of Coues deer hunters had hired Bill to take them on a horseback hunt in the Arizona mountains. The article described Bill's skill as a seasoned outdoorsman and painted him as a crusty old trapper—the kind of guy Jim knew he could relate to. Jim shot his buck in the first two hours of the first day of his six-day hunt. Although I didn't figure to have that kind of luck, Jim said that Bill knew his Coues deer stuff. Besides that, he was a great character to spend a week with.

I called Bill right away, and he had an opening that season. The season in that part of Arizona is split between December and January. According to Bill, the rut was still going strong in January. I booked the spot and started packing.

I flew to Phoenix, rented a car, and drove to Lakeside, Arizona, where I met Bill. He had camp already set up back in the Blue Mountains. I followed him in my car for several hours a long way back into the mountains and was truly surprised just how breathtaking the country was. Bill stopped at a viewpoint not far from camp, and we gazed out over the country we would be hunting. There was hardly a meadow or an open hillside. It was pretty much just timber as far as the eye could see. I could tell from the start that this was going to be an adventure in some truly wild country.

Bill's camp was a modest setup in a national forest campground. We slept and cooked in a motorhome, and his son, Bill Jr., helped with the chores and cooking. The horses were up the road a short way from camp in a set of Forest Service corrals. The area was huge and rough enough that the horses would save a lot of wear and tear on these old bones.

We went to Jim Van Norman's favorite tree stand, where he had shot his big buck. On the way there the main trail was riddled with wolf and lion tracks. Bill knew we would see very little in this basin because of the predators, but we decided to sit there for a day, just in case. We saw two deer on one of the hillsides nearby, but that was it.

*Bunkhouse under construction for future hunters, Sierra Madre Hunting Resort, Chihuahua City, Mexico, November 1997.*

The next day we rode in the opposite direction about eight miles back into the forest to one of Bill's favorite places. The country was almost enchanted. There were springs and creeks in almost every drainage we came to. At one spot Bill had a tree stand in the midst of old rock Indian ruins. There was distinct evidence of their stone houses near a big spring. Some of the trees standing there were fifteen feet around and eighty feet tall. If only they could tell the story of the Indian community they had guarded. Bill believes that the spirits of the Indian hunters are still here, guarding the springs. I almost hate to say it, but I could feel a presence of some sort myself. We hoped they approved of our hunting their old stomping grounds with a bow—although I'm sure they scoffed at compound bows.

We found a couple of scrapes, but there wasn't much recent action there, either. Again, a lot of wolf sign was present but very few deer. We actually had Mexican wolves (red wolves) come into our camp every night. A pair visited camp in broad daylight one day. A friend of Bill's, Wes Egg, was hunting the area and camping next to us. He had a little dog with him, and a female wolf attacked his dog right in camp. She tore the little dog up pretty bad. Wes reported the incident, and the feds came in the next day to investigate.

One of the federal agents said that they might have to shut the whole area down to hunting because of the wolves' importance to the ecosystem. It amazed me to hear a comment like that from an educated human being. Her take on this was that humans are interfering with the reintroduction of wolves to the area. The real problem was that these wolves had been fed by hand in the pens in which they were raised. They had not learned to kill on their own. The government should have turned live animals into the pen so that the wolves would know what to do when released into the wild. The way it was done, each time a wolf heard a human voice, it would come find the source and wait to be fed. Ridiculous!

We spent a couple more days looking for fresh scrapes and rubs in areas that Bill had previously scouted. The rutting activity had slowed to a standstill with the wolves touring the entire country. What deer were normally there had moved out. Finally, Bill's friend Wes had seen a red-hot scrape in an area he was hunting and had set up a tree stand. He decided that since Bill and I were having such poor luck, he would let me sit in his stand. I was taken aback by Wes's willingness to share his knowledge and to help with my goal. Sometimes we forget that there are still good people in this world. Among them are great hunters who are unselfish and seasoned enough to help their fellow man. Thank you, to a very special veteran and hunting friend.

The first day Bill and I sat there a small buck appeared out of nowhere around midmorning. He was big enough for me. I raised my 72-pound-pull Hoyt Defiant and waited for a clear shot. The buck wove around in the cover but didn't present a shot. He did walk within ten yards of Bill's position, though, and Bill got some good film of him. But he disappeared just as fast as he had appeared. I thought, *That may have been the only opportunity I'll get. So close and yet so far.*

It was pretty disappointing, but Bill assured me that the buck would be back in a day or two, checking the scrape again.

Bill, Wes, and I talked in camp that night about why we are tested so hard when we get close to the end of an undertaking. It seems that the powers that be decide nothing is worth having unless it comes with physical

*Bill Bishop in a tree stand filming Gary's hunt, Blue Mountains, Arizona, January 2000.*

and mental hardship. Just once I would like to have some quest of mine be like falling off a log. But I suppose I wouldn't appreciate it much if it came so easy. "Try me once," I mumbled, looking skyward. It was a long night. I tossed and turned and slept very little.

We were back in our tree stands at daylight. Bill was ready on the video camera, and I was watching the woods like a starving hawk. We had been there for about an hour and a half when, out of thin air, there stood the little whitetail ghost, almost in the same place as yesterday. He silently and carefully walked into a shooting lane a bit to my right. I had some distance flags hung in trees, and he stopped between two. My mind was racing whether to use one pin and hold high or another and hold low. I flip-flopped between the two notions until I finally had to tell myself to calm down. I drew and put the shorter distance pin on his vitals and held a bit high. I was shaking like a leaf. The pressure of the last critter in this monumental quest weighed heavy. The ACC 360 with a 100-grain NAP Shock Wave put the deer down immediately. I had misjudged the elevation, though, and the shot had hit him high. He was trying to get back up as I nocked another arrow. I couldn't get another clear shot before he got to his feet and stumbled out of sight over a bank.

I looked around at Bill in shock. He gave me a thumb's-up and signaled for me to sit down and relax for a while, to give the deer some time. We waited for about an hour and then eased out of our stands and stalked quietly over to where we last had seen the deer. There wasn't much blood, and we quickly found the arrow. We could see that the deer was having a hard time dragging itself along, but it was definitely on the move. Bill and I decided to leave the deer for a few more hours and go find Wes to help with the tracking.

We came back a few hours later and took up the trail. There was very little blood—we homed in on tiny specks and faint deer tracks. We would have to fan out when a deer trail forked, and spent most of our time on our hands and knees searching. The cover got thicker and thicker, and many times we crawled through Coues deer tunnels in the brush.

We jumped the buck twice, but I could never get a clear shot. As I look back now, I probably should have taken the flashing brush shot and tried to get another arrow in him. It finally got dark, so we flagged the last blood and started toward camp, climbing out of the canyon and back to the horses with

*The welcome sign that greeted me at the Sierra Madre Hunting Resort, November 1997.*

our flashlights. It was a long ride back to camp. I could tell that Bill and Wes were a bit down, too. But they encouraged me to keep a positive attitude. We would find him tomorrow. I wasn't so sure, remembering all the wolf and cat tracks we had seen.

We returned the following morning at daylight and started the search again. The scant trail led us to the edge of another canyon. The buck had gone over the edge but was falling from time to time. There were skid marks every few feet, small drops of blood, and hair. When we got to the bottom, believe it or not, I noticed an ear sticking out from beneath some deadfall. I hollered, "There he is!"

Bill and Wes yelled, "Where, where?"

We had been so intent with our eyes on the ground at our feet that we had forgotten to look ahead. The Coues buck lay almost in plain sight, right in front of us. "Right there," I said.

We all came completely unglued. I couldn't believe we had found him. Wes and Bill had proven themselves to be two of the best trackers I'd ever seen short of trackers in the jungles of Africa. This deer wasn't the biggest buck in the Arizona woods, but he was good enough for me.

The gray ghost had tested everything we had in our bag of tricks. And it had tested my nerves and emotions to the max. My personal quest was complete. My personal mountain had finally been climbed, and the feeling was overwhelming. It brought tears to my eyes and a strange feeling to my entire body. Then, a thank-you on bended knees. Without the friendship and help of those two dedicated hunters I would not have reached the hard-fought goal of the North American Twenty-Eight.

Without the help of all my guides, outfitters, their staffers, and families, I would never have been able to accomplish half of what I've done. No! Let me rephrase: what *we* have done! I'm proud of reaching the goal, the North American Twenty-Eight or Slam, but the kinships, friendships, and other bonds created between men, women, and children through all of these adventures are the most important of all my accomplishments.